THE 1989

Children Act

explained

CAROLINE GIBSON

JOANNA GRICE

REBECCA JAMES &

SHONA MULHOLLAND

London: The Stationery Office

© The Stationery Office 2000

Applications for reproduction should be made in writing to The Stationery Office Limited, St Crispins, Duke Street, Norwich NR3 1PD.

The information contained in this publication is believed to be correct at the time of manufacture. Whilst care has been taken to ensure that the information is accurate, the publisher can accept no responsibility for any errors or ommissions or for changes to the details given.

Caroline Gibson, Joanna Grice, Rebecca James and Shona Mulholland have asserted their moral rights under the Copyright, Designs and Patents Act 1988, to be identified as the authors of this work.

Crown copyright material reproduced with permission of Her Majestys Stationery Office

A CIP catalogue record for this book is available from the British Library
A Library of Congress CIP catalogue record has been applied for

First published 2000

ISBN 0 11 702385 X

Printed in the United Kingdom for the Stationery Office by
TJ000718 C10 04/00 9385 12257

Contents

The Children Act 1989, Explained

The "Children Act 1989, Explained", was written by Shona Mulholland, Rebecca James, Caroline Gibson and Joanna Grice, Barristers, of 1 King's Bench Walk, London.

All are members of the Family Law Bar Association and specialise in the area of Family and Children Law

Chambers of Anthony Hacking Q.C.
1 King's Bench Walk
Temple EC4Y 7DB
London
Tel : 0171 9361500
Fax :0171 936 1590
Web site: www.1KBW.co.uk.

Disclaimer

This publication is intended to provide a brief commentary on the Children Act 1989 and should not be relied upon by any party without taking further legal advice.

Introduction

The Children Act 1989 effected major changes in the way in which the courts deal with cases concerning children. Lord Mackay, the Lord Chancellor at the time of its passing by Parliament, called it, '[t]he most comprehensive and far-reaching reform of child law which has come before Parliament in living memory'.

The law concerning child care was in a confused and inadequate state in the early 1980s. There were far too many statutes dealing with children, leading to complex and at times contradictory rules. In addition, the law was out of date and clearly in need of reform. A number of reviews of the area were undertaken. Of particular importance in the genesis of the Children Act 1989 were the Department of Health and Social Security Review of Child Care Law, the White Paper The Law on Child Care and Family Services and the Law Commission report 'Review of Child Law: Guardianship and Custody'. It was from these reports that the Act grew.

Although the Act is divided into separate Parts, each dealing with a different aspect of child law, it must be remembered that the Act needs to be read as a whole. In particular, the principles set out in Pt I of the Act are of general application, especially the 'welfare check-list' as set out in s.1(3).

The Act was intended to provide a clear and comprehensive code for all children cases. It was envisaged that the balance of power between families and the State would be realigned to emphasise the importance of local authorities and parents working together. Further, the relative powers of the courts and local authorities were adjusted, in particular with the virtual abolition of wardship proceedings (see s.100). The extent to which the expressed aims of the Act have been achieved may be debated, but what cannot be disputed is that the law relating to child care is now radically different from that which the Act replaced.

The 12 Parts of the Act cover the following areas:

Part I - general principles to be applied in all cases

Part II - private law proceedings, where there is no local authority intervention

Part III - general services to be offered by local authorities to children in their jurisdiction

Part IV - rules concerning the granting of care and supervision orders

Part V - the investigation and protection of children at risk

Part VI - the regulation of community homes

Part VII - the regulation of voluntary homes

Part VIII - the regulation of children's homes

Part IX - the regulation of private fostering of children

Part X - the regulation of child minders and day care facilities

Part XI - the role of the Secretary of State

Part XII - general provisions dealing with incidental matters, such as courts' jurisdiction and interpretation

In addition, the Schedules provide important details concerning specific named areas. Numerous regulations have been made pursuant to the powers granted to the Secretary of State under the Act.

Since its implementation, the Act has been the subject of various judicial interpretations, both by the Court of Appeal and the House of Lords. However, it is important to remember that the law relating to child care is not restricted by 'black letter' interpretations of statutory rules. A flexible approach is necessary to ensure the welfare of the child will always be the paramount consideration.

Children Act 1989

The use of the words "to reform the law" and, "to amend the law", indicate that the law relating to children has been reformed by this Act. Prior to the Children Act 1989 there were a wide variety of acts dealing with these issues. They have all now been codified in this Act.

PART I

INTRODUCTORY

1 – (1) When a court determines any question with respect to–

(a) the upbringing of a child; or
(b) the administration of a child's property or the application of any income arising from it, the child's welfare shall be the court's paramount consideration.

> **Subsection (1)** *This subsection deals with, the first of a number of key principles behind the Children Act 1989. It sets out what is known as " the welfare principle". In all situations with which the court is concerned with a child, the child's welfare shall be the paramount consideration.*

(2) In any proceedings in which any question with respect to the upbringing of a child arises, the court shall have regard to the general principle that any delay in determining the question is likely to prejudice the welfare of the child.

> **Subsection (2)**
> *This subsection sets out the " delay" principle. In all proceedings concerning a child the court will always start from the position of considering that any delay in a case will not be good for the child.*

(3) In the circumstances mentioned in subsection (4), a court shall have regard in particular to–

(a) the ascertainable wishes and feelings of the child concerned (considered in the light of his age and understanding);
(b) his physical, emotional and educational needs;
(c) the likely effect on him of any change in his circumstances;
(d) his age, sex, background and any characteristics of his which the court considers relevant;
(e) any harm which he has suffered or is at risk of suffering;

   (f) how capable each of his parents, and any other person in relation to whom the court considers the question to be relevant, is of meeting his needs;

   (g) the range of powers available to the court under this Act in the proceedings in question.

> **Subsection (3)** *This subsection sets out the "welfare checklist". It is a checklist that the court must consider in every case of the type described in Subsection (4) (see below). There are seven categories for consideration, and a judge must consider each in turn. Often reports that are prepared for the court by, for example, court welfare officers or social workers, will have a section entitled " welfare checklist", in which they consider the categories and draw conclusions in order to assist the court.*

(4) The circumstances are that–

   (a) the court is considering whether to make, vary or discharge a section 8 order, and the making, variation or discharge of the order is opposed by any party to the proceedings; or

   (b) the court is considering whether to make, vary or discharge an order under Part IV.

> **Subsection (4)** *This sets out the circumstances in which the court must consider the welfare checklist. It must consider it when it is concerned with whether to make, vary or discharge an order under Section 8 of the Act, that is an order for residence, contact, specific issue, or prohibited steps (see below). It must also consider it when it is concerned with whether to make, vary or discharge an order under Part IV of the Act, that is an order for care or supervision of a child.(see below)*

(5) Where a court is considering whether or not to make one or more orders under this Act with respect to a child, it shall not make the order or any of the orders unless it considers that doing so would be better for the child than making no order at all.

> **Subsection (5)** *This subsection sets out what is known as the " No order" principle. The court must always ask itself whether making an order is better for the child than making no order in all the circumstances.*

2 – (1) Where a child's father and mother were married to each other at the time of his birth, they shall each have parental responsibility for the child.

Section 2

Subsection (1) Parents married to each other at the time of a child's birth will both have parental responsibility for that child. " Parental responsibility" was a new concept introduced for the first time in the Act. Previous thinking had been that parents had "rights", but this Act shifts the focus to the responsibilities of being a parent, and makes limited mention of parental rights with regard to children. This section explains who can have parental responsibility for a child.

(2) Where a child's father and mother were not married to each other at the time of his birth–

    (a) the mother shall have parental responsibility for the child;

    (b) the father shall not have parental responsibility for the child, unless he acquires it in accordance with the provisions of this Act.

Subsection (2) If the parents are unmarried when the child is born, the mother will have parental responsibility but the father does not have parental responsibility. If he wants to have parental responsibility he must take steps to "acquire" it.

(3) References in this Act to a child whose father and mother were, or (as the case may be) were not, married to each other at the time of his birth must be read with section 1 of the Family Law Reform Act 1987 (which extends their meaning).

Subsection (3) Section 1 of the Family Law Reform Act 1987 sets out the principle that in any legislation coming into force after it, the relationship between a person's parents i.e. married or unmarried, will not be of consequence, unless it is specifically set out. In Section 2 of the Children Act 1989 the question as to whether a child's parents were or were not married at the time of birth is specifically set out, and is therefore of consequence.

(4) The rule of law that a father is the natural guardian of his legitimate child is abolished.

Subsection (4) It is no longer the case that the father of a child born within marriage is the child's guardian, rather both parents share parental responsibility for the child, and can each appoint a guardian for the child.

(5) More than one person may have parental responsibility for the same child at the same time.

(6) A person who has parental responsibility for a child at any time shall not cease to have that responsibility solely because some other person subsequently acquires parental responsibility for the child.

> **Subsection (6)** *A person's parental responsibility does not cease when another person obtains parental responsibility*

(7) Where more than one person has parental responsibility for a child, each of them may act alone and without the other (or others) in meeting that responsibility; but nothing in this Part shall be taken to affect the operation of any enactment which requires the consent of more than one person in a matter affecting the child.

> **Subsection (7)** *If two people have parental responsibility for the same child, they do not need to act together in meeting the child's needs i.e. they do not need to consult each other on every issue, or obtain the other's consent. The exception to this is if there is a specific Act or piece of legislation which requires more than one person to consent to something concerning a child, in which case they must obtain the other's consent and cannot act unilaterally.*

(8) The fact that a person has parental responsibility for a child shall not entitle him to act in any way which would be incompatible with any order made with respect to the child under this Act.

(9) A person who has parental responsibility for a child may not surrender or transfer any part of that responsibility to another but may arrange for some or all of it to be met by one or more persons acting on his behalf.

> **Subsection (9)** *A person cannot surrender or transfer, in a permanent manner, his or her parental responsibility for a child. However if the person with parental responsibility needs someone else to assist them in order that they fulfil the requirements of parental responsibility, they may ask for assistance. For example, a person with parental responsibility may be unable to meet a child's health needs acting alone, and may require another to help. Or a person may delegate parental responsibility to a school or a camp, whilst the child is in the care of the school or camp.*

(10) The person with whom any such arrangement is made may himself be a person who already has parental responsibility for the child concerned.

Subsection (10) The situation as envisaged at subsection (9) above, may involve another person who has parental responsibility for the child in providing the assistance.

(11) The making of any such arrangement shall not affect any liability of the person making it which may arise from any failure to meet any part of his parental responsibility for the child concerned.

Subsection (11) Even if such delegation of parental responsibility takes place, the person with parental responsibility remains liable for any failure on his part to discharge his responsibilities to the child.

3 – (1) In this Act 'parental responsibility' means all the rights, duties, powers, responsibilities and authority which by law a parent of a child has in relation to the child and his property.

Section 3
Subsection (1) This subsection defines parental responsibility. The definition does not include a list of the responsibilities that a person might have for a child. This would be inappropriate as the Act must deal with children of all ages, levels of maturity, and in differing circumstances. The powers "which by law a parent of a child has", include, for example, the right to consent to that child's marriage. In general terms parental responsibility is taken to include decision making on issues such as a child's religion, medical needs and education.

(2) It also includes the rights, powers and duties which a guardian of the child's estate (appointed, before the commencement of section 5, to act generally) would have had in relation to the child and his property.

Subsection (2) The definition of parental responsibility includes the powers that a guardian held, prior to the Children Act 1989. These are defined further in subsection (3).

(3) The rights referred to in subsection (2) include, in particular, the right of the guardian to receive or recover in his own name, for the benefit of the child, property of whatever description and wherever situated which the child is entitled to receive or recover.

> **Subsection (3)** *The additional responsibilities that a guardian would have held on behalf of a child, would have been those of recovering property for the benefit of the child.*

(4) The fact that a person has, or does not have, parental responsibility for a child shall not affect–

    (a) any obligation which he may have in relation to the child (such as a statutory duty to maintain the child); or

    (b) any rights which, in the event of the child's death, he (or any other person) may have in relation to the child's property.

> **Subsection (4)** *This subsection demonstrates the working of section 2(3) above. Even if a child's parent does not have parental responsibility (due to being an unmarried father) that does not affect the child's entitlement to be maintained by his parents, nor does it affect the entitlement of the parent to inherit from the child's estate. It promotes equal status for all children regardless of their parent's marital status.*

(5) A person who–

    (a) does not have parental responsibility for a particular child; but

    (b) has care of the child,

    may (subject to the provisions of this Act) do what is reasonable in all the circumstances of the case for the purpose of safeguarding or promoting the child's welfare.

4 – (1) Where a child's father and mother were not married to each other at the time of his birth–

    (a) the court may, on the application of the father, order that he shall have parental responsibility for the child; or

    (b) the father and mother may by agreement ('a parental responsibility agreement') provide for the father to have parental responsibility for the child.

Section 4

Subsection (1) This section deals with the way in which a father who was not married to the mother at the time of the child's birth may acquire parental responsibility for that child. There are two ways for an unmarried father to acquire parental responsibility. Firstly, he may apply to the court and the court can order that he has parental responsibility. Secondly he may enter into a formal agreement with the child's mother that he will have parental responsibility.

(2) No parental responsibility agreement shall have effect for the purposes of this Act unless–

    (a) it is made in the form prescribed by regulations made by the Lord Chancellor; and

    (b) where regulations are made by the Lord Chancellor prescribing the manner in which such agreements must be recorded, it is recorded in the prescribed manner.

Subsection (2) A "parental responsibility agreement" will only have legal status if it is made and recorded, in the manner prescribed by the Lord Chancellor. The parents cannot simply draw up their own document of agreement, they must comply with the current Regulations.

(3) Subject to section 12(4), an order under subsection (1)(a), or a parental responsibility agreement, may only be brought to an end by an order of the court made on the application–

    (a) of any person who has parental responsibility for the child; or

    (b) with leave of the court, of the child himself.

Subsection (3) If an order is made for a father to have parental responsibility, or if he acquires it through a parental responsibility agreement, his parental responsibility can only be brought to an end by the order of a court following an application by any person with parental responsibility for the child, or if the court permits, an application by the child himself. The only exception to this is when a father has acquired parental responsibility by virtue of a residence order being made in his favour (see section 12 below), in which case the parental responsibility order cannot end whilst the residence order remains in force.

(4) The court may only grant leave under subsection (3)(b) if it is satisfied that the child has sufficient understanding to make the proposed application.

> **Subsection (4)** *The court will only permit a child to make an application to bring someone's parental responsibility to an end if it is satisfied that the child has sufficient understanding to make the application.*

5 – (1) Where an application with respect to a child is made to the court by any individual, the court may by order appoint that individual to be the child's guardian if–

    (a) the child has no parent with parental responsibility for him; or

    (b) a residence order has been made with respect to the child in favour of a parent or guardian of his who has died while the order was in force.

> **Section 5**
> **Subsection (1)** *If the child has either no parent with parental responsibility, or there is an existing residence order in respect of the child in favour of a parent or guardian who has died, the court can appoint as guardian a person who has made an application in respect of the child.*

(2) The power conferred by subsection (1) may also be exercised in any family proceedings if the court considers that the order should be made even though no application has been made for it.

> **Subsection (2)** *The court can appoint somebody to be a child's guardian even if no application has been made to the court for such an appointment.*

(3) A parent who has parental responsibility for his child may appoint another individual to be the child's guardian in the event of his death.

(4) A guardian of a child may appoint another individual to take his place as the child's guardian in the event of his death.

(5) An appointment under subsection (3) or (4) shall not have effect unless it is made in writing, is dated and is signed by the person making the appointment or–

    (a) in the case of an appointment made by a will which is not signed by the testator, is signed at the direction of the testator in accordance with the requirements of section 9 of the Wills Act 1837; or

(b) in any other case, is signed at the direction of the person making the appointment, in his presence and in the presence of two witnesses who each attest the signature.

Subsection (5) *If a person wishes to appoint someone else as the child's guardian should they die, then they must make the appointment in the correct format, as specified in this subsection.*

(6) A person appointed as a child's guardian under this section shall have parental responsibility for the child concerned.

Subsection (6) *A guardian appointed for a child under this section will have parental responsibility for the child.*

(7) Where–

(a) on the death of any person making an appointment under subsection (3) or (4), the child concerned has no parent with parental responsibility for him; or
(b) immediately before the death of any person making such an appointment, a residence order in his favour was in force with respect to the child,
    the appointment shall take effect on the death of that person.

(8) Where, on the death of any person making an appointment under subsection (3) or (4)–

(a) the child concerned has a parent with parental responsibility for him; and
(b) subsection (7)(b) does not apply,
    the appointment shall take effect when the child no longer has a parent who has parental responsibility for him.

(9) Subsections (1) and (7) do not apply if the residence order referred to in paragraph (b) of those subsections was also made in favour of a surviving parent of the child.

Subsection (7)(8)(9) *The appointment of a new guardian will only take effect immediately upon the death of the person who made the appointment if the following circumstance exists: that there is no longer living a parent with parental responsibility, or the person who died had a sole residence order in their favour in respect of the child, immediately before his or her death. If a parent with parental responsibility is alive then the appointment will only take place on the death of that parent.*

(10) Nothing in this section shall be taken to prevent an appointment under subsection (3) or (4) being made by two or more persons acting jointly.

> **Subsection (10)** *Two or more people can appoint a guardian for a child in the manner set out in subsections (3) and (4).*

(11) Subject to any provision made by rules of court, no court shall exercise the High Court's inherent jurisdiction to appoint a guardian of the estate of any child.

(12) Where the rules of court are made under subsection (11) they may prescribe the circumstances in which, and conditions subject to which, an appointment of such a guardian may be made.

> **Subsection (11) and (12)** *The High Court cannot appoint a person to be the guardian of a child's estate unless there are rules of court specifying the exact way in which this should happen.*

(13) A guardian of a child may only be appointed in accordance with the provisions of this section.

6 – (1) An appointment under section 5(3) or (4) revokes an earlier such appointment (including one made in an unrevoked will or codicil) made by the same person in respect of the same child, unless it is clear (whether as the result of an express provision in the later appointment or by any necessary implication) that the purpose of the later appointment is to appoint an additional guardian.

> **Subsection (1)** *If someone appoints a guardian in the way set out in section 5(3) or (4), then a later appointment will revoke any earlier appointment made in the same way. Only if the later appointment is clearly meant to be the appointment of an additional guardian will it not revoke an earlier appointment.*

(2) An appointment under section 5(3) or (4) (including one made in an unrevoked will or codicil) is revoked if the person who made the appointment revokes it by a written and dated instrument which is signed–

(a) by him; or
(b) at his direction, in his presence and in the presence of two witnesses who each attest the signature.

(3) An appointment under section 5(3) or (4) (other than one made in a will or codicil) is revoked if, with the intention of revoking the appointment, the person who made it–

    (a) destroys the instrument by which it was made; or
    (b) has some other person destroy that instrument in his presence.

(3A) An appointment under section 5(3) or (4) (including one made in an unrevoked will or codicil) is revoked if the person appointed is the spouse of the person who made the appointment and either–

    (a) a decree of a court of civil jurisdiction in England and Wales dissolves or annuls the marriage, or
    (b) the marriage is dissolved or annulled and the divorce or annulment is entitled to recognition in England and Wales by virtue of Part II of the Family Law Act 1986,
    unless a contrary intention appears by the appointment.

(4) For the avoidance of doubt, an appointment under section 5(3) or (4) made in a will or codicil is revoked if the will or codicil is revoked.

> *Subsection (2) (3)(3A)(4) These subsections set out the way in which a person can revoke an appointment they have made.*

(5) A person who is appointed as a guardian under section 5(3) or (4) may disclaim his appointment by an instrument in writing signed by him and made within a reasonable time of his first knowing that the appointment has taken effect.

(6) Where regulations are made by the Lord Chancellor prescribing the manner in which such disclaimers must be recorded, no such disclaimer shall have effect unless it is recorded in the prescribed manner.

> *Subsection (5)(6) If someone is appointed a guardian and does not wish to take up the appointment, they can disclaim it in writing, so long as they do so within a reasonable time of knowing the appointment has been made. If there are regulations in place stipulating the manner in which such a disclaimer should be recorded, then they must record it in the correct way in order for it to take effect.*

(7) Any appointment of a guardian under section 5 may be brought to an end at any time by order of the court–

    (a) on the application of any person who has parental responsibility for the child;
    (b) on the application of the child concerned, with leave of the court; or

(c) in any family proceedings, if the court considers that it should be brought to an end even though no application has been made.

> **Subsection (7)** *The court has the power to bring to an end the appointment of a person as a guardian, if any person with parental responsibility applies for it to do so. It may also do so if the child applies, with the court's permission, or if the court itself considers that it should do so.*

7 – (1) A court considering any question with respect to a child under this Act may–

(a) ask a probation officer; or
(b) ask a local authority to arrange for–
  (i) an officer of the authority; or
  (ii) such other person (other than a probation officer) as the authority considers appropriate, to report to the court on such matters relating to the welfare of that child as are required to be dealt with in the report.

> **Section 7**
> **Subsection (1)** *A "probation officer" in these circumstances is called a "court welfare officer".*

(2) The Lord Chancellor may make regulations specifying matters which, unless the court orders otherwise, must be dealt with in any report under this section.

(3) The report may be made in writing, or orally, as the court requires.

(4) Regardless of any enactment or rule of law which would otherwise prevent it from doing so, the court may take account of–

(a) any statement contained in the report; and
(b) any evidence given in respect of the matters referred to in the report, in so far as the statement or evidence is, in the opinion of the court, relevant to the question which it is considering.

> **Subsection (4)** *The court is not bound by the normal rules of evidence in dealing with such reports. The court may consider any matter included in the report that is relevant to the question it is considering.*

(5) It shall be the duty of the authority or probation officer to comply with any request for a report under this section.

PART II

ORDERS WITH RESPECT TO CHILDREN IN FAMILY PROCEEDINGS

GENERAL

8 – (1) In this Act–

'a contact order' means an order requiring the person with whom a child lives, or is to live, to allow the child to visit or stay with the person named in the order, or for that person and the child otherwise to have contact with each other;

'a prohibited steps order' means an order that no step which could be taken by a parent in meeting his parental responsibility for a child, and which is of a kind specified in the order, shall be taken by any person without the consent of the court;

'a residence order' means an order settling the arrangements to be made as to the person with whom a child is to live; and

'a specific issue order' means an order giving directions for the purpose of determining a specific question which has arisen, or which may arise, in connection with any aspect of parental responsibility for a child.

Section 8
Subsection (1) *This subsection provides the definitions of the four types of order, that the court can make in private law proceedings, that is proceedings that do not involve the local authority.*

(2) In this Act 'a section 8 order' means any of the orders mentioned in subsection (1) and any order varying or discharging such an order.

(3) For the purposes of this Act 'family proceedings' means any proceedings–

(a) under the inherent jurisdiction of the High Court in relation to children; and
(b) under the enactments mentioned in subsection (4),

but does not include proceedings on an application for leave under section 100(3).

Subsection (3) *"Family proceedings" do not include applications in wardship, under the inherent jurisdiction of the court by a local authority.*

(4) The enactments are–

    (a) Parts I, II and IV of this Act;
    (b) the Matrimonial Causes Act 1973;
    (c) ...
    (d) the Adoption Act 1976;
    (e) the Domestic Proceedings and Magistrates' Courts Act 1978;
    (f) ...
    (g) Part III of the Matrimonial and Family Proceedings Act 1984;
    (g) the Family Law Act 1996;
    (h) (i) sections 11 and 12 of the Crime and Disorder Act 1998.

9 – (1) No court shall make any section 8 order, other than a residence order, with respect to a child who is in the care of a local authority.

(2) No application may be made by a local authority for a residence order or contact order and no court shall make such an order in favour of a local authority.

(3) A person who is, or was at any time within the last six months, a local authority foster parent of a child may not apply for leave to apply for a section 8 order with respect to the child unless–

    (a) he has the consent of the authority;
    (b) he is relative of the child; or
    (c) the child has lived with him for at least three years preceding the application.

Section 9
Subsection (3) Some people need the leave of the court to make an application under Section 8. Foster parents fall into this category, and must therefore apply to the court for leave before making applications.(See section 10 below).

(4) The period of three years mentioned in subsection (3)(c) need not be continuous but must have begun not more than five years before the making of the application.

(5) No court shall exercise its powers to make a specific issue order or prohibited steps order–

    (a) with a view to achieving a result which could be achieved by making a residence or contact order; or
    (b) in any way which is denied to the High Court (by section 100(2)) in the exercise of its inherent jurisdiction with respect to children.

> **Subsection (5)** *The court must make residence or contact orders in preference to the other Section 8 orders, if the desired outcome can be achieved by those means.*

(6) No court shall make any section 8 order which is to have effect for a period which will end after the child has reached the age of sixteen unless it is satisfied that the circumstances of the case are exceptional.

(7) No court shall make any section 8 order, other than one varying or discharging such an order, with respect to a child who has reached the age of sixteen unless it is satisfied that the circumstances of the case are exceptional.

> **Subsection (6)(7)** *The general rule is that orders concerning children should only be made until the child reaches 16 years of age. The court is however provided with the power to make orders that last beyond the child attaining 16 years, in exceptional circumstances.*

10 – (1) In any family proceedings in which a question arises with respect to the welfare of any child, the court may make a section 8 order with respect to the child if–

    (a) an application for the order has been made by a person who–
        (i) is entitled to apply for a section 8 order with respect to the child; or
        (ii) has obtained the leave of the court to make the application; or
    (b) the court considers that the order should be made even though no such application has been made.

(2) The court may also make a section 8 order with respect to any child on the application of a person who–

    (a) is entitled to apply for a section 8 order with respect to the child; or
    (b) has obtained the leave of the court to make the application.

> **Section 10**
> *Subsection (1)(2) The court can make section 8 orders:*
> *i) on the application of a person entitled to make such an application (see subsection (4) below), or;*
> *ii) on the application of a non-entitled person, if the court grants them leave to make the application, or;*
> *iii) if the court itself decides that such an order should be made.*
> *Those entitled vary according to the order sought. (see subsection (5) below).*

(3) This section is subject to the restrictions imposed by section 9.

(4) The following persons are entitled to apply to the court for any section 8 order with respect to a child–

    (a) any parent or guardian of the child;

    (b) any person in whose favour a residence order is in force with respect to the child.

> *Subsection (4) Parents, guardians, and people with residence orders in respect of a child may apply for any section 8 order.*

(5) The following persons are entitled to apply for a residence or contact order with respect to a child–

    (a) any party to a marriage (whether or not subsisting) in relation to whom the child is a child of the family;

    (b) any person with whom the child has lived for a period of at least three years;

    (c) any person who–

        (i) in any case where a residence order is in force with respect to the child, has the consent of each of the persons in whose favour the order was made;

        (ii) in any case where the child is in the care of a local authority, has the consent of that authority; or

        (iii)in any other case, has the consent of each of those (if any) who have parental responsibility for the child.

Subsection (5) "*child of the family*" *in relation to the parties in a marriage, means either a child of both those parties, or any other child who has been treated by both of those parties as a child of the family. This can include step-children, but does not include a child who has been placed with the parents as foster parents by a local authority.*

(6) A person who would not otherwise be entitled (under the previous provisions of this section) to apply for the variation or discharge of a section 8 order shall be entitled to do so if–

(a) the order was made on his application; or
(b) in the case of a contact order, he is named in the order.

(7) Any person who falls within a category of person prescribed by rules of court is entitled to apply for any such section 8 order as may be prescribed in relation to that category of person.

(8) Where the person applying for leave to make an application for a section 8 order is the child concerned, the court may only grant leave if it is satisfied that he has sufficient understanding to make the proposed application for the section 8 order.

Subsection (8) A child may apply for leave to make an application under Section 8, but the court will again only grant leave if it is satisfied that he has sufficient understanding.

(9) Where the person applying for leave to make an application for a section 8 order is not the child concerned, the court shall, in deciding whether or not to grant leave, have particular regard to–

(a) the nature of the proposed application for the section 8 order;
(b) the applicant's connection with the child;
(c) any risk there might be of that proposed application disrupting the child's life to such an extent that he would be harmed by it; and
(d) where the child is being looked after by a local authority–
  (i) the authority's plans for the child's future; and
  (ii) the wishes and feelings of the child's parents.

Subsection (9) In considering an application for leave the court will take into account the welfare checklist, but it will give special consideration to the four issues set out in this subsection.

(10) The period of three years mentioned in subsection (5)(b) need not be continuous but must not have begun more than five years before, or ended more than three months before, the making of the application.

11 – (1) In proceedings in which any question of making a section 8 order, or any other question with respect to such an order, arises, the court shall (in the light of any rules made by virtue of subsection (2))–

(a) draw up a timetable with a view to determining the question without delay; and

(b) give such directions as it considers appropriate for the purpose of ensuring, so far as is reasonably practicable, that that timetable is adhered to.

(2) Rules of court may–

(a) specify periods within which specified steps must be taken in relation to proceedings in which such questions arise; and

(b) make other provision with respect to such proceedings for the purpose of ensuring, so far as is reasonably practicable, that such questions are determined without delay.

Section 11
Subsections (1)(2) These provisions are included in order to limit delay in any case. The court will strictly control the timetable of proceedings.

(3) Where a court has power to make a section 8 order, it may do so at any time during the course of the proceedings in question even though it is not in a position to dispose finally of those proceedings.

Subsection (3) The court has a very wide discretion to make any section 8 order in proceedings relating to a child, at any time. "Interim" orders can be made at a stage prior to the final hearing of a matter.

(4) Where a residence order is made in favour of two or more persons who do not themselves all live together, the order may specify the periods during which the child is to live in the different households concerned.

Subsection (4) This situation is known as joint or shared residence. The order can specify in detail how much time the child is to spend at each residence.

(5) Where–

    (a) a residence order has been made with respect to a child; and

    (b) as a result of the order the child lives, or is to live, with one of two parents who each have parental responsibility for him,

    the residence order shall cease to have effect if the parents live together for a continuous period of more than six months.

(6) A contact order which requires the parent with whom a child lives to allow the child to visit, or otherwise have contact with, his other parent shall cease to have effect if the parents live together for a continuous period of more than six months.

> **Subsection (5)(6)** *Contact and residence orders lapse after the child's parents live together for six months.*

(7) A section 8 order may–

    (a) contain directions about how it is to be carried into effect;

    (b) impose conditions which must be complied with by any person–

        (i) in whose favour the order is made;

        (ii) who is a parent of the child concerned;

        (iii) who is not a parent of his but who has parental responsibility for him; or

        (iv) with whom the child is living,

            and to whom the conditions are expressed to apply;

    (c) be made to have effect for a specified period, or contain provisions which are to have effect for a specified period;

    (d) make such incidental, supplemental or consequential provision as the court thinks fit.

12 – (1) Where the court makes a residence order in favour of the father of a child it shall, if the father would not otherwise have parental responsibility for the child, also make an order under section 4 giving him that responsibility.

(2) Where the court makes a residence order in favour of any person who is not the parent or guardian of the child concerned that person shall have parental responsibility for the child while the residence order remains in force.

(3) Where a person has parental responsibility for a child as a result of subsection (2), he shall not have the right–

    (a) to consent, or refuse to consent, to the making of an application with respect to the child under section 18 of the Adoption Act 1976;

    (b) to agree, or refuse to agree, to the making of an adoption order, or an order under section 55 of the Act of 1976, with respect to the child; or

    (c) to appoint a guardian for the child.

(4) Where subsection (1) requires the court to make an order under section 4 in respect of the father of a child, the court shall not bring that order to an end at any time while the residence order concerned remains in force.

Section 12
This section provides for a person with whom the child lives, under a residence order, to have parental responsibility for that child. If the residence order is in favour of the father of the child, a parental responsibility order is made. It is neither a limited nor a finite order. Where the person is not the parent or guardian of the child they have parental responsibility for the child, but there is no separate order and it will automatically come to an end once the residence order ceases to be in force. There are also a number of limitations on their rights, subsection (3).

13 – (1) Where a residence order is in force with respect to a child, no person may–

  (a) cause the child to be known by a new surname; or
  (b) remove him from the United Kingdom;

    without either the written consent of every person who has parental responsibility for the child or the leave of the court.

Section 13
Subsection (1) This subsection encourages those with parental responsibility to reach agreement on issues if at all possible, and to only resort to the court if consensus cannot be reached.

(2) Subsection (1)(b) does not prevent the removal of a child, for a period of less than one month, by the person in whose favour the residence order is made.

(3) In making a residence order with respect to a child the court may grant the leave required by subsection (1)(b), either generally or for specified purposes.

Section 13(3)
At the time of making a residence order the court can grant leave (give permission) for the child's name to be changed or for the child to be taken out of the UK. Once the order is made, further applications for leave will need to be made to the court if a person wishes for the child to be known by a different surname, or to take the child outside of the UK, and those with parental responsibility do not consent.

14 – (1) Where–

(a) a residence order is in force with respect to a child in favour of any person; and

(b) any other person (including one in whose favour the order is also in force) is in breach of the arrangements settled by that order,

the person mentioned in paragraph (a) may, as soon as the requirement in subsection (2) is complied with, enforce the order under section 63(3) of the Magistrates' Courts Act 1980 as if it were an order requiring the other person to produce the child to him.

(2) The requirement is that a copy of the residence order has been served on the other person.

(3) Subsection (1) is without prejudice to any other remedy open to the person in whose favour the residence order is in force.

Section 14
This enables a person to enforce a residence order in the Magistrates Court. If the original order was made in a higher court i.e. the County Court or High Court, then enforcement proceedings may be brought in a higher court.

15 – (1) Schedule 1 (which consists primarily of the re-enactment, with consequential amendments and minor modifications, of provisions of [section 6 of the Family Law Reform Act 1969], the Guardianship of Minors Acts 1971 and 1973, the Children Act 1975 and of sections 15 and 16 of the Family Law Reform Act 1987) makes provision in relation to financial relief for children.

(2) The powers of a magistrates' court under section 60 of the Magistrates' Courts Act 1980 to revoke, revive or vary an order for the periodical payment of money [and the power of a clerk of a magistrates' court to vary such an order] shall not apply in relation to an order made under Schedule 1.

Section 15
Prior to the making of the Children Act there were a number of acts that dealt with the issue of financial provision for children. These have now been codified in Schedule 1 of this Act.(see Schedule 1)

FAMILY ASSISTANCE ORDERS

16 – (1) Where, in any family proceedings, the court has power to make an order under this Part with respect to any child, it may (whether or not it makes such an order) make an order requiring–

(a) a probation officer to be made available; or

(b) a local authority to make an officer of the authority available,

to advise, assist and (where appropriate) befriend any person named in the order.

(2) The persons who may be named in an order under this section ('a family assistance order') are–

(a) any parent or guardian of the child;

(b) any person with whom the child is living or in whose favour a contact order is in force with respect to the child;

(c) the child himself.

(3) No court may make a family assistance order unless–

(a) it is satisfied that the circumstances of the case are exceptional; and

(b) it has obtained the consent of every person to be named in the order other than the child.

(4) A family assistance order may direct–

(a) the person named in the order; or

(b) such of the persons named in the order as may be specified in the order,

to take such steps as may be so specified with a view to enabling the officer concerned to be kept informed of the address of any person named in the order and to be allowed to visit any such person.

(5) Unless it specifies a shorter period, a family assistance order shall have effect for a period of six months beginning with the day on which it is made.

(6) Where–

(a) a family assistance order is in force with respect to a child; and

(b) a section 8 order is also in force with respect to the child,

the officer concerned may refer to the court the question whether the section 8 order should be varied or discharged.

(7) A family assistance order shall not be made so as to require a local authority to make an officer of theirs available unless–

(a) the authority agree; or

(b) the child concerned lives or will live within their area.

(8) Where a family assistance order requires a probation officer to be made available, the officer shall be selected in accordance with arrangements made by the probation committee for the area in which the child lives or will live.

(9) If the selected probation officer is unable to carry out his duties, or dies, another probation officer shall be selected in the same manner.

Section 16
Family Assistance Orders may be made in any proceedings where the court feels that it would benefit a child to have an officer of the local authority advise, assist and befriend, any person. The persons who may be named in such an order are set out in subsection (2). The order may only be made with the consent of the named person or person, and may last for no more than six months.

PART III

LOCAL AUTHORITY SUPPORT FOR CHILDREN AND FAMILIES

PROVISION OF SERVICES FOR CHILDREN AND THEIR FAMILIES

17 – (1) It shall be the general duty of every local authority (in addition to the other duties imposed on them by this Part)–

   (a) to safeguard and promote the welfare of children within their area who are in need; and

   (b) so far as is consistent with that duty, to promote the upbringing of such children by their families,by providing a range and level of services appropriate to those children's needs.

(2) For the purpose principally of facilitating the discharge of their general duty under this section, every local authority shall have the specific duties and powers set out in Part 1 of Schedule 2.

(3) Any service provided by an authority in the exercise of functions conferred on them by this section may be provided for the family of a particular child in need or for any member of his family, if it is provided with a view to safeguarding or promoting the child's welfare.

(4) The Secretary of State may by order amend any provision of Part I of Schedule 2 or add any further duty or power to those for the time being mentioned there.

(5) Every local authority–

   (a) shall facilitate the provision by others (including in particular voluntary organisations) of services which the authority have power to provide by virtue of this section, or section 18, 20, 23 or 24; and

   (b) may make such arrangements as they see fit for any person to act on their behalf in the provision of any such service.

(6) The services provided by a local authority in the exercise of functions conferred on them by this section may include giving assistance in kind or, in exceptional circumstances, in cash.

(7) Assistance may be unconditional or subject to conditions as to the repayment of the assistance or of its value (in whole or in part).

(8) Before giving any assistance or imposing any conditions, a local authority shall have regard to the means of the child concerned and of each of his parents.

(9) No person shall be liable to make any repayment of assistance or of its value at any time when he is in receipt of income support, [family credit or disability working allowance] under [Part VII of the Social Security Contributions and Benefits Act 1992] [or of an income-based jobseeker's allowance].

(10) For the purposes of this Part a child shall be taken to be in need if–

  (a) he is unlikely to achieve or maintain, or to have the opportunity of achieving or maintaining, a reasonable standard of health or development without the provision for him of services by a local authority under this Part;
  (b) his health or development is likely to be significantly impaired, or further impaired, without the provision for him of such services; or
  (c) he is disabled,

  and 'family', in relation to such a child, includes any person who has parental responsibility for the child and any other person with whom he has been living.

(11) For the purposes of this Part, a child is disabled if he is blind, deaf or dumb or suffers from mental disorder of any kind or is substantially and permanently handicapped by illness, injury or congenital deformity or such other disability as may be prescribed; and in this Part–

'development' means physical, intellectual, emotional, social or behavioural development; and

'health' means physical or mental health.

Section 17. Provision of services for children in need, their families and others. *This section deals in general terms with the duty of the local authority to needy children within its area and the services that may be provided to fulfil its obligations. See subsections (10) and (11) for definitions of 'child in need', 'disabled', 'family', 'development' and 'health'. It is important to note the emphasis again on the welfare principle and, at (17) (1) (b) on the local authority's obligation to keep the child with its family wherever possible. This is so much so that subsection (3) gives the local authority power to provide the services for any member of the child's family, as well as to the child alone, if it promotes the child welfare.*

18 – (1) Every local authority shall provide such day care for children in need within their area who are–

  (a) aged five or under; and
  (b) not yet attending schools,

    as is appropriate.

(2) A local authority may provide day care for children within their area who satisfy the conditions mentioned in subsection (1)(a) and (b) even though they are not in need.

(3) A local authority may provide facilities (including training, advice, guidance and counselling) for those–

(a) caring for children in day care; or
(b) who at any time accompany such children while they are in day care.

(4) In this section 'day care' means any form of care or supervised activity provided for children during the day (whether or not it is provided on a regular basis).

(5) Every local authority shall provide for children in need within their area who are attending any school such care or supervised activities as is appropriate–

(a) outside school hours; or
(b) during school holidays.

(6) A local authority may provide such care or supervised activities for children within their area who are attending any school even though those children are not in need.

(7) In this section 'supervised activity' means an activity supervised by a responsible person.

Section 18. Day care for pre-school and other children

This sets out the obligations placed on the local authority to provide day care or, as is appropriate, supervised activities and care outside school hours for children in need in its area. It also gives the local authority power to provide such care and services for children who are not in need. For definitions of 'day care' and 'supervised activity', see subsections (4) and (7) respectively.

19 – (1) Every local authority in England and Wales shall review–

(a) the provision which they make under section 18;
(b) the extent to which the services of child minders are available within their area with respect to children under the age of eight; and
(c) the provision for day care within their area made for children under the age of eight by persons other than the authority, required to register under section 71(1)(b).

(2) A review under subsection (1) shall be conducted–

(a) together with the appropriate local education authority; and
(b) at least once in every review period.

(3) (applies to Scotland only)

(4) In conducting any such review, the two authorities or, in Scotland, the authority shall have regard to the provision made with respect to children under the age of eight in relevant establishments within their area.

(5) In this section–

'relevant establishment' means any establishment which is mentioned in paragraphs 3 and 4 of Schedule 9 (hospitals, schools and other establishments exempt from the registration requirements which apply in relation to the provision of day care); and

'review period' means the period of one year beginning with the commencement of this section and each subsequent period of three years beginning with an anniversary of that commencement.

(6) Where a local authority have conducted a review under this section they shall publish the result of the review–

   (a) as soon as is reasonably practicable;
   (b) in such form as they consider appropriate; and
   (c) together with any proposals they may have with respect to the matters reviewed.

(7) The authorities conducting any review under this section shall have regard to–

   (a) any representations made to any one of them by any relevant [Health Authority, Special Health Authority] or health board; and
   (b) any other representations which they consider to be relevant.

(8) (applies to Scotland only)

Section 19. Review of provision for day care, child minding etc.
This sets out the requirement of the local authority, in conjunction with the local education authority, to review the provision for day care etc they make under section 18. It also provides for the provision of child minding services and day care by people other than the authority, for children under the age of eight in its area. The review period is defined by subsection (5). The local authority must publish a report setting out the results of the review as soon as is reasonably practicable after it has completed the review, (subsection (6)).

Provision of accommodation for children

20 – (1) Every local authority shall provide accommodation for any child in need within their area who appears to them to require accommodation as a result of–

   (a) there being no person who has parental responsibility for him;
   (b) his being lost or having been abandoned; or

(c) the person who has been caring for him being prevented (whether or not permanently, and for whatever reason) from providing him with suitable accommodation or care.

(2) Where a local authority provide accommodation under subsection (1) for a child who is ordinarily resident in the area of another local authority, that other local authority may take over the provision of accommodation for the child within–

(a) three months of being notified in writing that the child is being provided with accommodation; or
(b) such other longer period as may be prescribed.

(3) Every local authority shall provide accommodation for any child in need within their area who has reached the age of sixteen and whose welfare the authority consider is likely to be seriously prejudiced if they do not provide him with accommodation.

(4) A local authority may provide accommodation for any child within their area (even though a person who has parental responsibility for him is able to provide him with accommodation) if they consider that to do so would safeguard or promote the child's welfare.

(5) A local authority may provide accommodation for any person who has reached the age of sixteen but is under twenty-one in any community home which takes children who have reached the age of sixteen if they consider that to do so would safeguard or promote his welfare.

(6) Before providing accommodation under this section, a local authority shall, so far as is reasonably practicable and consistent with the child's welfare–

(a) ascertain the child's wishes regarding the provision of accommodation; and
(b) give due consideration (having regard to his age and understanding) to such wishes of the child as they have been able to ascertain.

(7) A local authority may not provide accommodation under this section for any child if any person who–

(a) has parental responsibility for him; and
(b) is willing and able to–
  (i) provide accommodation for him; or
  (ii) arrange for accommodation to be provided for him,
    objects.

(8) Any person who has parental responsibility for a child may at any time remove the child from accommodation provided by or on behalf of the local authority under this section.

(9) Subsections (7) and (8) do not apply while any person–

(a) in whose favour a residence order is in force with respect to the child; or
(b) who has care of the child by virtue of an order made in the exercise of the High Court's inherent jurisdiction with respect to children,

agrees to the child being looked after in accommodation provided by or on behalf of the local authority.

(10) Where there is more than one such person as is mentioned in subsection (9), all of them must agree

(11) Subsections (7) and (8) do not apply where a child who has reached the age of sixteen agrees to being provided with accommodation under this section.

Section 20. Provision of accommodation for children: general
This sets out the local authority's duties and powers as far as providing accommodation for the children in need in its area is concerned. This includes provision of accommodation for sixteen year olds and over (see subsections (3), (5) and (11)). Note the emphasis again on the child's wishes and feelings being ascertained and being given due consideration (subsection (6)). Note also that under this section the local authority can only accommodate with the consent of all those who have parental responsibility for the child, although the objection of any such person can be overridden by the consent of a person with a residence order for the child or who has care by virtue of an order made in the exercise of the High Court's inherent jurisdiction with respect to children (see subsection 9).

21 – (1) Every local authority shall make provision for the reception and accommodation of children who are removed or kept away from home under Part V.

(2) Every local authority shall receive, and provide accommodation for, children–

(a) in police protection whom they are requested to receive under section 46(3)(f);
(b) whom they are requested to receive under section 38(6) of the Police and Criminal Evidence Act 1984;
(c) who are–
  (i) on remand under [section 16(3A) or] 23(1) of the Children and Young Persons Act 1969; or
  (ii) the subject of a supervision order imposing a residence requirement under section 12AA of that Act,

and with respect to whom they are the designated authority.

(3) Where a child has been–

(a) removed under Part V; or
(b) detained under section 38 of the Police and Criminal Evidence Act 1984,

and he is not being provided with accommodation by a local authority or in a hospital vested in the Secretary of State [or otherwise made available pursuant to arrangements made by a [Health Authority]], any reasonable expenses of accommodating him shall be recoverable from the local authority in whose area he is ordinarily resident.

Section 21. Provision of accommodation for children in police protection or detention or on remand, etc
This relates also to the obligation on the local authority to provide accommodation for children removed from their families under emergency protection orders, or police protection orders.

Duties of local authorities in relation to children looked after by them

22 – (1) In this Act, any reference to a child who is looked after by a local authority is a reference to a child who is–

(a) in their care; or
(b) provided with accommodation by the authority in the exercise of any functions (in particular those under this Act) which stand referred to their social services committee under the Local Authority Social Services Act 1970.

Section 22. General duty of local authority in relation to children looked after by them.
Subsection (1) *A child is 'looked after' when it is in the care of the local authority or is being accommodated by it for longer than 24 hours.*

(2) In subsection (1) 'accommodation' means accommodation which is provided for a continuous period of more than 24 hours.

(3) It shall be the duty of a local authority looking after any child–

(a) to safeguard and promote his welfare; and
(b) to make such use of services available for children cared for by their own parents as appears to the authority reasonable in his case.

(4) Before making any decision with respect to a child whom they are looking after, or proposing to look after, a local authority shall, so far as is reasonably practicable, ascertain the wishes and feelings of–

(a) the child;
(b) his parents;

(c) any person who is not a parent of his but who has parental responsibility for him; and

(d) any other person whose wishes and feelings the authority consider to be relevant, regarding the matter to be decided.

(5) In making any such decision a local authority shall give due consideration–

(a) having regard to his age and understanding, to such wishes and feelings of the child as they have been able to ascertain;

(b) to such wishes and feelings of any person mentioned in subsection (4)(b) to (d) as they have been able to ascertain; and

(c) to the child's religious persuasion, racial origin and cultural and linguistic background.

Subsections (3)(4)(5) *The welfare principle and requirement to consult with the looked after/proposed looked after child and in particular his or her parents in the decision-making process are emphasised, as is the need to consider the child's background in all its aspects.*

(6) If it appears to a local authority that it is necessary, for the purposes of protecting members of the public from serious injury, to exercise their powers with respect to a child whom they are looking after in a manner which may not be consistent with their duties under this section, they may do so.

(7) If the Secretary of State considers it necessary, for the purpose of protecting members of the public from serious injury, to give directions to a local authority with respect to the exercise of their powers with respect to a child whom they are looking after, he may give such directions to the authority.

(8) Where any such directions are given to an authority they shall comply with them even though doing so is inconsistent with their duties under this section.

Subsections (6)(7)(8) *These override the requirement of the local authority to comply with its obligations under this section, where it appears to the authority or the Secretary of State necessary in order to protect members of the public from serious injury.*

23 – (1) It shall be the duty of any local authority looking after a child–

(a) when he is in their care, to provide accommodation for him; and

(b) to maintain him in other respects apart from providing accommodation for him.

(2) A local authority shall provide accommodation and maintenance for any child whom they are looking after by–

(a) placing him (subject to subsection (5) and any regulations made by the Secretary of State) with–
 (i) a family;
 (ii) a relative of his; or
 (iii) any other suitable person,

 on such terms as to payment by the authority and otherwise as the authority may determine;

(b) maintaining him in a community home;
(c) maintaining him in a voluntary home;
(d) maintaining him in a registered children's home;
(e) maintaining him in a home provided [in accordance with arrangements made] by the Secretary of State under section 82(5) on such terms as the Secretary of State may from time to time determine; or
(f) making such other arrangements as–
 (i) seem appropriate to them; and
 (ii) comply with any regulations made by the Secretary of State.

(3) Any person with whom a child has been placed under subsection (2)(a) is referred to in this Act as a local authority foster parent unless he falls within subsection (4).

(4) A person falls within this subsection if he is–

(a) a parent of the child;
(b) a person who is not a parent of the child but who has parental responsibility for him; or
(c) where the child is in care and there was a residence order in force with respect to him immediately before the care order was made, a person in whose favour the residence order was made.

(5) Where a child is in the care of a local authority, the authority may only allow him to live with a person who falls within subsection (4) in accordance with regulations made by the Secretary of State.

[(5A) For the purposes of subsection (5) a child shall be regarded as living with a person if he stays with that person for a continuous period of more than 24 hours.]

(6) Subject to any regulations made by the Secretary of State for the purposes of this subsection, any local authority looking after a child shall make arrangements to enable him to live with–

(a) a person falling within subsection (4); or
(b) a relative, friend or other person connected with him,
 unless that would not be reasonably practicable or consistent with his welfare.

(7) Where a local authority provide accommodation for a child whom they are looking after, they shall, subject to the provisions of this Part and so far as is reasonably practicable and consistent with his welfare, secure that–

(a) the accommodation is near his home; and
(b) where the authority are also providing accommodation for a sibling of his, they are accommodated together.

(8) Where a local authority provide accommodation for a child whom they are looking after and who is disabled, they shall, so far as is reasonably practicable, secure that the accommodation is not unsuitable to his particular needs.

(9) Part II of Schedule 2 shall have effect for the purposes of making further provision as to children looked after by local authorities and in particular as to the regulations that may be made under subsections (2)(a) and (f) and (5).

(10)

Section 23. Provision of accommodation and maintenance by local authority for children whom they are looking after.
This sets out the ways in which the local authority can provide accommodation for the children it is looking after. Note that the local authority can accommodate the child by placing him or her with his or her parents or relative, and subsection (6) obliges it to do so unless it 'would not be reasonably practicable or consistent with his welfare'. Note also the emphasis on providing accommodation near to the family home and keeping siblings together (subsection (7)).

Refer to Part II of Schedule 2 for further detail.

Advice and assistance for certain children

24 – (1) Where a child is being looked after by a local authority, it shall be the duty of the authority to advise, assist and befriend him with a view to promoting his welfare when he ceases to be looked after by them.

(2) In this Part 'a person qualifying for advice and assistance' means a person within the area of the authority who is under twenty-one and who was, at any time after reaching the age of sixteen but while still a child–

(a) looked after by a local authority;
(b) accommodated by or on behalf of a voluntary organisation;
(c) accommodated in a registered children's home;
(d) accommodated–
    (i) by any [Health Authority, Special Health Authority] or local education authority; or

(ii) in any residential care home, nursing home or mental nursing home [or in any accommodation provided by a National Health Service trust], for a consecutive period of at least three months; or

(e) privately fostered,

but who is no longer so looked after, accommodated or fostered.

(3) Subsection (2)(d) applies even if the period of three months mentioned there began before the child reached the age of sixteen.

(4) Where–

(a) a local authority know that there is within their area a person qualifying for advice and assistance;

(b) the conditions in subsection (5) are satisfied; and

(c) that person has asked them for help of a kind which they can give under this section, they shall (if he was being looked after by a local authority or was accommodated by or on behalf of a voluntary organisation) and may (in any other case) advise and befriend him.

(5) The conditions are that–

(a) it appears to the authority that the person concerned is in need of advice and being befriended;

(b) where that person was not being looked after by the authority, they are satisfied that the person by whom he was being looked after does not have the necessary facilities for advising or befriending him.

(6) Where as a result of this section a local authority are under a duty, or are empowered, to advise and befriend a person, they may also give him assistance.

(7) Assistance given under subsections (1) to (6) may be in kind or, in exceptional circumstances, in cash.

(8) A local authority may give assistance to any person who qualifies for advice and assistance by virtue of subsection (2)(a) by–

(a) contributing to expenses incurred by him in living near the place where he is, or will be–

(i) employed or seeking employment; or

(ii) receiving education or training; or

(b) making a grant to enable him to meet expenses connected with his education or training.

(9) Where a local authority are assisting the person under subsection (8) by making a contribution or grant with respect to a course of education or training, they may–

(a) continue to do so even though he reaches the age of twenty-one before completing the course; and

(b) disregard any interruption in his attendance on the course if he resumes it as soon as is reasonably practicable.

(10) Subsections (7) to (9) of section 17 shall apply in relation to assistance given under this section (otherwise than under subsection (8)) as they apply in relation to assistance given under that section.

(11) Where it appears to a local authority that a person whom they have been advising and befriending under this section, as a person qualifying for advice and assistance, proposes to live, or is living, in the area of another local authority, they shall inform that other local authority.

(12) Where a child who is accommodated–

(a) by a voluntary organisation or in a registered children's home;
(b) by any [Health Authority, Special Health Authority] or local education authority; or
(c) in any residential care home, nursing home or mental nursing home, [or any accommodation provided by a National Health Service trust,]

ceases to be so accommodated, after reaching the age of sixteen, the organisation, authority or (as the case may be) person carrying on the home shall inform the local authority within whose area the child proposes to live.

(13) Subsection (12) only applies, by virtue of paragraph (b) or (c), if the accommodation has been provided for a consecutive period of at least three months.

(14) Every local authority shall establish a procedure for considering any representations (including any complaint) made to them by a person qualifying for advice and assistance about the discharge of their functions under this Part in relation to him.

(15) In carrying out any consideration of representations under subsection (14), a local authority shall comply with any regulations made by the Secretary of State for the purposes of this subsection.]

Section 24. Advice and assistance for certain children
This deals with the local authorities obligations towards children it is looking after and other qualifying persons (see subsection (2)), to advise, befriend and assist with a view to promoting the child's or person's welfare post being looked after by the authority. This assistance can exceptionally take the form of cash (see subsection (6)).

Secure accommodation

25 – (1) Subject to the following provisions of this section, a child who is being looked after by a local authority may not be placed, and, if placed, may not be kept, in accommodation provided for the purpose of restricting liberty ('secure accommodation') unless it appears–

(a) that–
  (i) he has a history of absconding and is likely to abscond from any other description of accommodation; and
  (ii) if he absconds, he is likely to suffer significant harm; or
(b) that if he is kept in any other description of accommodation he is likely to injure himself or other persons.

(2) The Secretary of State may by regulations–

(a) specify a maximum period–
  (i) beyond which a child may not be kept in secure accommodation without the authority of the court; and
  (ii) for which the court may authorise a child to be kept in secure accommodation;
(b) empower the court from time to time to authorise a child to be kept in secure accommodation for such further period as the regulations may specify; and
(c) provide that applications to the court under this section shall be made only by local authorities.

(3) It shall be the duty of a court hearing an application under this section to determine whether any relevant criteria for keeping a child in secure accommodation are satisfied in his case.

(4) If a court determines that any such criteria are satisfied, it shall make an order authorising the child to be kept in secure accommodation and specifying the maximum period for which he may be so kept.

(5) On any adjournment of the hearing of an application under this section, a court may make an interim order permitting the child to be kept during the period of the adjournment in secure accommodation.

(6) No court shall exercise the powers conferred by this section in respect of a child who is not legally represented in that court unless, having been informed of his right to apply for legal aid [-] and having had the opportunity to do so, he refused or failed to apply.

(7) The Secretary of State may by regulations provide that–

(a) this section shall or shall not apply to any description of children specified in the regulations;
(b) this section shall have effect in relation to children of a description specified in the regulations subject to such modifications as may be so specified;
(c) such other provisions as may be so specified shall have effect for the purpose of determining whether a child of a description specified in the regulations may be placed or kept in secure accommodation.

(8) The giving of an authorisation under this section shall not prejudice any power of any court in England and Wales or Scotland to give directions relating to the child to whom the authorisation relates.

(9) This section is subject to section 20(8).

Section 25. Use of accommodation for restricting liberty.
This sort of accommodation is commonly referred to as 'secure accommodation'.

This section sets out the criteria under which the local authority may accommodate a child in a way that restricts his or her liberty. In practice a local authority rarely does this without a court order, because of objections raised on the child's behalf or by those who have parental responsibility for the child. The section clearly sets out the way the court should proceed in making such an order. This is a draconian order and therefore care must be taken to ensure that the criteria are fulfilled before making it.

Supplemental

26 – (1) The Secretary of State may make regulations requiring the case of each child who is being looked after by a local authority to be reviewed in accordance with the provisions of the regulations.

(2) The regulations may, in particular, make provision–

(a) as to the manner in which each case is to be reviewed;

(b) as to the considerations to which the local authority are to have regard in reviewing each case;

(c) as to the time when each case is first to be reviewed and the frequency of subsequent reviews;

(d) requiring the authority, before conducting any review, to seek the views of–
   (i) the child;
   (ii) his parents;
   (iii) any person who is not a parent of his but who has parental responsibility for him; and
   (iv) any other person whose views the authority consider to be relevant, including, in particular, the views of those persons in relation to any particular matter which is to be considered in the course of the review;

(e) requiring the authority to consider, in the case of a child who is in their care, whether an application should be made to discharge the care order;

(f) requiring the authority to consider, in the case of a child in accommodation provided by the authority, whether the accommodation accords with the requirements of this Part;

(g) requiring the authority to inform the child, so far as is reasonably practicable, of any steps he may take under this Act;

(h) requiring the authority to make arrangements, including arrangements with such other bodies providing services as it considers appropriate, to implement any decision which they propose to make in the course, or as a result, of the review;

(i) requiring the authority to notify details of the result of the review and of any decision taken by them in consequence of the review to–

    (i) the child;

    (ii) his parents;

    (iii) any person who is not a parent of his but who has parental responsibility for him; and

    (iv) any other person whom they consider ought to be notified;

(j) requiring the authority to monitor the arrangements which they have made with a view to ensuring that they comply with the regulations.

(3) Every local authority shall establish a procedure for considering any representations (including any complaint) made to them by–

(a) any child who is being looked after by them or who is not being looked after by them but is in need;

(b) a parent of his;

(c) any person who is not a parent of his but who has parental responsibility for him;

(d) any local authority foster parent;

(e) such other person as the authority consider has a sufficient interest in the child's welfare to warrant his representations being considered by them, about the discharge by the authority of any of their functions under this Part in relation to the child.

Section 26. Review of cases and inquiries into representations
Subsection (3) The local authority is obliged to establish a procedure for considering representations (normally complaints) made by those people specified as to the carrying out the authority's functions under Part III of the Act.

(4) The procedure shall ensure that at least one person who is not a member or officer of the authority takes part in–

(a) the consideration; and

(b) any discussions which are held by the authority about the action (if any) to be taken in relation to the child in the light of the consideration.

(5) In carrying out any consideration of representations under this section a local authority shall comply with any regulations made by the Secretary of State for the purpose of regulating the procedure to be followed.

(6) The Secretary of State may make regulations requiring local authorities to monitor the arrangements that they have made with a view to ensuring that they comply with any regulations made for the purposes of subsection (5).

(7) Where any representation has been considered under the procedure established by a local authority under this section, the authority shall–

(a) have due regard to the findings of those considering the representation; and
(b) take such steps as are reasonably practicable to notify (in writing)–
   (i) the person making the representation;
   (ii) the child (if the authority consider that he has sufficient understanding); and
   (iii) such other persons (if any) as appear to the authority to be likely to be affected,

of the authority's decision in the matter and their reasons for taking that decision and of any action which they have taken, or propose to take.

(8) Every local authority shall give such publicity to their procedure for considering representations under this section as they consider appropriate.

27– (1) Where it appears to a local authority that any authority ... mentioned in subsection (3) could, by taking any specified action, help in the exercise of any of their functions under this Part, they may request the help of that other authority ..., specifying the action in question.

(2) An authority whose help is so requested shall comply with the request if it is compatible with their own statutory or other duties and obligations and does not unduly prejudice the discharge of any of their functions.

(3) The [authorities] are–

(a) any local authority;
(b) any local education authority;
(c) any local housing authority;
(d) any [Health Authority, Special Health Authority] [or National Health Service trust]; and
(e) any person authorised by the Secretary of State for the purposes of this section.

(4) ...

28 – (1) Where–

(a) a child is being looked after by a local authority; and
(b) the authority propose to provide accommodation for him in an establishment at which education is provided for children who are accommodated there,

they shall, so far as is reasonably practicable, consult the appropriate local education authority before doing so.

(2) Where any such proposal is carried out, the local authority shall, as soon as is reasonably practicable, inform the appropriate local education authority of the arrangements that have been made for the child's accommodation.

(3) Where the child ceases to be accommodated as mentioned in subsection (1)(b), the local authority shall inform the appropriate local education authority.

(4) In this section 'the appropriate local education authority' means–

  (a) the local education authority within whose area the local authority's area falls; or

  (b) where the child has special educational needs and a statement of his needs is maintained under [Part IV of the Education Act 1996], the local education authority who maintain the statement.

29 – (1) Where a local authority provide any service under section 17 or 18, other than advice, guidance or counselling, they may recover from a person specified in subsection (4) such charge for the service as they consider reasonable.

(2) Where the authority are satisfied that that person's means are insufficient for it to be reasonably practicable for him to pay the charge, they shall not require him to pay more than he can reasonably be expected to pay.

(3) No person shall be liable to pay any charge under subsection (1) at any time when he is in receipt of income support[, family credit or disability working allowance] under [Part VII of the Social Security Contributions and Benefits Act 1992] [or of an income-based jobseeker's allowance].

(4) The persons are–

  (a) where the service is provided for a child under sixteen, each of his parents;

  (b) where it is provided for a child who has reached the age of sixteen, the child himself; and

  (c) where it is provided for a member of the child's family, that member.

(5) Any charge under subsection (1) may, without prejudice to any other method of recovery, be recovered summarily as a civil debt.

(6) Part III of Schedule 2 makes provision in connection with contributions towards the maintenance of children who are being looked after by local authorities and consists of the re-enactment with modifications of provisions in Part V of the Child Care Act 1980.

(7) Where a local authority provide any accommodation under section 20(1) for a child who was (immediately before they began to look after him) ordinarily resident within the area of another local authority, they may recover from that other authority any reasonable expenses incurred by them in providing the accommodation and maintaining him.

(8) Where a local authority provide accommodation under section 21(1) or (2)(a) or (b) for a child who is ordinarily resident within the area of another local authority and they are not maintaining him in–

  (a) a community home provided by them;

  (b) a controlled community home; or

  (c) a hospital vested in the Secretary of State, [or any other hospital made available pursuant to arrangements made by a [Health Authority]], they may recover from that other authority any reasonable expenses incurred by them in providing the accommodation and maintaining him.

(9) Where a local authority comply with any request under section 27(2) in relation to a child or other person who is not ordinarily resident within their area, they may recover from the local authority in whose area the child or person is ordinarily resident any [reasonable expenses] incurred by them in respect of that person.

Section 29. Recoupment of cost of providing services etc
This section empowers the local authority to recoup costs for providing services under section 17 and 18 from, amongst others, (and where appropriate) the parents of a child and the child him or herself where the child was over sixteen.

30 – (1) Nothing in this Part shall affect any duty imposed on a local authority by or under any other enactment.

(2) Any question arising under section 20(2), 21(3) or 29(7) to (9) as to the ordinary residence of a child shall be determined by agreement between the local authorities concerned or, in default of agreement, by the Secretary of State.

(3) Where the functions conferred on a local authority by this Part and the functions of a local education authority are concurrent, the Secretary of State may by regulations provide by which authority the functions are to be exercised.

(4) The Secretary of State may make regulations for determining, as respects any local education authority functions specified in the regulations, whether a child who is being looked after by a local authority is to be treated, for purposes so specified, as a child of parents of sufficient resources or as a child of parents without resources.

PART IV

CARE AND SUPERVISION

General

31 – (1) On the application of any local authority or authorised person, the court may make an order–

(a) placing the child with respect to whom the application is made in the care of a designated local authority; or
(b) putting him under the supervision of a designated local authority or of a probation officer.

Section 31 Care and supervision orders

Subsection (1) This subsection gives the court power to make a care or supervision order when an application has been made by a local authority or authorised person. An authorised person is defined in section 31(9) as being the National Society for the Prevention of Cruelty to Children and any of its officers, and any other person or officer of any other body authorised by order of the Secretary of State. No person or organisation other than the National Society for the Prevention of Cruelty to Children has yet been so authorised.

A designated local authority is defined in section 31(8) of the Act as being: "the authority in whose area the child is ordinarily resident or, where the child does not live in the area of a local authority, the area in which any circumstances arose in consequence of which the order is being made."

(2) A court may only make a care order or supervision order if it is satisfied–

    (a) that the child concerned is suffering, or is likely to suffer, significant harm; and

    (b) that the harm, or likelihood of harm, is attributable to–

        (i) the care given to the child, or likely to be given to him if the order were not made, not being what it would be reasonable to expect a parent to give to him; or

        (ii) the child's being beyond parental control.

Subsection (2) This sets out what are commonly referred to as the "threshold criteria" which must be met before the court can go on to consider whether or not to make a care or supervision order. The court must be satisfied, firstly, that the child, or children, who are the subjects of the application for a care or supervision order are suffering, or likely to suffer significant harm. The relevant time for this purpose is the date of the care order application or, if temporary protective measures have been continuously in place prior to the application for a care order, then the date that these were initiated. It is for the applicant, usually the local authority, to prove that the child is suffering, or likely to suffer, significant harm on the balance of probabilities. Generally speaking the more serious the allegation the more cogent the evidence required to prove it. Harm is defined at s.31(9) of the Act as meaning ill-treatment or the impairment of health or development. To establish the threshold criteria the court must be satisfied that the child is suffering, or likely to suffer, significant harm as a result either of the inadequacy of the parent's care, and it matters not whether this is deliberate or as a result of the parent's own inadequacies, or as a result of the child being beyond parental control.

(3) No care order or supervision order may be made with respect to a child who has reached the age of seventeen (or sixteen, in the case of a child who is married).

> *Subsection (3)* *This subsection is largely self-explanatory. A care order when made lasts until the child attains the age of eighteen but this subsection prevents applications being made in respect of seventeen year olds or sixteen year olds who are married. This, no doubt, is for practical reasons as given the length of time before the application could be dealt with it would be bordering on futile to make an application in respect of a seventeen year old. Further, it is hard to imagine any situations were such an order would be appropriate.*

(4) An application under this section may be made on its own or in any other family proceedings.

> *Subsection (4)* *This section confirms that an application can be made as a free-standing application or, in any other family proceedings. The most usual situation for an order to be made in other family proceedings would be where in a private law dispute between parents, such as a dispute as to where the child should reside, a local authority has been ordered to investigate the family's situation and concludes that care proceedings are required. Family proceedings are defined in section 8 (3) of the Act.*

(5) The court may–

    (a) on an application for a care order, make a supervision order;
    (b) on an application for a supervision order, make a care order.

> *Subsection (5)* *When the court is dealing with an application for a care order it can, of its own volition, make a supervision order and vice versa, whether or not this is requested by any of the parties to the proceedings.*

(6) Where an authorised person proposes to make an application under this section he shall–

    (a) if it is reasonably practicable to do so; and
    (b) before making the application,

consult the local authority appearing to him to be the authority in whose area the child concerned is ordinarily resident.

(7) An application made by an authorised person shall not be entertained by the court if, at the time when it is made, the child concerned is–

(a) the subject of an earlier application for a care order, or supervision order, which has not been disposed of; or
(b) subject to–
(i) a care order or supervision order;
(ii) an order under section 7(7)(b) of the Children and Young Persons Act 1969; or
(iii)(applies to Scotland only)

Subsection (7) *This subsection is designed to prevent duplication of proceedings in respect of the same child, and further to prevent the making of any application for a care or supervision order in respect of a child who is already subject to a care or supervision order, or the equivalent.*

(8) The local authority designated in a care order must be–

(a) the authority within whose area the child is ordinarily resident; or
(b) where the child does not reside in the area of a local authority, the authority within whose area any circumstances arose in consequence of which the order is being made.

Subsection (8) *Section 31(8)(b) should read " where the child does not ordinarily reside in the area of a local authority" in order to make sense. Ordinary residence is determined by reference to where the child was living before being placed in interim care. It is possible for more than one authority to qualify for designation under s 31(8) (b), and where this is the case the court has a choice of area, taking into account where the circumstances arose that carry the case over the s 31 threshold. In s. 31(8)(b) "any circumstances" can include events that have taken place before the birth of the child.*

(9) In this section–

'authorised person' means–

(a) the National Society for the Prevention of Cruelty to Children and any of its officers; and
(b) any person authorised by order of the Secretary of State to bring proceedings under this section and any officer of a body which is so authorised;

'harm' means ill-treatment or the impairment of health or development;

'development' means physical, intellectual, emotional, social or behavioural development;

'health' means physical or mental health; and

'ill-treatment' includes sexual abuse and forms of ill-treatment which are not physical.

Subsection (9) *This section is concerned with the definition of various terms used elsewhere in section 31. The wide definition of the meaning of "harm" should be noted.*

(10) Where the question of whether harm suffered by a child is significant turns on the child's health or development, his health or development shall be compared with that which could reasonably be expected of a similar child.

Subsection (10) *This subsection would be relevant, for example, where the child, who is the subject of the proceedings, has an inherent condition such as dyslexia or down's syndrome. It confirms that the development of such a child should be compared with that which could reasonably be expected of a child with the same underlying condition, and not the average child.*

(11) In this Act–

'a care order' means (subject to section 105(1)) an order under subsection (1)(a) and (except where express provision to the contrary is made) includes an interim care order made under section 38; and

'a supervision order' means an order under subsection (1)(b) and (except where express provision to the contrary is made) includes an interim supervision order made under section 38.

32 – (1) A court hearing an application for an order under this Part shall (in the light of any rules made by virtue of subsection (2))–

(a) draw up a timetable with a view to disposing of the application without delay; and

(b) give such directions as it considers appropriate for the purpose of ensuring, so far as is reasonably practicable, that that timetable is adhered to.

Subsection (1) *The court, at an early stage in the proceedings, and following representations by the parties to the proceedings, sets out a timetable to deal with the filing of evidence, (including any expert assessments of the parents and/or child considered necessary), and the listing of the final hearing, if at all possible. Delay is generally considered prejudicial to the welfare of the child (see s 1(2) of the Act) but this consideration has to be balanced against the need, in the interest of the child's welfare, for a proper investigation of the child's circumstances. It is possible at any stage of the proceedings for any of the parties to the proceedings to apply for further directions if any problems arise in relation to the original timetable. The guardian ad litem is under a duty to review the file regularly, and if necessary take out a summons for directions to avoid unnecessary delay.*

(2) Rules of court may–

   (a) specify periods within which specified steps must be taken in relation to such proceedings; and

   (b) make other provision with respect to such proceedings for the purpose of ensuring, so far as is reasonably practicable, that they are disposed of without delay.

Subsection (2) *The rules of court referred to are contained in the Family Proceedings Rules 1991 rule 4.14.*

Care orders

33 – (1) Where a care order is made with respect to a child it shall be the duty of the local authority designated by the order to receive the child into their care and to keep him in their care while the order remains in force.

Subsection (1) *The local authority named in the order is under a duty to keep the child in its care in accordance with the provisions of s 23 of the Act while the order remains in force. This means that the child remains in local authority care either until attaining the age of 18, or until the care order is discharged by further order of the court, whichever is the sooner. The child can be placed with his parents under a care order.*

(2) Where–

    (a) a care order has been made with respect to a child on the application of an authorised person; but

    (b) the local authority designated by the order was not informed that that person proposed to make the application,

the child may be kept in the care of that person until received into the care of the authority.

> **Subsection (2)** *For " authorised person" see s 31(9) of the Act. At present the only organisation falling into this category is the National Society for the Prevention of Cruelty to Children.*

(3) While a care order is in force with respect to a child, the local authority designated by the order shall–

    (a) have parental responsibility for the child; and

    (b) have the power (subject to the following provisions of this section) to determine the extent to which a parent or guardian of the child may meet his parental responsibility for him.

> **Subsection (3)** *Parental Responsibility is defined at s 3(1) of the Act as meaning, "all the rights, duties, powers, responsibilities and authority which by law a parent of a child has in relation to the child and his property". When a care order is in force parental responsibility is shared between any parent with parental responsibility and the local authority but, as s 33(3)(b) establishes, the local authority can override the exercise of parental responsibility by a parent subject to subsection (4) and subsection (6) below.*

(4) The authority may not exercise the power in subsection (3)(b) unless they are satisfied that it is necessary to do so in order to safeguard or promote the child's welfare.

> **Subsection (4)** *The local authority should not override the parent's exercise of parental responsibility unless satisfied that this is necessary in the interests of the child's welfare. This emphasis on intervention only where necessary to an extent echoes the no order principle set out in s1(5) of the Act and is a theme which runs throughout the Act.*

(5) Nothing in subsection (3)(b) shall prevent a parent or guardian of the child who has care of him from doing what is reasonable in all the circumstances of the case for the purpose of safeguarding or promoting his welfare.

> **Subsection (5)** *This subsection enables a parent or guardian who has the child in his care to take reasonable steps to safeguard or promote the child's welfare even though a care order is in force.*

(6) While a care order is in force with respect to a child, the local authority designated by the order shall not–

   (a) cause the child to be brought up in any religious persuasion other than that in which he would have been brought up if the order had not been made; or
   (b) have the right–
      (i) to consent or refuse to consent to the making of an application with respect to the child under section 18 of the Adoption Act 1976;
      (ii) to agree or refuse to agree to the making of an adoption order, or an order under section 55 of the Act of 1976, with respect to the child; or
      (iii) to appoint a guardian for the child.

> **Subsection (6)** *This section limits the local authority's exercise of parental responsibility for the child who is the subject of the care order. The local authority is not permitted to allow the child to be brought up in any religious persuasion other than that of its parents (note this section does not impose any mandatory duty to bring the child up in accordance with his parents' religious belief). Section 33(6)(b) further circumscribes the exercise of parental responsibility by the local authority and confirms that, unlike a parent with parental responsibility, the local authority can not consent to a child's adoption; freeing for adoption under s 18 of the Adoption Act 1976; adoption abroad under s 55 of the Adoption Act 1976, or appoint a guardian for the child.*

(7) While a care order is in force with respect to a child, no person may–

   (a) cause the child to be known by a new surname; or
   (b) remove him from the United Kingdom,

without either the written consent of every person who has parental responsibility for the child or the leave of the court.

(8) Subsection (7)(b) does not–

   (a) prevent the removal of such a child, for a period of less than one month, by the authority in whose care he is; or

(b) apply to arrangements for such a child to live outside England and Wales (which are governed by paragraph 19 of Schedule 2).

Subsection (8) The ability of the local authority to take a child out of the United Kingdom for up to a month mirrors the permission to remove for the same period that is automatically given to the holder of a residence order under s 8 of the Act. Paragraph 19 of Schedule 2 includes provision that arrangements for a child to live outside England and Wales can only be made with the approval of the court.

(9) The power in subsection (3)(b) is subject (in addition to being subject to the provisions of this section) to any right, duty, power, responsibility or authority which a parent or guardian of the child has in relation to the child and his property by virtue of any other enactment.

Subsection (9) One effect of this subsection is that parents retain their right to inherit on the child's intestacy.

34 – (1) Where a child is in the care of a local authority, the authority shall (subject to the provisions of this section) allow the child reasonable contact with–

(a) his parents;

(b) any guardian of his;

(c) where there was a residence order in force with respect to the child immediately before the care order was made, the person in whose favour the order was made; and

(d) where, immediately before the care order was made, a person had care of the child by virtue of an order made in the exercise of the High Court's inherent jurisdiction with respect to children, that person.

34 Parental contact etc with children in care
Subsection (1) A presumption in favour of contact to anyone falling within the definitions set out at (a) to (d) is created by this subsection. This presumption can be overriden in accordance with the various provisions of this section. The local authority is under a general duty to promote contact between a child and his family and other persons connected with the child see Schedule 2 paragraph 15 of the Act.

(2) On an application made by the authority or the child, the court may make such order as it considers appropriate with respect to the contact which is to be allowed between the child and any named person.

> *Subsection (2) It should be noted that the child may himself apply for contact. This reflects the view that contact is the right of the child. The court has power on an application under this subsection to order that there be no contact between the child and any named person. A contact order is only binding on the local authority and can not be used to compel the person named in the order to have contact with the child.*

(3) On an application made by–

(a) any person mentioned in paragraphs (a) to (d) of subsection (1); or
(b) any person who has obtained the leave of the court to make the application,

the court may make such order as it considers appropriate with respect to the contact which is to be allowed between the child and that person.

> *Subsection (3) This gives the court a wide discretion as to the type of order for contact, it can make. If it is appropriate, the court can make an order for indirect contact by way of letters and cards. Section 34(3)(b) provides that any person who falls outside the categories listed in 1(a) to (d) can apply for leave to make an application for contact to a child in care. The court in considering whether to grant leave will look at the connection between the applicant and the child, the nature of the contact sought, whether the proposed application would seriously disrupt the child, and will also consider the wishes of the child's parents and the local authority. The test is then, considering these factors, whether or not it can be said that the applicant has a good arguable case for contact with the child.*

(4) On an application made by the authority or the child, the court may make an order authorising the authority to refuse to allow contact between the child and any person who is mentioned in paragraphs (a) to (d) of subsection (1) and named in the order.

> *Subsection (4) This provision allows the court to permit the local authority to refuse contact to any of the groups of people listed in subsection (1). Once such an order is made the local authority still has a discretion to allow contact.*

(5) When making a care order with respect to a child, or in any family proceedings in connection with a child who is in the care of a local authority, the court may make an order under this section, even though no application for such an order has been made with respect to the child, if it considers that the order should be made.

Subsection (5) *This subsection enables the court to make an order for contact, or an order refusing contact, of its own volition in proceedings concerning the child.*

(6) An authority may refuse to allow the contact that would otherwise be required by virtue of subsection (1) or an order under this section if–

(a) they are satisfied that it is necessary to do so in order to safeguard or promote the child's welfare; and
(b) the refusal–
   (i) is decided upon as a matter of urgency; and
   (ii) does not last for more than seven days.

Subsection (6) *This gives a local authority an emergency power to withhold contact even where an order for contact is in existence. After the 7 day period in (ii) the local authority would be obliged, if it still wished to withhold contact, to seek the court's authorisation by making an application under s.34(4).*

(7) An order under this section may impose such conditions as the court considers appropriate.

(8) The Secretary of State may by regulations make provision as to–

(a) the steps to be taken by a local authority who have exercised their powers under subsection (6);
(b) the circumstances in which, and conditions subject to which, the terms of any order under this section may be departed from by agreement between the local authority and the person in relation to whom the order is made;
(c) notification by a local authority of any variation or suspension of arrangements made (otherwise than under an order under this section) with a view to affording any person contact with a child to whom this section applies.

Subsection (8) *The regulations referred to are the Contact with Children Regulations 1991 SI 1991/891.*

(9) The court may vary or discharge any order made under this section on the application of the authority, the child concerned or the person named in the order.

(10) An order under this section may be made either at the same time as the care order itself or later.

Subsection (10) Orders can be made at any time after a care order has been made. An order for contact can therefore be made when the child is freed for adoption (s 18 of the Adoption Act 1978).

(11) Before making a care order with respect to any child the court shall–

(a) consider the arrangements which the authority have made, or propose to make, for affording any person contact with a child to whom this section applies; and

(b) invite the parties to the proceedings to comment on those arrangements.

Subsection (11) This subsection obliges the court to consider the arrangements for contact for the child before making a care order. If the care plan is unsatisfactory in this respect the court can invite the local authority to reconsider the proposals for contact and to amend the care plan, and if they refuse to do so the court can make orders for contact.

Supervision orders

35 – (1) While a supervision order is in force it shall be the duty of the supervisor–

(a) to advise, assist and befriend the supervised child;
(b) to take such steps as are reasonably necessary to give effect to the order; and
(c) where–
   (i) the order is not wholly complied with; or
   (ii) the supervisor considers that the order may no longer be necessary,

to consider whether or not to apply to the court for its variation or discharge.

Subsection (1) A supervision order places the named child under the supervision of a designated local authority (see s.31(8) of the Act) or a probation officer. The duties of the supervisor are set out in paragraphs (a) to (c). The threshold criteria (see s.31 of the Act) must be met before a supervision order is made. The court also has power to make an interim supervision order (for further detail as to interim orders see s.38).

(2) Parts I and II of Schedule 3 make further provision with respect to supervision orders.

> **Subsection (2)** *Part I of Schedule 3 makes provision for the supervisor to give certain directions to the supervised child, and allows imposition of certain obligations on the child's parents, or other person with whom the child is living, but only with their consent. It also makes provision for psychiatric and medical examination and treatment of the child. Part II deals with the periods of time for which a supervision order can be made. In the first place a supervision order can be made for a maximum of one year and thereafter can be extended up to a maximum period of 3 years.*

36 – (1) On the application of any local education authority, the court may make an order putting the child with respect to whom the application is made under the supervision of a designated local education authority.

> **36 Education supervision orders**
> **Subsection (1)** *Education supervision orders are designed to deal with non-attendance at school. Guidance in respect of education supervision orders has been issued by the Department of Health in the Children Act 1989 Guidance and Regulations Volume 7, Chapter 3. Before applying for an education supervision order all reasonable efforts should be made to solve any attendance problem without legal sanctions.*

(2) In this Act 'an education supervision order' means an order under subsection (1).

(3) A court may only make an education supervision order if it is satisfied that the child concerned is of compulsory school age and is not being properly educated.

> **Subsection (3)** *Compulsory school age is defined in the Education Act 1996 s 8 as being following a child's fifth birthday until the age of 16. Before making an education supervision order the court must be satisfied, on the balance of probabilities, that the child is of compulsory school age.*

(4) For the purposes of this section, a child is being properly educated only if he is receiving efficient full-time education suitable to his age, ability and aptitude and any special educational needs he may have.

Subsection (4) *This echoes the provisions of s.7 of the Education Act 1996 which imposes a duty on parents to ensure that their child receives full-time education suitable to his age, ability and aptitude and any special needs he may have. A parent who fails under this duty can be served with a school attendance order under the provisions of the Education Act 1996. Failure to comply with a school attendance order is an offence. The court dealing with the criminal case can direct the local authority to institute proceedings for an education supervision order, but it is not necessary for there to be any proceedings for a school attendance order in place before the court can make an education supervision order.*

(5) Where a child is–

   (a) the subject of a school attendance order which is in force under [section 437 of the Education Act 1996] and which has not been complied with; or
   (b) a registered pupil at a school which he is not attending regularly within the meaning of [section 444] of that Act,

then, unless it is proved that he is being properly educated, it shall be assumed that he is not.

Subsection (5) *If a child is either the subject of a school attendance order, or not attending school regularly in accordance with the provisions of the Education Act 1996, then a presumption is created that the child is not being properly educated with the burden of disproving the presumption being on the child's carer.*

(6) An education supervision order may not be made with respect to a child who is in the care of a local authority.

Subsection (6) *Where a child is in care it is expected that the local authority will be able to make proper arrangements for his education making an education supervision order unnecessary.*

(7) The local education authority designated in an education supervision order must be–

   (a) the authority within whose area the child concerned is living or will live; or
   (b) where–
       (i) the child is a registered pupil at a school; and

(ii) the authority mentioned in paragraph (a) and the authority within whose area the school is situated agree,

the latter authority.

> **Subsection (7)** *The designated local education authority will normally be the authority where the child lives, unless he goes to school elsewhere and the two authorities agree.*

(8) Where a local education authority propose to make an application for an education supervision order they shall, before making the application, consult the ... appropriate local authority.

> **Subsection (8)** *There is no requirement for the local authority's agreement to the proposed application, but this subsection ensures that the local education authority is better informed as to the child's circumstances before deciding whether to make an application.*

(9) The 'appropriate local authority' is–

(a) in the case of a child who is being provided with accommodation by, or on behalf of, a local authority, that authority; and

(b) in any other case, the local authority within whose area the child concerned lives, or will live.

(10) Part III of Schedule 3 makes further provision with respect to education supervision orders.

> **Subsection (10)** *The supervisor is under a duty to advise, assist, and befriend the supervised child and his parents. Reference should be made to Part III of Schedule 3 for the detail of these provisions.*

Powers of court

37 – (1) Where, in any family proceedings in which a question arises with respect to the welfare of any child, it appears to the court that it may be appropriate for a care or supervision order to be made with respect to him, the court may direct the appropriate authority to undertake an investigation of the child's circumstances.

37 Powers of court in certain family proceedings

Subsection (1) For the definition of family proceedings see s 8(3) of the Act. This is a useful power that enables the court to direct the local authority to investigate the circumstances of a child about whom the court is concerned. This power should, however, only be used where it may be appropriate to make a care or supervision order. It should not be used as a means of speeding up a welfare report where the preparation of reports by the court welfare service is taking a long time, or simply to enable a guardian ad litem to be appointed in private law proceedings. The local authority officer who conducts the investigation usually prepares a written report for the court.

(2) Where the court gives a direction under this section the local authority concerned shall, when undertaking the investigation, consider whether they should–

    (a) apply for a care order or for a supervision order with respect to the child;
    (b) provide services or assistance for the child or his family; or
    (c) take any other action with respect to the child.

Subsection (2) This subsection obliges the local authority to give consideration to the matters listed when investigating the child's circumstances. This is echoed by the local authority's duties in respect of the provision of services for children within their area set out in Schedule 2 to the Act.

(3) Where a local authority undertake an investigation under this section, and decide not to apply for a care order or supervision order with respect to the child concerned, they shall inform the court of–

    (a) their reasons for so deciding;
    (b) any service or assistance which they have provided, or intend to provide, for the child and his family; and
    (c) any other action which they have taken, or propose to take, with respect to the child.

Subsection (3) This is largely self explanatory. The matters set out at (a) to (c) would usually be explored in a written report.

(4) The information shall be given to the court before the end of the period of eight weeks beginning with the date of the direction, unless the court otherwise directs.

Subsection (4) *This subsection gives the court flexibility as to the timescale for a report by a local authority under s 36. There might be situations where it is necessary for a local authority to report urgently, within a matter of days, as to the circumstances of a child. In this situation the report would probably be given orally. The usual period of 8 weeks is intended to give the local authority sufficient time to investigate the child's situation thoroughly while ensuring there is no unnecessary delay which is generally considered prejudicial to the child's welfare.*

(5) The local authority named in a direction under subsection (1) must be–

   (a) the authority in whose area the child is ordinarily resident; or
   (b) where the child [is not ordinarily resident] in the area of a local authority, the authority within whose area any circumstances arose in consequence of which the direction is being given.

Subsection (5) *This repeats the criteria as to which local authority should be the "designated" local authority at s 31 (8).*

(6) If, on the conclusion of any investigation or review under this section, the authority decide not to apply for a care order or supervision order with respect to the child–

   (a) they shall consider whether it would be appropriate to review the case at a later date; and
   (b) if they decide that it would be, they shall determine the date on which that review is to begin.

Subsection (6) *It should be noted that the court has no power to compel a local authority to make an application for a care or supervision order. This subsection places the local authority under a duty to consider whether it would be appropriate to reconsider the child's circumstances on a specified future date.*

38 – (1) Where–

   (a) in any proceedings on an application for a care order or supervision order, the proceedings are adjourned; or
   (b) the court gives a direction under section 37(1),

the court may make an interim care order or an interim supervision order with respect to the child concerned.

38 Interim Orders

Subsection (1) *This subsection allows the court to make interim (i.e. short term) care or supervision orders to safeguard the welfare of the child while the court is in the process of investigating whether or not a full order is required.*

(2) A court shall not make an interim care order or interim supervision order under this section unless it is satisfied that there are reasonable grounds for believing that the circumstances with respect to the child are as mentioned in section 31(2).

Subsection (2) *In order to make an interim care or supervision order the court must be satisfied that there are reasonable grounds to believe that the child has suffered or is likely to suffer significant harm (see s 31(2) of the Act). The test of " reasonable grounds to believe", is different to establishing on the balance of probabilities, that the child has suffered or is likely to suffer significant harm, which is the test which must be satisfied before a final care order can be made.*

(3) Where, in any proceedings on an application for a care order or supervision order, a court makes a residence order with respect to the child concerned, it shall also make an interim supervision order with respect to him unless satisfied that his welfare will be satisfactorily safeguarded without an interim order being made.

Subsection (3) *This subsection places an obligation on the court to make an interim supervision order if it makes a residence order in proceedings for a care or supervision order, unless satisfied that the child's welfare does not require this. It should be noted that at the interim stage a residence order should not be made unless the court can be confident that following a substantive hearing a full residence order is likely to be made.*

(4) An interim order made under or by virtue of this section shall have effect for such period as may be specified in the order, but shall in any event cease to have effect on whichever of the following events first occurs–

   (a) the expiry of the period of eight weeks beginning with the date on which the order is made;

(b) if the order is the second or subsequent such order made with respect to the same child in the same proceedings, the expiry of the relevant period;

(c) in a case which falls within subsection (1)(a), the disposal of the application;

(d) in a case which falls within subsection (1)(b), the disposal of an application for a care order or supervision order made by the authority with respect to the child;

(e) in a case which falls within subsection (1)(b) and in which–

  (i) the court has given a direction under section 37(4), but

  (ii) no application for a care order or supervision order has been made with respect to the child,

the expiry of the period fixed by that direction.

Subsection (4) This subsection sets out the various maximum periods for the duration of interim orders. The relevant period referred to in (b) is 4 weeks. The court can, of course, make shorter interim orders where this is appropriate. Where the parents have not had sufficient time to fully prepare their opposition to the making of an interim order the court might feel it appropriate to make a short order to give them the opportunity to present their arguments in full at an early opportunity.

(5) In subsection (4)(b) 'the relevant period' means–

  (a) the period of four weeks beginning with the date on which the order in question is made; or

  (b) the period of eight weeks beginning with the date on which the first order was made if that period ends later than the period mentioned in paragraph (a).

Subsection (5) The maximum period for the first interim order is 8 weeks. If the court on the first hearing of an application for an interim order makes an order for a shorter period than 8 weeks, i.e. for two weeks, then, on the second hearing the court can make an order for a maximum period of 6 weeks thereby making up the difference to 8 weeks.

(6) Where the court makes an interim care order, or interim supervision order, it may give such directions (if any) as it considers appropriate with regard to the medical or psychiatric examination or other assessment of the child; but if the child is of sufficient understanding to make an informed decision he may refuse to submit to the examination or other assessment.

> **Subsection (6)** *A court may direct an assessment of the child, which may include assessment of the child's parents, under this subsection. The court can direct such an assessment, including a residential assessment, even though the local authority objects but the court has to take account of the costs involved and the limits of local authority funding. The assessment must be just that, assessment, and not a package directed more to therapeutic intervention. It is normal for the expert who is to undertake any assessment or examination of the child to be identified prior to the court agreeing to a direction for examination or assessment.*

(7) A direction under subsection (6) may be to the effect that there is to be–

    (a) no such examination or assessment; or

    (b) no such examination or assessment unless the court directs otherwise.

> **Subsection (7)** *This subsection is designed to protect the child from being exposed to too many examinations or assessments that might be detrimental to his welfare.*

(8) A direction under subsection (6) may be–

    (a) given when the interim order is made or at any time while it is in force; and

    (b) varied at any time on the application of any person falling within any class of person prescribed by rules of court for the purposes of this subsection.

> **Subsection (8)** *As to "class of person prescribed by rules of court" see the Family Proceedings Rules 1991 r 4.2(1) which defines the class of person as the parties to the proceedings and any person named in such a direction. This subsection enables directions for assessment and examination to be made and varied with a degree of flexibility.*

(9) Paragraphs 4 and 5 of Schedule 3 shall not apply in relation to an interim supervision order.

> **Subsection (9)** *Paragraphs 4 and 5 of Schedule 3 require the supervised child, in certain circumstances, to submit to psychiatric and medical examination and treatment.*

(10) Where a court makes an order under or by virtue of this section it shall, in determining the period for which the order is to be in force, consider whether any party who was, or might have been, opposed to the making of the order was in a position to argue his case against the order in full.

> **Subsection (10)** *Often interim orders are made on relatively short notice. This subsection requires the court to consider whether a party was able to argue his case in full against the order when deciding the length of an interim order. Although the court has power to make an initial interim care or supervision order for an 8 week period, this subsection recognises that there are occasions when a shorter order might be more appropriate.*

38A – (1) Where–

(a) on being satisfied that there are reasonable grounds for believing that the circumstances with respect to a child are as mentioned in section 31(2)(a) and (b)(i), the court makes an interim care order with respect to a child, and

(b) the conditions mentioned in subsection (2) are satisfied,
     the court may include an exclusion requirement in the interim care order.

> **38A Power to include exclusion requirement in interim care order**
> **Subsection (1)** *When the court is satisfied that there are reasonable grounds to believe the child is suffering or likely to suffer significant harm, as a result of the care given to the child, or likely to be given if the order were not made, not being what it would be reasonable to expect a parent to give a child and, subject to the conditions in subsection (2), the court can make an order excluding any person who is putting the child at risk from the child's home.*

(2) The conditions are–

(a) that there is reasonable cause to believe that, if a person ('the relevant person') is excluded from a dwelling-house in which the child lives, the child will cease to suffer, or cease to be likely to suffer, significant harm, and

(b) that another person living in the dwelling-house (whether a parent of the child or some other person)–
     (i) is able and willing to give to the child the care which it would be reasonable to expect a parent to give him, and
     (ii) consents to the inclusion of the exclusion requirement.

Subsection (2) *This subsection sets out the various conditions that must be met before an order excluding any person from the child's home is made. This allows the court to create a potentially safer environment for the child to remain at home, for example, where the child's mother is a parent capable of giving the child good enough parenting, but she is living with a partner who is a risk to the child. The consent of the person who remains in the home to look after the child to the exclusion order, must be obtained before the exclusion order can be made.*

(3) For the purposes of this section an exclusion requirement is any one or more of the following–

    (a) a provision requiring the relevant person to leave a dwelling-house in which he is living with the child,

    (b) a provision prohibiting the relevant person from entering a dwelling-house in which the child lives, and

    (c) a provision excluding the relevant person from a defined area in which a dwelling-house in which the child lives is situated.

Subsection (3) *As can be seen the court has power to exclude a person from entering the child's home, or indeed from entering a defined zone around the child's home. Care should be taken to ensure clarity when defining an area around the home.*

(4) The court may provide that the exclusion requirement is to have effect for a shorter period than the other provisions of the interim care order.

(5) Where the court makes an interim care order containing an exclusion requirement, the court may attach a power of arrest to the exclusion requirement.

Subsection (5) *A power of arrest is a useful sanction to ensure compliance with the exclusion order. If a person breaches the order he can be arrested by the police and brought before the court.*

(6) Where the court attaches a power of arrest to an exclusion requirement of an interim care order, it may provide that the power of arrest is to have effect for a shorter period than the exclusion requirement.

(7) Any period specified for the purposes of subsection (4) or (6) may be extended by the court (on one or more occasions) on an application to vary or discharge the interim care order.

(8) Where a power of arrest is attached to an exclusion requirement of an interim care order by virtue of subsection (5), a constable may arrest without warrant any person whom he has reasonable cause to believe to be in breach of the requirement.

(9) Sections 47(7), (11) and (12) and 48 of, and Schedule 5 to, the Family Law Act 1996 shall have effect in relation to a person arrested under subsection (8) of this section as they have effect in relation to a person arrested under section 47(6) of that Act.

> **Subsection (9)** *The sections of the Family Law Act 1996 referred to in this subsection relate to the provisions for bringing an arrested person before the court, and the various powers to remand in custody or on bail subject, if required, to various conditions.*

(10) If, while an interim care order containing an exclusion requirement is in force, the local authority have removed the child from the dwelling-house from which the relevant person is excluded to other accommodation for a continuous period of more than 24 hours, the interim care order shall cease to have effect in so far as it imposes the exclusion requirement.]

> **Subsection (10)** *Under this subsection if the child has been removed from his home by the local authority the part of the interim care order excluding the named person ceases to have effect after the child has been removed for a period in excess of 24 hours. An exclusion order clearly interferes with the named person's liberty and so should no longer be effective when there is no longer any need to keep him out of the child's home.*

38B – (1) In any case where the court has power to include an exclusion requirement in an interim care order, the court may accept an undertaking from the relevant person.

> **38B Undertakings relating to interim care orders**
> **Subsection (1)** *This subsection enables a person to give a solemn promise to the court that he will not enter the dwelling house in which the child is living, but only in circumstances where the court would have power to make an exclusion order.*

(2) No power of arrest may be attached to any undertaking given under subsection (1).

(3) An undertaking given to a court under subsection (1)–

(a) shall be enforceable as if it were an order of the court, and

(b) shall cease to have effect if, while it is in force, the local authority have removed the child from the dwelling-house from which the relevant person is excluded to other accommodation for a continuous period of more than 24 hours.

> **Subsection (3)** *This confirms that an undertaking has the same effect as an order made under section 38A, and a person who breaks an undertaking can be sent to prison for contempt of court if he is found to have breached his undertaking.*

(4) This section has effect without prejudice to the powers of the High Court and county court apart from this section.

> **Subsection (4)** *This refers to the inherent jurisdiction of the High Court (see section 100 of the Act).*

(5) In this section 'exclusion requirement' and 'relevant person' have the same meaning as in section 38A.

39 – (1) A care order may be discharged by the court on the application of–

(a) any person who has parental responsibility for the child;

(b) the child himself; or

(c) the local authority designated by the order.

> **39 Discharge and variation etc of care orders and supervision orders.**
> **Subsection (1)** *This lists the categories of people who can apply to discharge a care order. Parental responsibility is held by the child's mother, the married father of the child, the unmarried father who has acquired parental responsibility through a court order or agreement with the child's mother, or the child's guardian under section 5(6) of the Act. A person without parental responsibility, such as an unmarried father, who wishes to end a care order cannot apply for discharge under this section but must apply for a residence order under s 10 of the Act instead. On an application to discharge a care order the applicant has the burden of showing that the child's welfare will be met if the order is revoked.*

(2) A supervision order may be varied or discharged by the court on the application of–

(a) any person who has parental responsibility for the child;
(b) the child himself; or
(c) the supervisor.

(3) On the application of a person who is not entitled to apply for the order to be discharged, but who is a person with whom the child is living, a supervision order may be varied by the court in so far as it imposes a requirement which affects that person.

> **Subsection (3)** *The requirements which can be imposed under a supervision order are set out in Schedule 3 to the Act.*

(3A) On the application of a person who is not entitled to apply for the order to be discharged, but who s a person to whom an exclusion requirement contained in the order applies, an interim care order may be varied or discharged by the court in so far as it imposes the exclusion requirement.

> **Subsection (3A)** *A person who has been excluded from a dwelling- house in which the child lives pursuant to s 38A can apply to have the exclusion requirement either lifted or varied. It is unclear whether the other potential categories of applicant listed under subsection (1) can apply to vary an exclusion requirement.*

(3B) Where a power of arrest has been attached to an exclusion requirement of an interim care order, the court may, on the application of any person entitled to apply for the discharge of the order so far as it imposes the exclusion requirement, vary or discharge the order in so far as it confers a power of arrest (whether or not any application has been made to vary or discharge any other provision of the order).

(4) Where a care order is in force with respect to a child the court may, on the application of any person entitled to apply for the order to be discharged, substitute a supervision order for the care order.

> **Subsection (4)** *This enables the court to discharge a care order and replace it with a supervision order. This can occur even if the applicant does not request the making of a supervision order.*

(5) When a court is considering whether to substitute one order for another under subsection (4) any provision of this Act which would otherwise require section 31(2) to be satisfied at the time when the proposed order is substituted or made shall be disregarded.

> **Subsection (5)** *When deciding whether to replace a care order with a supervision order the court does not have to find that the threshold criteria (that the child is suffering or likely to suffer significant harm) are met for a second time.*

40 – (1) Where–

   (a) a court dismisses an application for a care order; and
   (b) at the time when the court dismisses the application, the child concerned is the subject of an interim care order,

the court may make a care order with respect to the child to have effect subject to such directions (if any) as the court may see fit to include in the order.

> **40 Orders pending appeals in cases about care or supervision orders**
> **Subsection (1)** *This subsection enables the court to order that a child who is subject to an interim care order should remain in care until the determination of any appeal against refusal to make a care order. This provision is designed to ensure that the court has power to preserve the status quo until the appeal is dealt with so that the child's welfare can be safeguarded. It should be noted that the court has a discretion to order that the child remain in care, and that this is not automatic. The court may include such directions as it sees fit, for example, in relation to contact with the parents.*

(2) Where–

   (a) a court dismisses an application for a care order, or an application for a supervision order; and
   (b) at the time when the court dismisses the application, the child concerned is the subject of an interim supervision order,

the court may make a supervision order with respect to the child to have effect subject to such directions (if any) as the court may see fit to include in the order.

Subsection (2) This subsection gives the court power to make a supervision order pending appeal where the court has rejected an application for a care or supervision order, and where an interim supervision order was in place at the time.

(3) Where a court grants an application to discharge a care order or supervision order, it may order that–

    (a) its decision is not to have effect; or

    (b) the care order, or supervision order, is to continue to have effect but subject to such directions as the court sees fit to include in the order.

Subsection (3) As above, the court can either order that an order discharging a care or supervision order is not to have effect, or continue such orders pending the determination of any appeal.

(4) An order made under this section shall only have effect for such period, not exceeding the appeal period, as may be specified in the order.

Subsection (4) An order can be made for up to the period within which an appeal can be lodged (14 days in the Family Proceedings Court, and 28 days in the High or County Courts) or, once the appeal is lodged, up to its determination. An order under this subsection can not extend beyond the determination of the appeal. The court has a discretion as to the length of the order.

(5) Where–

    (a) an appeal is made against any decision of a court under this section; or

    (b) any application is made to the appellate court in connection with a proposed appeal against that decision,

the appellate court may extend the period for which the order in question is to have effect, but not so as to extend it beyond the end of the appeal period.

Subsection (5) This subsection gives the appellate court power to extend a care or supervision order pending appeal.

(6) In this section 'the appeal period' means–

    (a) where an appeal is made against the decision in question, the period between the making of that decision and the determination of the appeal; and

    (b) otherwise, the period during which an appeal may be made against the decision.

Subsection (6) This defines "appeal period"(see the note to subsection (4) for the relevant time limits).

Guardians ad litem

41 – (1) For the purpose of any specified proceedings, the court shall appoint a guardian ad litem for the child concerned unless satisfied that it is not necessary to do so in order to safeguard his interests.

41 Representation of child and his interests in certain proceedings
Subsection (1) "The child concerned" means the child who is the subject of the proceedings. It is very unusual for a child in proceedings for a care or supervision order not to be represented by a guardian ad litem.

(2) The guardian ad litem shall–

    (a) be appointed in accordance with rules of court; and

    (b) be under a duty to safeguard the interests of the child in the manner prescribed by such rules.

Subsection (2) The rules referred to are the Family Proceedings Rules r 4.10 and r 4.11 and the Family Proceedings Courts (Children Act 1989) Rules 1991 r.10 and 11. The guardian ad litem will normally be selected from the panel of guardian ad litems but may unusually be the Official Solicitor.

(3) Where–

    (a) the child concerned is not represented by a solicitor; and

    (b) any of the conditions mentioned in subsection (4) is satisfied,
       the court may appoint a solicitor to represent him.

> **Subsection (3)** *The power contained in this subsection relates only to "specified" proceedings (involving a local authority) as defined in subsection (6) below, and not to private law proceedings (between individuals), for example, for a residence or contact order.*

(4) The conditions are that–

   (a) no guardian ad litem has been appointed for the child;
   (b) the child has sufficient understanding to instruct a solicitor and wishes to do so;
   (c) it appears to the court that it would be in the child's best interests for him to be represented by a solicitor.

> **Subsection (4)** *This sets out the conditions one of which must be met before the court can appoint a solicitor to act for the child. The subject of whether or not the child has "sufficient understanding to instruct a solicitor" has been considered in a number of cases. Reference should be made to r.9.2 A of the Family Proceedings Rules 1991 for the circumstances in which it is appropriate for a child to begin, prosecute, or defend proceedings without a next friend or guardian ad litem.*

(5) Any solicitor appointed under or by virtue of this section shall be appointed, and shall represent the child, in accordance with rules of court.

> **Subsection (5)** *The rules of court referred to are r 4.12 of the Family Proceedings Rules 1991 and the Family Proceedings Court (Children Act 1989) Rules 1991, r 10.*

(6) In this section 'specified proceedings' means any proceedings–

   (a) on an application for a care order or supervision order;
   (b) in which the court has given a direction under section 37(1) and has made, or is considering whether to make, an interim care order;
   (c) on an application for the discharge of a care order or the variation or discharge of a supervision order;
   (d) on an application under section 39(4);
   (e) in which the court is considering whether to make a residence order with respect to a child who is the subject of a care order;

(f) with respect to contact between a child who is the subject of a care order and any other person;

(g) under Part V;

(h) on an appeal against–

    (i) the making of, or refusal to make, a care order, supervision order or any order under section 34;

    (ii) the making of, or refusal to make, a residence order with respect to a child who is the subject of a care order; or

    (iii) the variation or discharge, or refusal of an application to vary or discharge, an order of a kind mentioned in sub-paragraph (i) or (ii);

    (iv) the refusal of an application under section 39(4);

    (v) the making of, or refusal to make, an order under Part V; or

    (i) which are specified for the time being, for the purposes of this section, by rules of court.

Subsection (6) This subsection sets out the various categories of proceedings that fall under the classification of specified proceedings. It should be noted in relation to (b) where the court has given a direction for a report under s 37 (1) that this should not be used as a device to appoint a guardian ad litem for the child in a difficult case. The appointment of a guardian in such cases should be where the court has made an interim care order, or where the circumstances go beyond the court simply wishing to investigate whether a care order is likely to be necessary.

(7) The Secretary of State may by regulations provide for the establishment of panels of persons from whom guardians ad litem appointed under this section must be selected.

Subsection (7) Reference should be made to the Guardian ad Litem and Reporting Officers (Panels) Regulations 1991.

(8) Subsection (7) shall not be taken to prejudice the power of the Lord Chancellor to confer or impose duties on the Official Solicitor under section 90(3) of the Supreme Court Act 1981.

Subsection (8) *A direction has been given under this subsection to prescribe the duties and functions of the Official Solicitor under the Act. Exceptional circumstances are required before the Official Solicitor is appointed to act as the child's guardian ad litem, rather than a guardian from the panel established under s 41 (7) above, such as where there is a foreign element to the case which may require enquiries to be made outside the jurisdiction.*

(9) The regulations may, in particular, make provision–

  (a) as to the constitution, administration and procedures of panels;
  (b) requiring two or more specified local authorities to make arrangements for the joint management of a panel;
  (c) for the defrayment by local authorities of expenses incurred by members of panels;
  (d) for the payment by local authorities of fees and allowances for members of panels;
  (e) as to the qualifications for membership of a panel;
  (f) as to the training to be given to members of panels;
  (g) as to the co-operation required of specified local authorities in the provision of panels in specified areas; and
  (h) for monitoring the work of guardians ad litem.

(10) Rules of court may make provision as to–

  (a) the assistance which any guardian ad litem may be required by the court to give to it;
  (b) the consideration to be given by any guardian ad litem, where an order of a specified kind has been made in the proceedings in question, as to whether to apply for the variation or discharge of the order;
  (c) the participation of guardians ad litem in reviews, of a kind specified in the rules, which are conducted by the court.

Subsection (10) *The Rules referred to are rule 11 of the Family Proceedings Court (Children Act 1989) Rules 1991 and rule 4.11 of the Family Proceedings Rules 1991. These rules oblige the guardian ad litem to carry out a thorough investigation of the child's circumstances having regard to the welfare checklist set out in s 1(3) of the Act. The guardian interviews the child (where appropriate), his family, professionals involved in caring for the child, and the social workers. The guardian then prepares a written report for the Court.*

(11) Regardless of any enactment or rule of law which would otherwise prevent it from doing so, the court may take account of–

    (a) any statement contained in a report made by a guardian ad litem who is appointed under this section for the purpose of the proceedings in question; and

    (b) any evidence given in respect of the matters referred to in the report, in so far as the statement or evidence is, in the opinion of the court, relevant to the question which the court is considering.

> **Subsection (11)** *The guardian in his, or her, written report and evidence to the court is not confined by the usual rules of evidence. The court has still to weigh up the relevance of the statement or evidence in deciding whether or not it is admissible, and also can still take a view on what weight should attach to the evidence.*

(12) The Secretary of State may, with the consent of the Treasury, make such grants with respect to expenditure of any local authority–

    (a) in connection with the establishment and administration of guardian ad litem panels in accordance with this section;

    (b) in paying expenses, fees, allowances and in the provision of training for members of such panels,

as he considers appropriate.

42 – (1) Where a person has been appointed as a guardian ad litem under this Act he shall have the right at all reasonable times to examine and take copies of–

    (a) any records of, or held by, a local authority [or an authorised person] which were compiled in connection with the making, or proposed making, by any person of any application under this Act with respect to the child concerned;
    ...

    (b) any ... records of, or held by, a local authority which were compiled in connection with any functions which stand referred to their social services committee under the Local Authority Social Services Act 1970, so far as those records relate to that child[; or

    (c) any records of, or held by, an authorised person which were compiled in connection with the activities of that person, so far as those records relate to that child.

42 Right of guardian ad litem to have access to local authority records
Subsection (1) The rights granted by this subsection are only available to guardians appointed under s 41 of the Act. This subsection gives such a guardian wide powers to inspect the specified records in so far as they relate to the child for whom the guardian acts.

(2) Where a guardian ad litem takes a copy of any record which he is entitled to examine under this section, that copy or any part of it shall be admissible as evidence of any matter referred to in any–

(a) report which he makes to the court in the proceedings in question; or
(b) evidence which he gives in those proceedings.

(3) Subsection (2) has effect regardless of any enactment or rule of law which would otherwise prevent the record in question being admissible in evidence.

Subsection (3) This provision prevents the hearsay rule from applying in relation to the admissibility in evidence of documents that the guardian is entitled to take copies of under subsection 1.

(4) In this section 'authorised person' has the same meaning as in section 31].

Subsection (4) The relevant subsection is s 31(9). The only "authorised person" is the National Society for the Prevention of Cruelty to Children.

PART V

PROTECTION OF CHILDREN

43 – (1) On the application of a local authority or authorised person for an order to be made under this section with respect to a child, the court may make the order if, but only if, it is satisfied that–

(a) the applicant has reasonable cause to suspect that the child is suffering, or is likely to suffer, significant harm;
(b) an assessment of the state of the child's health or development, or of the way in which he has been treated, is required to enable the applicant to determine whether or not the child is suffering, or is likely to suffer, significant harm; and

(c) it is unlikely that such an assessment will be made, or be satisfactory, in the absence of an order under this section.

Section 43 - Child Assessment Orders
Subsection (1) A Child Assessment Order is an order for assessment of a child's health or development or the way in which he has been treated. Its purpose is to allow the Local Authority to ascertain enough about the child's health /development to see if any further action is required. It is not needed where a Care Order is in force, as an assessment can be arranged without need for a further order. The paramountcy principle applies to any application under this section [see s1(1)]. It is used primarily to assist the Applicant in whether to initiate Care Proceedings; in practice it is little used. Some uses may be to arrange a general examination by a GP, psychologist or educational psychologist.

An "authorised person" is someone authorised for the purposes of s31 ie NSPCC or any officer or anyone authorised by the Secretary of State.

Subsection (1)(A) "He has reasonable cause" is a subjective belief. Contrast with the test for granting Interim Care Orders or Interim Supervision Orders - see s38(2).

"significant harm" has the same meaning as s 31.

(2) In this Act 'a child assessment order' means an order under this section.

(3) A court may treat an application under this section as an application for an emergency protection order.

Subsection (3) This means that if the court is satisfied that grounds exist for an Emergency Protection Order, it may make one - see generally s44 and subsection 4 below.

(4) No court shall make a child assessment order if it is satisfied–

(a) that there are grounds for making an emergency protection order with respect to the child; and

(b) that it ought to make such an order rather than a child assessment order.

Subsection (4) A Child Assessment Order is less interventionist than an Emergency Protection Order, Interim Care Order or Interim Supervision Order, and should not be used where one of these orders is more appropriate

(5) A child assessment order shall–

  (a) specify the date by which the assessment is to begin; and
  (b) have effect for such period, not exceeding 7 days beginning with that date, as may be specified in the order.

> **Subsection (5)(b)** *A Child Assessment Order can be for a shorter but not longer period than 7 days*

(6) Where a child assessment order is in force with respect to a child it shall be the duty of any person who is in a position to produce the child–

  (a) to produce him to such person as may be named in the order; and
  (b) to comply with such directions relating to the assessment of the child as the court thinks fit to specify in the order.

(7) A child assessment order authorises any person carrying out the assessment, or any part of the assessment, to do so in accordance with the terms of the order.

(8) Regardless of subsection (7), if the child is of sufficient understanding to make an informed decision he may refuse to submit to a medical or psychiatric examination or other assessment.

> **Subsection (8)** *Parental control does not extend to a child reaching the age of 18. It yields to the child's right to make a decision when he is of sufficient understanding and intelligence to be able to make up his own mind on a matter requiring his decision. Such a child is commonly described as "Gillick-competent". Where a child is "Gillick competent" he should be invited to comment on assessment even if parents don't agree. The more mature the child, the more care should be taken to consider his wishes and feelings.*

(9) The child may only be kept away from home–

  (a) in accordance with directions specified in the order;
  (b) if it is necessary for the purposes of the assessment; and
  (c) for such period or periods as may be specified in the order.

> **Subsection (9)** *If the child is to be kept away from home for the duration of the order, the Applicant must obtain directions to that effect, which will only be granted if reasons fall within s9(b) and (c), and subject to s43(10) concerning contact. A Guardian ad litem must be appointed unless unnecessary [S41].*

(10) Where the child is to be kept away from home, the order shall contain such directions as the court thinks fit with regard to the contact that he must be allowed to have with other persons while away from home.

(11) Any person making an application for a child assessment order shall take such steps as are reasonably practicable to ensure that notice of the application is given to–

    (a) the child's parents;

    (b) any person who is not a parent of his but who has parental responsibility for him;

    (c) any other person caring for the child;

    (d) any person in whose favour a contact order is in force with respect to the child;

    (e) any person who is allowed to have contact with the child by virtue of an order under section 34; and

    (f) the child,

before the hearing of the application.

(12) Rules of court may make provision as to the circumstances in which–

    (a) any of the persons mentioned in subsection (11); or

    (b) such other person as may be specified in the rules,

may apply to the court for a child assessment order to be varied or discharged.

(13) In this section 'authorised person' means a person who is an authorised person for the purposes of section 31.

44 – (1) Where any person ('the applicant') applies to the court for an order to be made under this section with respect to a child, the court may make the order if, but only if, it is satisfied that–

    (a) there is reasonable cause to believe that the child is likely to suffer significant harm if–

      (i) he is not removed to accommodation provided by or on behalf of the applicant; or

      (ii) he does not remain in the place in which he is then being accommodated;

    (b) in the case of an application made by a local authority–

      (i) enquiries are being made with respect to the child under section 47(1)(b); and

(ii) those enquiries are being frustrated by access to the child being unreasonably refused to a person authorised to seek access and that the applicant has reasonable cause to believe that access to the child is required as a matter of urgency; or

(c) in the case of an application made by an authorised person–

   (i) the applicant has reasonable cause to suspect that a child is suffering, or is likely to suffer, significant harm;

   (ii) the applicant is making enquiries with respect to the child's welfare; and

   (iii) those enquiries are being frustrated by access to the child being unreasonably refused to a person authorised to seek access and the applicant has reasonable cause to believe that access to the child is required as a matter of urgency.

Section 44 Emergency Protection Order
Subsection (1)(A)
Contrast this wording with s43(1)(a) with reference to "reasonable cause".

Subsection (1) An Emergency Protection Order vests parental responsibility in the Applicant for the duration of the Order. The Applicant may be the Local Authority or an "authorised person" eg NSPCC officer or other person appointed by the Secretary of State [see s 31(9)] or a police officer who is "designated" - see s46(3)(e). The section allows ANY PERSON to apply, but if asking for removal, there must be suitable accommodation for the child. In practice, it is usually the Local Authority or the police who apply. "Significant harm" has the same meaning as s31(10). Grounds to be satisfied depend on the type of applicant. Any applicant can rely on the "common ground" set out at s44(1)(a)(i) and (ii). The Local Authority may also rely on the "frustrated access" ground at s44(1)(b). An "authorised person" may rely on the "frustrated access" ground at s44(1)(c).

(2) In this section–

   (a) 'authorised person' means a person who is an authorised person for the purposes of section 31; and

   (b) 'a person authorised to seek access' means–

      (i) in the case of an application by a local authority, an officer of the local authority or a person authorised by the authority to act on their behalf in connection with the enquiries; or

      (ii) in the case of an application by an authorised person, that person.

(3) Any person–

   (a) seeking access to a child in connection with enquiries of a kind mentioned in subsection (1); and

   (b) purporting to be a person authorised to do so,

shall, on being asked to do so, produce some duly authenticated document as evidence that he is such a person.

(4) While an order under this section ('an emergency protection order') is in force it–

(a) operates as a direction to any person who is in a position to do so to comply with any request to produce the child to the applicant;

(b) authorises–

(i) the removal of the child at any time to accommodation provided by or on behalf of the applicant and his being kept there; or

(ii) the prevention of the child's removal from any hospital, or other place, in which he was being accommodated immediately before the making of the order; and

(c) gives the applicant parental responsibility for the child.

> *Subsection (4) The effect of the order is to authorise the Applicant to remove the child or prevent his removal from a location. The effect of this subsection is to make anyone who obstructs removal or prevents removal of a child guilty of a criminal offence. (See also s.44(15) and s.44(16))*

(5) Where an emergency protection order is in force with respect to a child, the applicant–

(a) shall only exercise the power given by virtue of subsection (4)(b) in order to safeguard the welfare of the child;

(b) shall take, and shall only take, such action in meeting his parental responsibility for the child as is reasonably required to safeguard or promote the welfare of the child (having regard in particular to the duration of the order); and

(c) shall comply with the requirements of any regulations made by the Secretary of State for the purposes of this subsection.

> *Subsection (5) The effect can also be to act as a direction to anyone to comply with a request to produce the child.*

(6) Where the court makes an emergency protection order, it may give such directions (if any) as it considers appropriate with respect to–

(a) the contact which is, or is not, to be allowed between the child and any named person;

(b) the medical or psychiatric examination or other assessment of the child.

(7) Where any direction is given under subsection (6)(b), the child may, if he is of sufficient understanding to make an informed decision, refuse to submit to the examination or other assessment.

(8) A direction under subsection (6)(a) may impose conditions and one under subsection (6)(b) may be to the effect that there is to be–

(a) no such examination or assessment; or
(b) no such examination or assessment unless the court directs otherwise.

(9) A direction under subsection (6) may be–

(a) given when the emergency protection order is made or at any time while it is in force; and
(b) varied at any time on the application of any person falling within any class of person prescribed by rules of court for the purposes of this subsection.

(10) Where an emergency protection order is in force with respect to a child and–

(a) the applicant has exercised the power given by subsection (4)(b)(i) but it appears to him that it is safe for the child to be returned; or
(b) the applicant has exercised the power given by subsection (4)(b)(ii) but it appears to him that it is safe for the child to be allowed to be removed from the place in question,

he shall return the child or (as the case may be) allow him to be removed.

(11) Where he is required by subsection (10) to return the child the applicant shall–

(a) return him to the care of the person from whose care he was removed; or
(b) if that is not reasonably practicable, return him to the care of–
    (i) a parent of his;
    (ii) any person who is not a parent of his but who has parental responsibility for him; or
    (iii) such other person as the applicant (with the agreement of the court) considers appropriate.

(12) Where the applicant has been required by subsection (10) to return the child, or to allow him to be removed, he may again exercise his powers with respect to the child (at any time while the emergency protection order remains in force) if it appears to him that a change in the circumstances of the case makes it necessary for him to do so.

(13) Where an emergency protection order has been made with respect to a child, the applicant shall, subject to any direction given under subsection (6), allow the child reasonable contact with–

(a) his parents;
(b) any person who is not a parent of his but who has parental responsibility for him;

(c) any person with whom he was living immediately before the making of the order;

(d) any person in whose favour a contact order is in force with respect to him;

(e) any person who is allowed to have contact with the child by virtue of an order under section 34; and

(f) any person acting on behalf of any of those persons.

> **Subsection (13)** *During the Emergency Protection Order the Applicant must allow reasonable contact to the child by those specified in this subsection.*

(14) Wherever it is reasonably practicable to do so, an emergency protection order shall name the child; and where it does not name him it shall describe him as clearly as possible.

(15) A person shall be guilty of an offence if he intentionally obstructs any person exercising the power under subsection (4)(b) to remove, or prevent the removal of, a child.

(16) A person guilty of an offence under subsection (15) shall be liable on summary conviction to a fine not exceeding level 3 on the standard scale.

44A – (1) Where–

(a) on being satisfied as mentioned in section 44(1)(a), (b) or (c), the court makes an emergency protection order with respect to a child, and

(b) the conditions mentioned in subsection (2) are satisfied,

the court may include an exclusion requirement in the emergency protection order.

(2) The conditions are–

(a) that there is reasonable cause to believe that, if a person ('the relevant person') is excluded from a dwelling-house in which the child lives, then–

(i) in the case of an order made on the ground mentioned in section 44(1)(a), the child will not be likely to suffer significant harm, even though the child is not removed as mentioned in section 44(1)(a)(i) or does not remain as mentioned in section 44(1)(a)(ii), or

(ii) in the case of an order made on the ground mentioned in paragraph (b) or (c) of section 44(1), the enquiries referred to in that paragraph will cease to be frustrated, and

(b) that another person living in the dwelling-house (whether a parent of the child or some other person)–

(i) is able and willing to give to the child the care which it would be reasonable to expect a parent to give him, and

(ii) consents to the inclusion of the exclusion requirement.

(3) For the purposes of this section an exclusion requirement is any one or more of the following–

(a) a provision requiring the relevant person to leave a dwelling-house in which he is living with the child,

(b) a provision prohibiting the relevant person from entering a dwelling-house in which the child lives, and

(c) a provision excluding the relevant person from a defined area in which a dwelling-house in which the child lives is situated.

(4) The court may provide that the exclusion requirement is to have effect for a shorter period than the other provisions of the order.

(5) Where the court makes an emergency protection order containing an exclusion requirement, the court may attach a power of arrest to the exclusion requirement.

(6) Where the court attaches a power of arrest to an exclusion requirement of an emergency protection order, it may provide that the power of arrest is to have effect for a shorter period than the exclusion requirement.

(7) Any period specified for the purposes of subsection (4) or (6) may be extended by the court (on one or more occasions) on an application to vary or discharge the emergency protection order.

(8) Where a power of arrest is attached to an exclusion requirement of an emergency protection order by virtue of subsection (5), a constable may arrest without warrant any person whom he has reasonable cause to believe to be in breach of the requirement.

(9) Sections 47(7), (11) and (12) and 48 of, and Schedule 5 to, the Family Law Act 1996 shall have effect in relation to a person arrested under subsection (8) of this section as they have effect in relation to a person arrested under section 47(6) of that Act.

(10) If, while an emergency protection order containing an exclusion requirement is in force, the applicant has removed the child from the dwelling-house from which the relevant person is excluded to other accommodation for a continuous period of more than 24 hours, the order shall cease to have effect in so far as it imposes the exclusion requirement.]

44B – (1) In any case where the court has power to include an exclusion requirement in an emergency protection order, the court may accept an undertaking from the relevant person.

(2) No power of arrest may be attached to any undertaking given under subsection (1).

(3) An undertaking given to a court under subsection (1)–

(a) shall be enforceable as if it were an order of the court, and

(b) shall cease to have effect if, while it is in force, the applicant has removed the child from the dwelling-house from which the relevant person is excluded to other accommodation for a continuous period of more than 24 hours.

(4) This section has effect without prejudice to the powers of the High Court and county court apart from this section.

(5) In this section 'exclusion requirement' and 'relevant person' have the same meaning as in section 44A.

45 – (1) An emergency protection order shall have effect for such period, not exceeding eight days, as may be specified in the order.

> **Section 45**
> *Subsection (1) An Emergency Protection Order may be made for a maximum of 8 days and may be extended once for a period not exceeding 7 days subject to the provisions set out in s45(2)(a) and (b) and s45(3) if relevant.*

(2) Where–

(a) the court making an emergency protection order would, but for this subsection, specify a period of eight days as the period for which the order is to have effect; but

(b) the last of those eight days is a public holiday (that is to say, Christmas Day, Good Friday, a bank holiday or a Sunday),

the court may specify a period which ends at noon on the first later day which is not such a holiday.

(3) Where an emergency protection order is made on an application under section 46(7), the period of eight days mentioned in subsection (1) shall begin with the first day on which the child was taken into police protection under section 46.

(4) Any person who–

(a) has parental responsibility for a child as the result of an emergency protection order; and

(b) is entitled to apply for a care order with respect to the child,

may apply to the court for the period during which the emergency protection order is to have effect to be extended.

(5) On an application under subsection (4) the court may extend the period during which the order is to have effect by such period, not exceeding seven days, as it thinks fit, but may do so only if it has reasonable cause to believe that the child concerned is likely to suffer significant harm if the order is not extended.

(6) An emergency protection order may only be extended once.

(7) Regardless of any enactment or rule of law which would otherwise prevent it from doing so, a court hearing an application for, or with respect to, an emergency protection order may take account of–

   (a) any statement contained in any report made to the court in the course of, or in connection with, the hearing; or

   (b) any evidence given during the hearing,

which is, in the opinion of the court, relevant to the application.

(8) Any of the following may apply to the court for an emergency protection order to be discharged–

   (a) the child;

   (b) a parent of his;

   (c) any person who is not a parent of his but who has parental responsibility for him; or

   (d) any person with whom he was living immediately before the making of the order.

(8A) On the application of a person who is not entitled to apply for the order to be discharged, but who is a person to whom an exclusion requirement contained in the order applies, an emergency protection order may be varied or discharged by the court in so far as it imposes the exclusion requirement.

(8B) Where a power of arrest has been attached to an exclusion requirement of an emergency protection order, the court may, on the application of any person entitled to apply for the discharge of the order so far as it imposes the exclusion requirement, vary or discharge the order in so far as it confers a power of arrest (whether or not any application has been made to vary or discharge any other provision of the order).]

(9) No application for the discharge of an emergency protection order shall be heard by the court before the expiry of the period of 72 hours beginning with the making of the order.

(10) No appeal may be made against–

   (a) the making of, or refusal to make, an emergency protection order;

   (b) the extension of, or refusal to extend, the period during which such an order is to have effect;

   (c) the discharge of, or refusal to discharge, such an order; or

   (d) the giving of, or refusal to give, any direction in connection with such an order.

(11) Subsection (8) does not apply –

   (a) where the person who would otherwise be entitled to apply for the emergency protection order to be discharged–

     (i) was given notice (in accordance with rules of court) of the hearing at which the order was made; and

     (ii) was present at that hearing; or

   (b) to any emergency protection order the effective period of which has been extended under subsection (5).

(12) A court making an emergency protection order may direct that the applicant may, in exercising any powers which he has by virtue of the order, be accompanied by a registered medical practitioner, registered nurse or registered health visitor, if he so chooses.

46 – (1) Where a constable has reasonable cause to believe that a child would otherwise be likely to suffer significant harm, he may–

   (a) remove the child to suitable accommodation and keep him there; or
   (b) take such steps as are reasonable to ensure that the child's removal from any hospital, or other place, in which he is then being accommodated is prevented.

Section 46 Police Protection
Subsection (1) This section provides for the protection of children in an emergency by a police officer taking children into police protection, without a court order, for a maximum of 72 hours. Once taken into Police Protection, the Local Authority is under a duty to receive the child and provide accommodation for him [s21(2)(a)].

(2) For the purposes of this Act, a child with respect to whom a constable has exercised his powers under this section is referred to as having been taken into police protection.

(3) As soon as is reasonably practicable after taking a child into police protection, the constable concerned shall–

   (a) inform the local authority within whose area the child was found of the steps that have been, and are proposed to be, taken with respect to the child under this section and the reasons for taking them;
   (b) give details to the authority within whose area the child is ordinarily resident ('the appropriate authority') of the place at which the child is being accommodated;
   (c) inform the child (if he appears capable of understanding)–
      (i) of the steps that have been taken with respect to him under this section and of the reasons for taking them; and
      (ii) of the further steps that may be taken with respect to him under this section;
   (d) take such steps as are reasonably practicable to discover the wishes and feelings of the child;
   (e) secure that the case is inquired into by an officer designated for the purposes of this section by the chief officer of the police area concerned; and
   (f) where the child was taken into police protection by being removed to accommodation which is not provided–
      (i) by or on behalf of a local authority; or

(ii) as a refuge, in compliance with the requirements of section 51,
secure that he is moved to accommodation which is so provided.

> **Subsection (3)** *Sets out the action that must be taken by a constable who takes the child into Police Protection including the referral of the case to a designated officer [see s46(9)(b)].*

(4) As soon as is reasonably practicable after taking a child into police protection, the constable concerned shall take such steps as are reasonably practicable to inform–

(a) the child's parents;
(b) every person who is not a parent of his but who has parental responsibility for him; and
(c) any other person with whom the child was living immediately before being taken into police protection,

of the steps that he has taken under this section with respect to the child, the reasons for taking them and the further steps that may be taken with respect to him under this section.

(5) On completing any inquiry under subsection (3)(e), the officer conducting it shall release the child from police protection unless he considers that there is still reasonable cause for believing that the child would be likely to suffer significant harm if released.

(6) No child may be kept in police protection for more than 72 hours.

(7) While a child is being kept in police protection, the designated officer may apply on behalf of the appropriate authority for an emergency protection order to be made under section 44 with respect to the child.

> **Subsection (7)** *This subsection enables the provisions of s44 in relation to Emergency Protection Orders to be used. If a child is to be kept, or removed, at the expiry of the 72 hour period, an Emergency Protection Order [s44] or a Care Order [s31] must be applied for.*

(8) An application may be made under subsection (7) whether or not the authority know of it or agree to its being made.

(9) While a child is being kept in police protection–

(a) neither the constable concerned nor the designated officer shall have parental responsibility for him; but

> **Subsection (9)(a)** *The police officer does not acquire parental responsibility [ss2-4] for the child: compare with an Emergency Protection Order [s44], a Child Assessment Order [s43], Care Order [s31] or Interim Care Order [s38].*

    (b) the designated officer shall do what is reasonable in all the circumstances of the case for the purpose of safeguarding or promoting the child's welfare (having regard in particular to the length of the period during which the child will be so protected).

> **Subsection (9)(b)** *This subsection sets out the duties of the designated officer. A Chief Officer for each police area must designate officers for the purposes of the Children Act to whom children taken into Police Protection must be referred by the acting constable.*

(10) Where a child has been taken into police protection, the designated officer shall allow–

    (a) the child's parents;

    (b) any person who is not a parent of the child but who has parental responsibility for him;

    (c) any person with whom the child was living immediately before he was taken into police protection;

    (d) any person in whose favour a contact order is in force with respect to the child;

    (e) any person who is allowed to have contact with the child by virtue of an order under section 34; and

    (f) any person acting on behalf of any of those persons,
to have such contact (if any) with the child as, in the opinion of the designated officer, is both reasonable and in the child's best interests.

(11) Where a child who has been taken into police protection is in accommodation provided by, or on behalf of, the appropriate authority, subsection (10) shall have effect as if it referred to the authority rather than to the designated officer.

47 – (1) Where a local authority–

    (a) are informed that a child who lives, or is found, in their area–

        (i) is the subject of an emergency protection order; or

        (ii) is in police protection; or

        [(iii)has contravened a ban imposed by a curfew notice within the meaning of Chapter I of Part I of the Crime and Disorder Act 1998; or]

    (b) have reasonable cause to suspect that a child who lives, or is found, in their area is suffering, or is likely to suffer, significant harm, the authority shall make, or cause to be made, such enquiries as they consider necessary to enable them to decide whether they should take any action to safeguard or promote the child's welfare.

[In the case of a child falling within paragraph (a)(iii) above, the enquiries shall be commenced as soon as practicable and, in any event, within 48 hours of the authority receiving the information.

(2) Where a local authority have obtained an emergency protection order with respect to a child, they shall make, or cause to be made, such enquiries as they consider necessary to enable them to decide what action they should take to safeguard or promote the child's welfare.

(3) The enquiries shall, in particular, be directed towards establishing–

(a) whether the authority should make any application to the court, or exercise any of their other powers under this Act [or section 11 of the Crime and Disorder Act 1998 (child safety orders)], with respect to the child;

Section 47 Duty to Investigate
Subsection (3)(a) This subsection requires the Local Authority to consider whether it ought to institute care proceedings in respect of a child [for care orders see s31] or to make an application for an Emergency Protection Order [see s44]. It is primarily aimed at emergency situations.

(b) whether, in the case of a child–
　(i) with respect to whom an emergency protection order has been made; and
　(ii) who is not in accommodation provided by or on behalf of the authority,

it would be in the child's best interests (while an emergency protection order remains in force) for him to be in such accommodation; and

(c) whether, in the case of a child who has been taken into police protection, it would be in the child's best interests for the authority to ask for an application to be made under section 46(7).

(4) Where enquiries are being made under subsection (1) with respect to a child, the local authority concerned shall (with a view to enabling them to determine what action, if any, to take with respect to him) take such steps as are reasonably practicable–

(a) to obtain access to him; or
(b) to ensure that access to him is obtained, on their behalf, by a person authorised by them for the purpose,

unless they are satisfied that they already have sufficient information with respect to him.

(5) Where, as a result of any such enquiries, it appears to the authority that there are matters connected with the child's education which should be investigated, they shall consult the relevant local education authority.

(6) Where, in the course of enquiries made under this section–

   (a) any officer of the local authority concerned; or
   (b) any person authorised by the authority to act on their behalf in connection with those enquiries–
       (i) is refused access to the child concerned; or
       (ii) is denied information as to his whereabouts,

   the authority shall apply for an emergency protection order, a child assessment order, a care order or a supervision order with respect to the child unless they are satisfied that his welfare can be satisfactorily safeguarded without their doing so.

> **Subsection (6)** *See the provisions governing applications for Child Assessment Orders [s43], Emergency Protection Orders [s44] and Care/Supervision Orders [s31].*

(7) If, on the conclusion of any enquiries or review made under this section, the authority decide not to apply for an emergency protection order, a care order, a child assessment order or a supervision order they shall–

   (a) consider whether it would be appropriate to review the case at a later date; and
   (b) if they decide that it would be, determine the date on which that review is to begin.

(8) Where, as a result of complying with this section, a local authority conclude that they should take action to safeguard or promote the child's welfare they shall take that action (so far as it is both within their power and reasonably practicable for them to do so).

> **Subsection (8)** *This subsection, for example, requires the Local Authority to either take court action, or offer services to a child/family. Examples of services may include advice or counselling, day care, home help, travel assistance, financial help or as set out in Schedule 2 Part I paragraphs 1-11 and ss17-19 of the Act.*

(9) Where a local authority are conducting enquiries under this section, it shall be the duty of any person mentioned in subsection (11) to assist them with those

enquiries (in particular by providing relevant information and advice) if called upon by the authority to do so.

(10) Subsection (9) does not oblige any person to assist a local authority where doing so would be unreasonable in all the circumstances of the case.

(11) The persons are–

   (a) any local authority;
   (b) any local education authority;
   (c) any local housing authority;
   (d) any [Health Authority, Special Health Authority] [or National Health Service trust]; and
   (e) any person authorised by the Secretary of State for the purposes of this section.

(12) Where a local authority are making enquiries under this section with respect to a child who appears to them to be ordinarily resident within the area of another authority, they shall consult that other authority, who may undertake the necessary enquiries in their place.

48 – (1) Where it appears to a court making an emergency protection order that adequate information as to the child's whereabouts–

   (a) is not available to the applicant for the order; but
   (b) is available to another person,

it may include in the order a provision requiring that other person to disclose, if asked to do so by the applicant, any information that he may have as to the child's whereabouts.

(2) No person shall be excused from complying with such a requirement on the ground that complying might incriminate him or his spouse of an offence; but a statement or admission made in complying shall not be admissible in evidence against either of them in proceedings for any offence other than perjury.

(3) An emergency protection order may authorise the applicant to enter premises specified by the order and search for the child with respect to whom the order is made.

(4) Where the court is satisfied that there is reasonable cause to believe that there may be another child on those premises with respect to whom an emergency protection order ought to be made, it may make an order authorising the applicant to search for that other child on those premises.

(5) Where–

   (a) an order has been made under subsection (4);
   (b) the child concerned has been found on the premises; and
   (c) the applicant is satisfied that the grounds for making an emergency protection order exist with respect to him,

the order shall have effect as if it were an emergency protection order.

> **Section 48 Power to assist in Emergency Protection Orders**
> *Subsections (4),(5) If another child is found upon the premises in addition to the subject of an Emergency Protection Order and the Applicant is satisfied that grounds exist for an Emergency Protection Order, then the Applicant is entitled to remove that child and the Order applies as if it were to both [all] children, on condition that an order has been made authorising the Applicant to search for the additional child/ children.*

(6) Where an order has been made under subsection (4), the applicant shall notify the court of its effect.

(7) A person shall be guilty of an offence if he intentionally obstructs any person exercising the power of entry and search under subsection (3) or (4).

(8) A person guilty of an offence under subsection (7) shall be liable on summary conviction to a fine not exceeding level 3 on the standard scale.

(9) Where, on an application made by any person for a warrant under this section, it appears to the court–

    (a) that a person attempting to exercise powers under an emergency protection order has been prevented from doing so by being refused entry to the premises concerned or access to the child concerned; or

    (b) that any such person is likely to be so prevented from exercising any such powers,

it may issue a warrant authorising any constable to assist the person mentioned in paragraph (a) or (b) in the exercise of those powers, using reasonable force if necessary.

(10) Every warrant issued under this section shall be addressed to, and executed by, a constable who shall be accompanied by the person applying for the warrant if–

    (a) that person so desires; and

    (b) the court by whom the warrant is issued does not direct otherwise.

(11) A court granting an application for a warrant under this section may direct that the constable concerned may, in executing the warrant, be accompanied by a registered medical practitioner, registered nurse or registered health visitor if he so chooses.

(12) An application for a warrant under this section shall be made in the manner and form prescribed by rules of court.

(13) Wherever it is reasonably practicable to do so, an order under subsection (4), an application for a warrant under this section and any such warrant shall name the child; and where it does not name him it shall describe him as clearly as possible.

> **Subsection (9) -(13)** *These subsections deal with the granting of warrants to enable someone attempting to exercise powers under an Emergency Protection Order to exercise those powers. The warrant itself must be executed by a constable, and may contain directions for its execution.*

49 – (1) A person shall be guilty of an offence if, knowingly and without lawful authority or reasonable excuse, he–

(a) takes a child to whom this section applies away from the responsible person;

(b) keeps such a child away from the responsible person; or

(c) induces, assists or incites such a child to run away or stay away from the responsible person.

(2) This section applies in relation to a child who is–

(a) in care;

(b) the subject of an emergency protection order; or

(c) in police protection,

and in this section 'the responsible person' means any person who for the time being has care of him by virtue of the care order, the emergency protection order, or section 46, as the case may be.

(3) A person guilty of an offence under this section shall be liable on summary conviction to imprisonment for a term not exceeding six months, or to a fine not exceeding level 5 on the standard scale, or to both.

> **Section 49 Recovery Orders**
> *This section creates criminal offences in respect of those who remove or keep children from responsible persons under a Care Order [s31], Emergency Protection Order [s44] or Police Protection [s46] or incite such children to run or stay away from that responsible person under those provisions.*

50 – (1) Where it appears to the court that there is reason to believe that a child to whom this section applies–

(a) has been unlawfully taken away or is being unlawfully kept away from the responsible person;

(b) has run away or is staying away from the responsible person; or

(c) is missing,

the court may make an order under this section ('a recovery order').

> **Section 50 Abduction**
> *Subsection (1) A Recovery Order may be applied for without giving notice of the application to anyone else. It is not time-limited and therefore may last until such time as the child is recovered. This section allows the court to make a Recovery Order where a child in care [s31] or subject to an Emergency Protection Order [s44] or in Police Protection [s46] is missing or has been unlawfully kept or taken or has run away or is staying away.*

(2) This section applies to the same children to whom section 49 applies and in this section 'the responsible person' has the same meaning as in section 49.

(3) A recovery order–

    (a) operates as a direction to any person who is in a position to do so to produce the child on request to any authorised person;

    (b) authorises the removal of the child by any authorised person;

    (c) requires any person who has information as to the child's whereabouts to disclose that information, if asked to do so, to a constable or an officer of the court;

    (d) authorises a constable to enter any premises specified in the order and search for the child, using reasonable force if necessary.

(4) The court may make a recovery order only on the application of–

    (a) any person who has parental responsibility for the child by virtue of a care order or emergency protection order; or

    (b) where the child is in police protection, the designated officer.

(5) A recovery order shall name the child and–

    (a) any person who has parental responsibility for the child by virtue of a care order or emergency protection order; or

    (b) where the child is in police protection, the designated officer.

> **Subsections (4), (5)**
> *In the case of a Care Order [s31] the Local Authority will have Parental Responsibility [ss2-4]. In the case of an Emergency Protection Order, the applicant will have Parental Responsibility.*

(6) Premises may only be specified under subsection (3)(d) if it appears to the court that there are reasonable grounds for believing the child to be on them.

(7) In this section–

'an authorised person' means–

(a) any person specified by the court;
(b) any constable;
(c) any person who is authorised–
   (i) after the recovery order is made; and
   (ii) by a person who has parental responsibility for the child by virtue of a care order or an emergency protection order,

to exercise any power under a recovery order; and

'the designated officer' means the officer designated for the purposes of section 46.

(8) Where a person is authorised as mentioned in subsection (7)(c)–

(a) the authorisation shall identify the recovery order; and
(b) any person claiming to be so authorised shall, if asked to do so, produce some duly authenticated document showing that he is so authorised.

(9) A person shall be guilty of an offence if he intentionally obstructs an authorised person exercising the power under subsection (3)(b) to remove a child.

(10) A person guilty of an offence under this section shall be liable on summary conviction to a fine not exceeding level 3 on the standard scale.

(11) No person shall be excused from complying with any request made under subsection (3)(c) on the ground that complying with it might incriminate him or his spouse of an offence; but a statement or admission made in complying shall not be admissible in evidence against either of them in proceedings for an offence other than perjury.

(12) Where a child is made the subject of a recovery order whilst being looked after by a local authority, any reasonable expenses incurred by an authorised person in giving effect to the order shall be recoverable from the authority.

(13) (applies to Scotland only)

(14) In this section 'the court', in relation to Northern Ireland, means a magistrates' court within the meaning of the Magistrates' Courts (Northern Ireland) Order 1981.

Section 51 Refuges for Children at Risk

Any person who provides refuge for a child who has run away from parents or carers or from accommodation while in care [s31] or from Police Protection [s46] or who is subject to an Emergency Protection Order [s44] may be guilty of a criminal offence. Section 51 generally provides that certain persons fulfilling this role are not liable to prosecution under s49 or other legislation provided that such refuge is offered at places in respect of which the Secretary of State has issued a certificate. The purpose is to assist bona fide organisations which assist runaways who have made up their own mind. It is not clear under the Act at what age a child may lawfully leave home/his accommodation and therefore be entitled to refuse to return [whether subject to a Care Order [s31] or Emergency Protection Order [s44].

51 – (1) Where it is proposed to use a voluntary home or registered children's home to provide a refuge for children who appear to be at risk of harm, the Secretary of State may issue a certificate under this section with respect to that home.

(2) Where a local authority or voluntary organisation arrange for a foster parent to provide such a refuge, the Secretary of State may issue a certificate under this section with respect to that foster parent.

(3) In subsection (2) 'foster parent' means a person who is, or who from time to time is, a local authority foster parent or a foster parent with whom children are placed by a voluntary organisation.

(4) The Secretary of State may by regulations–

 (a) make provision as to the manner in which certificates may be issued;
 (b) impose requirements which must be complied with while any certificate is in force; and
 (c) provide for the withdrawal of certificates in prescribed circumstances.

(5) Where a certificate is in force with respect to a home, none of the provisions mentioned in subsection (7) shall apply in relation to any person providing a refuge for any child in that home.

(6) Where a certificate is in force with respect to a foster parent, none of those provisions shall apply in relation to the provision by him of a refuge for any child in accordance with arrangements made by the local authority or voluntary organisation.

(7) The provisions are–

 (a) section 49;
 (b) sections 82 (recovery of certain fugitive children) and 83 (harbouring) of the Children (Scotland) Act 1995, so far as they apply in relation to anything done in England and Wales;]

(c) section 32(3) of the Children and Young Persons Act 1969 (compelling, persuading, inciting or assisting any person to be absent from detention, etc), so far as it applies in relation to anything done in England and Wales;

(d) section 2 of the Child Abduction Act 1984.

52 – (1) Without prejudice to section 93 or any other power to make such rules, rules of court may be made with respect to the procedure to be followed in connection with proceedings under this Part.

(2) The rules may in particular make provision–

(a) as to the form in which any application is to be made or direction is to be given;

(b) prescribing the persons who are to be notified of–

    (i) the making, or extension, of an emergency protection order; or

    (ii) the making of an application under section 45(4) or (8) or 46(7); and

(c) as to the content of any such notification and the manner in which, and person by whom, it is to be given.

(3) The Secretary of State may by regulations provide that, where–

(a) an emergency protection order has been made with respect to a child;

(b) the applicant for the order was not the local authority within whose area the child is ordinarily resident; and

(c) that local authority are of the opinion that it would be in the child's best interests for the applicant's responsibilities under the order to be transferred to them,

that authority shall (subject to their having complied with any requirements imposed by the regulations) be treated, for the purposes of this Act, as though they and not the original applicant had applied for, and been granted, the order.

(4) Regulations made under subsection (3) may, in particular, make provision as to–

(a) the considerations to which the local authority shall have regard in forming an opinion as mentioned in subsection (3)(c); and

(b) the time at which responsibility under any emergency protection order is to be treated as having been transferred to a local authority.

Part VI

Community Homes

53 – (1) Every local authority shall make such arrangements as they consider appropriate for securing that homes ('community homes') are available–

(a) for the care and accommodation of children looked after by them; and

(b) for purposes connected with the welfare of children (whether or not looked after by them),

and may do so jointly with one or more other local authorities.

Section 53. Provision of community homes by local authorities
Subsection (1) 'Community homes' is effectively a blanket term for homes in the local authority's area. This subsection imposes an obligation on the local authority to provide homes in its area for the accommodation of children it is looking after and also for other purposes as to children's welfare. (In the latter case, the children do not have to be being looked after by the local authority.)

(2) In making such arrangements, a local authority shall have regard to the need for ensuring the availability of accommodation–

(a) of different descriptions; and

(b) which is suitable for different purposes and the requirements of different descriptions of children.

Subsection (2) The local authority must ensure that there is a variety of accommodation available in its area and that it can fit the varying requirements of the children in the area.

(3) A community home may be a home–

(a) provided, [equipped, maintained and (subject to subsection (3A)) managed] by a local authority; or

(b) provided by a voluntary organisation but in respect of which a local authority and the organisation–

(i) propose that, in accordance with an instrument of management, the [equipment, maintenance and (subject to subsection (3B)) management] of the home shall be the responsibility of the local authority; or

(ii) so propose that the management, equipment and maintenance of the home shall be the responsibility of the voluntary organisation.

> **Subsection (3)** *The definition of a community home is such that it can be provided either by a local authority or a voluntary organisation, and can be managed by either, but in the case of management by the voluntary organisation, the local authority must give its agreement.*

(3A) A local authority may make arrangements for the management by another person of accommodation provided by the local authority for the purpose of restricting the liberty of children.

(3B) Where a local authority are to be responsible for the management of a community home provided by a voluntary organisation, the local authority may, with the consent of the body of managers constituted by the instrument of management for the home, make arrangements for the management by another person of accommodation provided for the purpose of restricting the liberty of children.

> **Subsections (3A) (3B)** *Where the local authority is managing a community home whether provided by itself or by a voluntary organisation and the accommodation is to be used for restricting the children's liberty, the local authority may appoint another person to manage it.*

(4) Where a local authority are to be responsible for the management of a community home provided by a voluntary organisation, the authority shall designate the home as a controlled community home.

> **Subsection (4)** *A community home provided by the voluntary organisation, but managed by the local authority is to be designated a 'controlled' community home.*

(5) Where a voluntary organisation are to be responsible for the management of a community home provided by the organisation, the local authority shall designate the home as an assisted community home.

> **Subsection (5)** *A community home provided and managed by the voluntary organisation is to be designated by the local authority as an 'assisted' community home.*
>
> *See Schedule 4 for further information.*

(6) Schedule 4 shall have effect for the purpose of supplementing the provisions of this Part.

54 – (1) Where it appears to the Secretary of State that–

(a) any premises used for the purposes of a community home are unsuitable for those purposes; or

(b) the conduct of a community home–

(i) is not in accordance with regulations made by him under paragraph 4 of Schedule 4; or

(ii) is otherwise unsatisfactory,

he may, by notice in writing served on the responsible body, direct that as from such date as may be specified in the notice the premises shall not be used for the purposes of a community home.

(2) Where–

(a) the Secretary of State has given a direction under subsection (1); and

(b) the direction has not been revoked,

he may at any time by order revoke the instrument of management for the home concerned.

(3) For the purposes of subsection (1), the responsible body–

(a) in relation to a community home provided by a local authority, is that local authority;

(b) in relation to a controlled community home, is the local authority specified in the home's instrument of management; and

(c) in relation to an assisted community home, is the voluntary organisation by which the home is provided.

Section 54. Directions that premises be no longer used for community home
This sets out the powers of the Secretary of State to direct that a place no longer be used as a community home. Any such direction should be served on the body managing the home, where it is the local authority or the voluntary organisation, and in other cases, the local authority.

55 – (1) Where any dispute relating to a controlled community home arises between the local authority specified in the home's instrument of management and–

(a) the voluntary organisation by which the home is provided; or

(b) any other local authority who have placed, or desire or are required to place, in the home a child who is looked after by them,

the dispute may be referred by either party to the Secretary of State for his determination.

(2) Where any dispute relating to an assisted community home arises between the voluntary organisation by which the home is provided and any local authority who have placed, or desire to place, in the home a child who is looked after by them, the dispute may be referred by either party to the Secretary of State for his determination.

(3) Where a dispute is referred to the Secretary of State under this section he may, in order to give effect to his determination of the dispute, give such directions as he thinks fit to the local authority or voluntary organisation concerned.

(4) This section applies even though the matter in dispute may be one which, under or by virtue of Part II of Schedule 4, is reserved for the decision, or is the responsibility, of–

(a) the local authority specified in the home's instrument of management; or
(b) (as the case may be) the voluntary organisation by which the home is provided.

(5) Where any trust deed relating to a controlled or assisted community home contains provision whereby a bishop or any other ecclesiastical or denominational authority has power to decide questions relating to religious instruction given in the home, no dispute which is capable of being dealt with in accordance with that provision shall be referred to the Secretary of State under this section.

(6) In this Part 'trust deed', in relation to a voluntary home, means any instrument (other than an instrument of management) regulating–

(a) the maintenance, management or conduct of the home; or
(b) the constitution of a body of managers or trustees of the home.

Section 55. Determination of disputes relating to controlled and assisted community homes.
This deals with the power of the Secretary of State to decide disputes arising between the local authority and voluntary organisation, or another local authority in certain cases. This is subject to powers set out in any trust deed for the home given to 'a bishop or any other ecclesiastical or denominational authority' specifically to decide disputes relating to religious instruction in the home. (See s. 55(5))

56 – (1) The voluntary organisation by which a controlled or assisted community home is provided shall not cease to provide the home except after giving to the Secretary of State and the local authority specified in the home's instrument of management not less than two years' notice in writing of their intention to do so.

(2) A notice under subsection (1) shall specify the date from which the voluntary organisation intend to cease to provide the home as a community home.

(3) Where such a notice is given and is not withdrawn before the date specified in it, the home's instrument of management shall cease to have effect on that date and the home shall then cease to be a controlled or assisted community home.

(4) Where a notice is given under subsection (1) and the home's managers give notice in writing to the Secretary of State that they are unable or unwilling to continue as its managers until the date specified in the subsection (1) notice, the Secretary of State may by order–

(a) revoke the home's instrument of management; and

(b) require the local authority who were specified in that instrument to conduct the home until–

(i) the date specified in the subsection (1) notice; or

(ii) such earlier date (if any) as may be specified for the purposes of this paragraph in the order,

as if it were a community home provided by the local authority.

(5) Where the Secretary of State imposes a requirement under subsection (4)(b)–

(a) nothing in the trust deed for the home shall affect the conduct of the home by the local authority;

(b) the Secretary of State may by order direct that for the purposes of any provision specified in the direction and made by or under any enactment relating to community homes (other than this section) the home shall, until the date or earlier date specified as mentioned in subsection (4)(b), be treated as a controlled or assisted community home;

(c) except in so far as the Secretary of State so directs, the home shall until that date be treated for the purposes of any such enactment as a community home provided by the local authority; and

(d) on the date or earlier date specified as mentioned in subsection (4)(b) the home shall cease to be a community home.

Section 56. Discontinuance by voluntary organisation of controlled or assisted community home
This deals with the method by which the voluntary organisation can cease to provide a community home. Note that a notice period of two years has to be given by the organisation of its intention to cease to provide the home, although there are powers given to the Secretary of State to direct the local authority to take over the provision and management of such a home, should the organisation be unable to provide throughout the notice period.

57 – (1) The local authority specified in the instrument of management for a controlled or assisted community home may give–

(a) the Secretary of State; and

(b) the voluntary organisation by which the home is provided,

not less than two years' notice in writing of their intention to withdraw their designation of the home as a controlled or assisted community home.

(2) A notice under subsection (1) shall specify the date ('the specified date') on which the designation is to be withdrawn.

(3) Where–

(a) a notice is given under subsection (1) in respect of a controlled or assisted community home;

(b) the home's managers give notice in writing to the Secretary of State that they are unable or unwilling to continue as managers until the specified date; and

(c) the managers' notice is not withdrawn,

the Secretary of State may by order revoke the home's instrument of management from such date earlier than the specified date as may be specified in the order.

(4) Before making an order under subsection (3), the Secretary of State shall consult the local authority and the voluntary organisation.

(5) Where a notice has been given under subsection (1) and is not withdrawn, the home's instrument of management shall cease to have effect on–

(a) the specified date; or

(b) where an earlier date has been specified under subsection (3), that earlier date,

and the home shall then cease to be a community home.

Section 57. Closure by local authority of controlled or assisted community home
This sets out the method by which a local authority may withdraw its designation of 'controlled' or 'assisted' community home. Note it must give both the voluntary organisation by which the home is provided, and the Secretary of State two years' notice of its intention. However, if the managers of the home do not wish to continue, the Secretary of State may revoke the home's instrument of management earlier.

58 – (1) Where–

(a) the instrument of management for a controlled or assisted community home is revoked or otherwise ceases to have effect under section 54(2), 56(3) or (4)(a) or 57(3) or (5); or

(b) any premises used for the purposes of such a home are (at any time after 13th January 1987) disposed of, or put to use otherwise than for those purposes,

the proprietor shall become liable to pay compensation ('the appropriate compensation') in accordance with this section.

(2) Where the instrument of management in force at the relevant time relates–

(a) to a controlled community home; or

(b) to an assisted community home which, at any time before the instrument came into force, was a controlled community home,

the appropriate compensation is a sum equal to that part of the value of any premises which is attributable to expenditure incurred in relation to the premises, while the home was a controlled community home, by the authority who were then the responsible authority.

(3) Where the instrument of management in force at the relevant time relates–

(a) to an assisted community home; or

(b) to a controlled community home which, at any time before the instrument came into force, was an assisted community home,

the appropriate compensation is a sum equal to that part of the value of the premises which is attributable to the expenditure of money provided by way of grant under section 82, section 65 of the Children and Young Persons Act 1969 or section 82 of the Child Care Act 1980.

(4) Where the home is, at the relevant time, conducted in premises which formerly were used as an approved school or were an approved probation hostel or home, the appropriate compensation is a sum equal to that part of the value of the premises which is attributable to the expenditure–

(a) of sums paid towards the expenses of the managers of an approved school under section 104 of the Children and Young Persons Act 1933; or

(b) of sums paid under section 51(3)(c) of the Powers of Criminal Courts Act 1973 [or section 20(1)(c) of the Probation Service Act 1993] in relation to expenditure on approved probation hostels or homes.

(5) The appropriate compensation shall be paid–

(a) in the case of compensation payable under subsection (2), to the authority who were the responsible authority at the relevant time; and

(b) in any other case, to the Secretary of State.

(6) In this section–

'disposal' includes the grant of a tenancy and any other conveyance, assignment, transfer, grant, variation or extinguishment of an interest in or right over land, whether made by instrument or otherwise;

'premises' means any premises or part of premises (including land) used for the purposes of the home and belonging to the proprietor;

'the proprietor' means–

(a) the voluntary organisation by which the home is, at the relevant time, provided; or

(b) if the premises are not, at the relevant time, vested in that organisation, the persons in whom they are vested;

'the relevant time' means the time immediately before the liability to pay arises under subsection (1); and

'the responsible authority' means the local authority specified in the instrument of management in question.

(7) For the purposes of this section an event of a kind mentioned in subsection (1)(b) shall be taken to have occurred–

(a) in the case of a disposal, on the date on which the disposal was completed or, in the case of a disposal which is effected by a series of transactions, the date on which the last of those transactions was completed;

(b) in the case of premises which are put to different use, on the date on which they first begin to be put to their new use.

(8) The amount of any sum payable under this section shall be determined in accordance with such arrangements–

(a) as may be agreed between the voluntary organisation by which the home is, at the relevant time, provided and the responsible authority or (as the case may be) the Secretary of State;

or

(b) in default of agreement, as may be determined by the Secretary of State.

(9) With the agreement of the responsible authority or (as the case may be) the Secretary of State, the liability to pay any sum under this section may be discharged, in whole or in part, by the transfer of any premises.

(10) This section has effect regardless of–

(a) anything in any trust deed for a controlled or assisted community home;

(b) the provisions of any enactment or instrument governing the disposition of the property of a voluntary organisation.

Section 58. Financial provisions applicable on cessation of controlled or assisted community home or disposal etc of premises.
This deals with compensation payable by the proprietor on revocation of instrument of management or on dealing with the premises for purposes other than as a home, to either the local authority or the Secretary of State.

PART VII

VOLUNTARY HOMES AND VOLUNTARY ORGANISATIONS

59 – (1) Where a voluntary organisation provide accommodation for a child, they shall do so by–

(a) placing him (subject to subsection (2)) with–
   (i) a family;
   (ii) a relative of his; or
   (iii) any other suitable person,

   on such terms as to payment by the organisation and otherwise as the organisation may determine;

(b) maintaining him in a voluntary home;
(c) maintaining him in a community home;
(d) maintaining him in a registered children's home;
(e) maintaining him in a home provided by the Secretary of State under section 82(5) on such terms as the Secretary of State may from time to time determine; or
(f) making such other arrangements (subject to subsection (3)) as seem appropriate to them.

Section 59. Provision of accommodation by voluntary organisations
Subsection (1) This sets out the ways in which a voluntary organisation might accommodate a child. Voluntary organisation: the definition is as set out in section 105 ('a body (other than a public or local authority) whose activities are not carried on for profit')

(2) The Secretary of State may make regulations as to the placing of children with foster parents by voluntary organisations and the regulations may, in particular, make provision which (with any necessary modifications) is similar to the provision that may be made under section 23(2)(a).

(3) The Secretary of State may make regulations as to the arrangements which may be made under subsection (1)(f) and the regulations may in particular make provision which (with any necessary modifications) is similar to the provision that may be made under section 23(2)(f).

Subsections (2) (3)
These subsections indicate that the voluntary organisation is subject to regulations made by the Secretary of State when placing a child with foster parents or using their discretion as to making appropriate arrangements for a child which are not specified by statute.

(4) The Secretary of State may make regulations requiring any voluntary organisation who are providing accommodation for a child–

(a) to review his case; and
(b) to consider any representations (including any complaint) made to them by any person falling within a prescribed class of person,

in accordance with the provisions of the regulations.

(5) Regulations under subsection (4) may in particular make provision which (with any necessary modifications) is similar to the provision that may be made under section 26.

Subsections (4) (5)
These subsections deal with the voluntary organisation's obligations as to review of the position of a child who is being accommodated by the organisation, and places the organisation under similar regulations and obligations in its review process as a local authority accommodating a child.

(6) Regulations under subsections (2) to (4) may provide that any person who, without reasonable excuse, contravenes or fails to comply with a regulation shall be guilty of an offence and liable on summary conviction to a fine not exceeding level 4 on the standard scale.

Subsection (6) *This allows the Secretary of State power in making regulations under ss (2) and (4) to create a criminal offence, punishable by fine, of a contravention of a regulation.*

60 – (1) No voluntary home shall be carried on unless it is registered in a register to be kept for the purposes of this section by the Secretary of State.

Section 60. Registration and regulation of voluntary homes.
Subsection (1) This makes it compulsory for all voluntary homes to be registered with the Secretary of State, before they can operate as such.

(2) The register may be kept by means of a computer.

(3) In this Act 'voluntary home' means any home or other institution providing care and accommodation for children which is carried on by a voluntary organisation but does not include–

(a) a nursing home, mental nursing home or residential care home [(other than a small home)];
(b) a school;
(c) any health service hospital;
(d) any community home;
(e) any home or other institution provided, equipped and maintained by the Secretary of State; or
(f) any home which is exempted by regulations made for the purposes of this section by the Secretary of State.

Subsection (3) This sets out the definition of 'voluntary home', specifically excluding certain institutions. All required definitions for these institutions can be found at s.105(1) of the Act, with the exception of 'community home' the definition of which can be found at s.53.

(4) Schedule 5 shall have effect for the purpose of supplementing the provisions of this Part.

Subsection (4) Reference needs to be made to Schedule 5 of the Act for more information as to the process of registration and regulation of voluntary homes.

61 – (1) Where a child is accommodated by or on behalf of a voluntary organisation, it shall be the duty of the organisation–

(a) to safeguard and promote his welfare;
(b) to make such use of the services and facilities available for children cared for by their own parents as appears to the organisation reasonable in his case; and
(c) to advise, assist and befriend him with a view to promoting his welfare when he ceases to be so accommodated.

Section 61. Duties of voluntary organisations
Subsection (1) This imposes three general duties on the organisation to a child accommodated by the organisation. These are promotion of the child's welfare, reasonable provision of services for a child who remains with his or her own parents, and continuing advice and assistance to the child after ceasing to be accommodated. This last duty means that the organisation has continuing obligations to the child, even though it no longer has specific responsibility for his or her full time care.

(2) Before making any decision with respect to any such child the organisation shall, so far as is reasonably practicable, ascertain the wishes and feelings of–

(a) the child;
(b) his parents;
(c) any person who is not a parent of his but who has parental responsibility for him; and
(d) any other person whose wishes and feelings the organisation consider to be relevant,

regarding the matter to be decided.

Subsection (2) This sets out the consultation process necessary before making decisions in respect of any child who the organisation is accommodating. It is similar in nature to the consultation process that a local authority has to undergo when accommodating or caring for a child.

(3) In making any such decision the organisation shall give due consideration–

(a) having regard to the child's age and understanding, to such wishes and feelings of his as they have been able to ascertain;
(b) to such other wishes and feelings mentioned in subsection (2) as they have been able to ascertain; and
(c) to the child's religious persuasion, racial origin and cultural and linguistic background.

Subsection (3) This obliges the voluntary organisation to take into account the consultations it has made according to s.61(2) and also the child's background when actually making the decision in respect of the child. The voluntary organisation would be expected to show that its decision making process was in order with the statute, were there to be any query or complaint as regards the action taken.

62 – (1) Every local authority shall satisfy themselves that any voluntary organisation providing accommodation–

(a) within the authority's area for any child; or
(b) outside that area for any child on behalf of the authority,

are satisfactorily safeguarding and promoting the welfare of the children so provided with accommodation.

Section 62. Duties of local authorities
Subsection (1) The local authority has to make sure that the voluntary organisation is acting in accordance with the welfare principle. This section sets out the overriding responsibility the local authority still has for the children from its area, even if a voluntary organisation is providing accommodation for them. The local authority has a supervisory role as far as the voluntary organisation is concerned and should be proactive in carrying out that role.

(2) Every local authority shall arrange for children who are accommodated within their area by or on behalf of voluntary organisations to be visited, from time to time, in the interests of their welfare.

(3) The Secretary of State may make regulations–

(a) requiring every child who is accommodated within a local authority's area, by or on behalf of a voluntary organisation, to be visited by an officer of the authority–
    (i) in prescribed circumstances; and
    (ii) on specified occasions or within specified periods; and
(b) imposing requirements which must be met by any local authority, or officer of a local authority, carrying out functions under this section.

Subsections (2) (3) These subsections impose a duty upon the local authority to visit any child accommodated by a voluntary organisation, in order to check that their welfare is being safeguarded and promoted. They also give power for regulations to be made that prescribe times and frequency for such visits, and also that set out requirements for the local authority in carrying out its duties under this section.

(4) Subsection (2) does not apply in relation to community homes.

(5) Where a local authority are not satisfied that the welfare of any child who is accommodated by or on behalf of a voluntary organisation is being satisfactorily

safeguarded or promoted they shall–

(a) unless they consider that it would not be in the best interests of the child, take such steps as are reasonably practicable to secure that the care and accommodation of the child is undertaken by–

(i) a parent of his;

(ii) any person who is not a parent of his but who has parental responsibility for him; or

(iii) a relative of his; and

(b) consider the extent to which (if at all) they should exercise any of their functions with respect to the child.

> **Subsection (5)** *This sets out the action that a local authority must take if it believes that a voluntary organisation is not promoting and safeguarding the welfare of a child from its area.*

(6) Any person authorised by a local authority may, for the purpose of enabling the authority to discharge their duties under this section–

(a) enter, at any reasonable time, and inspect any premises in which children are being accommodated as mentioned in subsection (1) or (2);

(b) inspect any children there;

(c) require any person to furnish him with such records of a kind required to be kept by regulations made under paragraph 7 of Schedule 5 (in whatever form they are held), or allow him to inspect such records, as he may at any time direct.

(7) Any person exercising the power conferred by subsection (6) shall, if asked to do so, produce some duly authenticated document showing his authority to do so.

(8) Any person authorised to exercise the power to inspect records conferred by subsection (6)–

(a) shall be entitled at any reasonable time to have access to, and inspect and check the operation of, any computer and any associated apparatus or material which is or has been in use in connection with the records in question; and

(b) may require–

(i) the person by whom or on whose behalf the computer is or has been so used; or

(ii) any person having charge of, or otherwise concerned with the operation of, the computer, apparatus or material,

to afford him such assistance as he may reasonably require.

Subsections (6) (7) (8)
These deal with the powers of an officer of the local authority to inspect premises, children and records held by a voluntary organisation (including the computer and other such apparatus on which the records are kept and the people operating such apparatus), and the need for the officer to be able to provide written evidence of his or her authority to inspect, should a request for such be made.

(9) Any person who intentionally obstructs another in the exercise of any power conferred by subsection (6) or (8) shall be guilty of an offence and liable on summary conviction to a fine not exceeding level 3 on the standard scale.

Subsection (9) *This creates a criminal offence of intentional obstruction of a local authority officer trying to inspect.*

Part VIII

Registered Children's Homes

63 – (1) No child shall be cared for and provided with accommodation in a children's home unless the home is registered under this Part.

(2) The register may be kept by means of a computer.

Section 63. Children not to be cared for and accommodated in unregistered children's homes
Subsections (1) (2) *Children's homes must be registered to be able to operate.*

(3) For the purposes of this Part, 'a children's home'–

    (a) means a home which provides (or usually provides or is intended to provide) care and accommodation wholly or mainly for more than three children at any one time; but

    (b) does not include a home which is exempted by or under any of the following provisions of this section or by regulations made for the purposes of this subsection by the Secretary of State.

(4) A child is not cared for and accommodated in a children's home when he is cared for and accommodated by–

(a) a parent of his;

(b) a person who is not a parent of his but who has parental responsibility for him; or

(c) any relative of his.

(5) A home is not a children's home for the purposes of this Part if it is–

(a) a community home;

(b) a voluntary home;

(c) a residential care home [(other than a small home)], nursing home or mental nursing home;

(d) a health service hospital;

(e) a home provided, equipped and maintained by the Secretary of State; or

(f) a school (but subject to subsection (6)).

Subsections (3) (4) (5)
These deal in more detail with the definition of a 'children's home' and certain types of organisation that do not qualify as 'children's homes' even though ostensibly they might fit the criteria.

(6) An independent school is a children's home at any time if at that time accommodation is provided for children at the school and either–

(a) in each year that fell within the period of two years ending at that time accommodation was provided for more than three of the children at the school, or under arrangements made by the proprietor of the school, for more than 295 days in that year, or

(b) it is intended to provide accommodation for more than three of the children at the school, or under arrangements made by the proprietor of the school, for more than 295 days in any year,

unless the school is approved by the Secretary of State under section 347(1) of the Education Act 1996 (approval of independent schools for children with statements); and in this subsection 'year' means a period of twelve months and 'proprietor' has the same meaning as in that Act.

Subsection (6) *This sets out the limited circumstances in which an independent school can qualify as a 'children's home'.*

(7) A child shall not be treated as cared for and accommodated in a children's home when–

(a) any person mentioned in subsection (4)(a) or (b) is living at the home; or

(b) the person caring for him is doing so in his personal capacity and not in the course of carrying out his duties in relation to the home.

(8) In this Act 'a registered children's home' means a children's home registered under this Part.

(9) In this section 'home' includes any institution.

(10) Where any child is at any time cared for and accommodated in a children's home which is not a registered children's home, the person carrying on the home shall be–

(a) guilty of an offence; and

(b) liable to a fine not exceeding level 5 on the standard scale,

unless he has a reasonable excuse.

> **Subsection (10)** *This makes it a criminal offence to care for a child in a children's home, if that home is not registered and there is no reasonable excuse for non-registration.*

(11) Schedule 6 shall have effect with respect to children's homes.

(12) Schedule 7 shall have effect for the purpose of setting out the circumstances in which a person may foster more than three children without being treated as carrying on a children's home.

> **Subsections (11) (12)** *Reference should be made to schedules 6 and 7 for more detail as to registration of and qualification of a children's home.*

64 – (1) Where a child is accommodated in a children's home, it shall be the duty of the person carrying on the home to–

(a) safeguard and promote the child's welfare;

(b) make such use of the services and facilities available for children cared for by their own parents as appears to that person reasonable in the case of the child; and

(c) advise, assist and befriend him with a view to promoting his welfare when he ceases to be so accommodated.

(2) Before making any decision with respect to any such child the person carrying on the home shall, so far as is reasonably practicable, ascertain the wishes and feelings of–

(a) the child;

(b) his parents;

(c) any other person who is not a parent of his but who has parental responsibility for him; and

(d) any person whose wishes and feelings the person carrying on the home considers to be relevant,

regarding the matter to be decided.

(3) In making any such decision the person concerned shall give due consideration–

(a) having regard to the child's age and understanding, to such wishes and feelings of his as he has been able to ascertain;

(b) to such other wishes and feelings mentioned in subsection (2) as he has been able to ascertain; and

(c) to the child's religious persuasion, racial origin and cultural and linguistic background.

Section 64. Welfare of children in children's homes
Subsections (1) (2) (3) This section indicates that persons carrying on children's homes have the same obligations to the child as those set out for a voluntary organisation in section 61.

(4) Section 62, except subsection (4), shall apply in relation to any person who is carrying on a children's home as it applies in relation to any voluntary organisation.

Subsection (4) This imposes similar obligations on the local authority in respect of children from its area accommodated in children's homes as those imposed on the authority in respect of children accommodated by voluntary organisations.

65 – (1) A person who is disqualified (under section 68) from fostering a child privately shall not carry on, or be otherwise concerned in the management of, or have any financial interest in, a children's home unless he has–

(a) disclosed to the responsible authority the fact that he is so disqualified; and

(b) obtained their written consent.

(2) No person shall employ a person who is so disqualified in a children's home unless he has–

(a) disclosed to the responsible authority the fact that that person is so disqualified; and

(b) obtained their written consent.

(3) Where an authority refuse to give their consent under this section, they shall inform the applicant by a written notice which states–

    (a) the reason for the refusal;

    (b) the applicant's right to appeal against the refusal to a Registered Homes Tribunal under paragraph 8 of Schedule 6; and

    (c) the time within which he may do so.

Section 65. Persons disqualified from carrying on, or being empoyed in, children's homes.
Subsections (1) (2) (3) This section shows that disqualification from privately fostering a child prevents a person from carrying on a children's home or from being employed in a children's home, unless the local authority, with knowledge of the fact, gives its written consent.

(4) Any person who contravenes subsection (1) or (2) shall be guilty of an offence and liable on summary conviction to imprisonment for a term not exceeding six months or to a fine not exceeding level 5 on the standard scale or to both.

(5) Where a person contravenes subsection (2) he shall not be guilty of an offence if he proves that he did not know, and had no reasonable grounds for believing, that the person whom he was employing was disqualified under section 68.

Subsections (4) (5) These subsections make it a criminal offence to carry on a children's home when disqualified from fostering privately and also to employ a disqualified person in a children's home, except where the employing person had no reason to believe that the employee might be disqualified.

PART IX

PRIVATE ARRANGEMENTS FOR FOSTERING CHILDREN

66 – (1) In this Part–

    (a) 'a privately fostered child' means a child who is under the age of sixteen and who is cared for, and provided with accommodation by, someone other than–

        (i) a parent of his;

        (ii) a person who is not a parent of his but who has parental responsibility for him; or

        (iii) a relative of his; and

(b) 'to foster a child privately' means to look after the child in circumstances in which he is a privately fostered child as defined by this section.

66 Privately fostered children

Subsection (1) This subsection sets out the definition of "privately fostered child". Private fostering arrangements are subject to the Children (Private Arrangements for Fostering) Regulations 1991 and guidance from the Department of Health given in the Children Act 1989 Guidance and Regulations, Volume 8, Private Fostering and Miscellaneous, Chapters 1 and 2. A person under (ii) who is not a parent but who has parental responsibility would include a person who has acquired parental responsibility through a residence order. A relative under (iii) is defined at s.105 of the Act as a grandparent, brother, sister, uncle or aunt(whether full-blood or half-blood or by affinity, ie by marriage) or step-parent.

(2) A child is not a privately fostered child if the person caring for and accommodating him–

(a) has done so for a period of less than 28 days; and
(b) does not intend to do so for any longer period.

Subsection (2) This excludes situations, for example, where the child is staying with someone who is not a parent, person with parental responsibility, or a relative for a holiday. The period of 28 days does not have to be continuous, so that if the child visited it's parents on occasion this would not affect the calculation.

(3) Subsection (1) is subject to–

(a) the provisions of section 63; and
(b) the exceptions made by paragraphs 1 to 5 of Schedule 8.

Subsection (3) This makes subsection (1) subject to s 63 which creates a prohibition on a child being cared for and provided with accommodation in an unregistered children's home. Reference should be made to Schedule 8 which sets out a series of exceptions to subsection (1) such as where a child is at boarding school or in hospital.

(4) In the case of a child who is disabled, subsection (1)(a) shall have effect as if for 'sixteen' there were substituted 'eighteen'.

> ***Subsection (4)** The definition of "disabled" is set out at s 17 (11) of the Act.*

(5) Schedule 8 shall have effect for the purposes of supplementing the provision made by this Part.

67 – (1) It shall be the duty of every local authority to satisfy themselves that the welfare of children who are privately fostered within their area is being satisfactorily safeguarded and promoted and to secure that such advice is given to those caring for them as appears to the authority to be needed.

> **67 Welfare of privately fostered children**
> ***Subsection (1)** The local authority is placed under a duty to consider the welfare of any privately fostered child in its area. Where the local authority is not satisfied as to the welfare of a privately fostered child it must exercise its powers under subsection (5) which can range from offering advice to the foster parents to improve the situation, to removing the child.*

(2) The Secretary of State may make regulations–

    (a) requiring every child who is privately fostered within a local authority's area to be visited by an officer of the authority–
       (i) in prescribed circumstances; and
       (ii) on specified occasions or within specified periods; and
    (b) imposing requirements which are to be met by any local authority, or officer of a local authority, in carrying out functions under this section.

> ***Subsection (2)** The regulations referred to are the Children (Private Arrangements for Fostering) Regulations 1991.*

(3) Where any person who is authorised by a local authority to visit privately fostered children has reasonable cause to believe that–

    (a) any privately fostered child is being accommodated in premises within the authority's area; or
    (b) it is proposed to accommodate any such child in any such premises,

he may at any reasonable time inspect those premises and any children there.

(4) Any person exercising the power under subsection (3) shall, if so required, produce some duly authenticated document showing his authority to do so.

(5) Where a local authority are not satisfied that the welfare of any child who is privately fostered within their area is being satisfactorily safeguarded or promoted they shall–

(a) unless they consider that it would not be in the best interests of the child, take such steps as are reasonably practicable to secure that the care and accommodation of the child is undertaken by–
  (i) a parent of his;
  (ii) any person who is not a parent of his but who has parental responsibility for him; or
  (iii) a relative of his; and

(b) consider the extent to which (if at all) they should exercise any of their functions under this Act with respect to the child.

> **Subsection (5)** *The local authority should, if the child is not being looked after properly, take steps first to see if the child could be returned to a parent of his, a person with parental responsibility for the child, or relative, and if this is not possible or would be contrary to the child's welfare, consider use of its statutory powers, for example, to take care proceedings.*

68 – (1) Unless he has disclosed the fact to the appropriate local authority and obtained their written consent, a person shall not foster a child privately if he is disqualified from doing so by regulations made by the Secretary of State for the purposes of this section.

> **68 Persons disqualified from being private foster parents**
> *Subsection (1) Reference should be made to the Disqualification from Caring for Children Regulations 1991, SI 1991/2094. This disqualifies certain people from acting as private foster parents because of their personal circumstances or background.*

(2) The regulations may, in particular, provide for a person to be so disqualified where–

(a) an order of a kind specified in the regulations has been made at any time with respect to him;

(b) an order of a kind so specified has been made at any time with respect to any child who has been in his care;

(c) a requirement of a kind so specified has been imposed at any time with respect to any such child, under or by virtue of any enactment;

(d) he has been convicted of any offence of a kind so specified, or has been placed on probation or discharged absolutely or conditionally for any such offence;

(e) a prohibition has been imposed on him at any time under section 69 or under any other specified enactment;

(f) his rights and powers with respect to a child have at any time been vested in a specified authority under a specified enactment.

Subsection (2) Reference should be made to the regulations mentioned in the notes to subsection 1.

(3) Unless he has disclosed the fact to the appropriate local authority and obtained their written consent, a person shall not foster a child privately if–

(a) he lives in the same household as a person who is himself prevented from fostering a child by subsection (1); or

(b) he lives in a household at which any such person is employed.

Subsection (3) This section allows the local authority to control not only the class of people who can foster privately, but also the people who reside or are employed at the home in which the child lives.

(4) Where an authority refuse to give their consent under this section, they shall inform the applicant by a written notice which states–

(a) the reason for the refusal;

(b) the applicant's right under paragraph 8 of Schedule 8 to appeal against the refusal; and

(c) the time within which he may do so.

Subsection (4) The time limit for appeal is 14 days from the notification of the refusal. The appeal is to the magistrates court from which there is the usual right of appeal.

(5) In this section–

'the appropriate authority' means the local authority within whose area it is proposed to foster the child in question; and 'enactment' means any enactment having effect, at any time, in any part of the United Kingdom.

69 – (1) This section applies where a person–

(a) proposes to foster a child privately; or
(b) is fostering a child privately.

> **69   Power to prohibit private fostering**
> *Subsection (1) This confirms that the power to prohibit private fostering relates not only to a proposal to foster but where the child is already fostered and may have been with the foster parents for some time.*

(2) Where the local authority for the area within which the child is proposed to be, or is being, fostered are of the opinion that–

(a) he is not a suitable person to foster a child;
(b) the premises in which the child will be, or is being, accommodated are not suitable; or
(c) it would be prejudicial to the welfare of the child for him to be, or continue to be, accommodated by that person in those premises,

the authority may impose a prohibition on him under subsection (3).

> *Subsection (2) If one of the grounds set out at (a) to (c) are made out the local authority has a discretion to impose a prohibition on the foster parent fostering or continuing to foster any child.*

(3) A prohibition imposed on any person under this subsection may prohibit him from fostering privately–

(a) any child in any premises within the area of the local authority; or
(b) any child in premises specified in the prohibition;
(c) a child identified in the prohibition, in premises specified in the prohibition.

> *Subsection (3) This subsection gives the local authority flexibility as to exactly what it can prohibit if, for example, their concern is not in respect of the foster parent but their accommodation.*

(4) A local authority who have imposed a prohibition on any person under subsection (3) may, if they think fit, cancel the prohibition–

(a) of their own motion; or
(b) on an application made by that person,

if they are satisfied that the prohibition is no longer justified.

> **Subsection (4)** *The local authority can cancel a prohibition made under subsection (3) above but only if they are satisfied that it is no longer justified.*

(5) Where a local authority impose a requirement on any person under paragraph 6 of Schedule 8, they may also impose a prohibition on him under subsection (3).

(6) Any prohibition imposed by virtue of subsection (5) shall not have effect unless–

(a) the time specified for compliance with the requirement has expired; and
(b) the requirement has not been complied with.

> **Subsection (6)** *This enables a local authority to enforce a requirement placed on a foster parent by imposing a prohibition on him in any of the forms specified in subsection (3), which comes into effect when the time limit imposed for complying with the requirement has expired.*

(7) A prohibition imposed under this section shall be imposed by notice in writing addressed to the person on whom it is imposed and informing him of–

(a) the reason for imposing the prohibition;
(b) his right under paragraph 8 of Schedule 8 to appeal against the prohibition; and
(c) the time within which he may do so.

70 – (1) A person shall be guilty of an offence if–

(a) being required, under any provision made by or under this Part, to give any notice or information–
  (i) he fails without reasonable excuse to give the notice within the time specified in that provision; or
  (ii) he fails without reasonable excuse to give the information within a reasonable time; or
  (iii) he makes, or causes or procures another person to make, any statement in the notice or information which he knows to be false or misleading in a material particular;

(b) he refuses to allow a privately fostered child to be visited by a duly authorised officer of a local authority;

(c) he intentionally obstructs another in the exercise of the power conferred by section 67(3);

(d) he contravenes section 68;

(e) he fails without reasonable excuse to comply with any requirement imposed by a local authority under this Part;

(f) he accommodates a privately fostered child in any premises in contravention of a prohibition imposed by a local authority under this Part;

(g) he knowingly causes to be published, or publishes, an advertisement which he knows contravenes paragraph 10 of Schedule 8.

(2) Where a person contravenes section 68(3), he shall not be guilty of an offence under this section if he proves that he did not know, and had no reasonable ground for believing, that any person to whom section 68(1) applied was living or employed in the premises in question.

(3) A person guilty of an offence under subsection (1)(a) shall be liable on summary conviction to a fine not exceeding level 5 on the standard scale.

(4) A person guilty of an offence under subsection (1)(b), (c) or (g) shall be liable on summary conviction to a fine not exceeding level 3 on the standard scale.

(5) A person guilty of an offence under subsection (1)(d) or (f) shall be liable on summary conviction to imprisonment for a term not exceeding six months, or to a fine not exceeding level 5 on the standard scale, or to both.

(6) A person guilty of an offence under subsection (1)(e) shall be liable on summary conviction to a fine not exceeding level 4 on the standard scale.

(7) If any person who is required, under any provision of this Part, to give a notice fails to give the notice within the time specified in that provision, proceedings for the offence may be brought at any time within six months from the date when evidence of the offence came to the knowledge of the local authority.

(8) Subsection (7) is not affected by anything in section 127(1) of the Magistrates' Courts Act 1980 (time limit for proceedings).

70 Offences
This section is largely self-explanatory. It creates a number of offences in relation to private fostering and details the various penalties. The burden of proving that the foster parent has a reasonable excuse is on the foster parent. Under (g) an advert which contravenes paragraph 10 of Schedule 8 is one which does not state the name and address of the person arranging or undertaking private fostering.

Part X

Child Minding and Day Care for Young Children

71 – (1) Every local authority shall keep a register of–

(a) persons who act as child minders on domestic premises within the authority's area; and

(b) persons who provide day care for children under the age of eight on premises (other than domestic premises) within that area.

---

71 Registration

Subsection (1) This subsection imposes a mandatory duty on every local authority to keep a register of child minders and persons providing day care for children. The definitions of "child minder" and "day care" are set out in subsection (2).

---

(2) For the purposes of this Part–

(a) a person acts as a child minder if–
   (i) he looks after one or more children under the age of eight, for reward; and
   (ii) the period, or the total of the periods, which he spends so looking after children in any day exceeds two hours; and

(b) a person does not provide day care for children unless the period, or the total of the periods, during which children are looked after exceeds two hours in any day.

Subsection (2) " For reward" arguably requires an element of profit so friends who look after each others children on an exchange basis would not fall under the definition of a child minder.

---

(3) Where a person provides day care for children under the age of eight on different premises situated within the area of the same local authority, that person shall be separately registered with respect to each of those premises.

(4) A person who–

(a) is the parent, or a relative, of a child;

(b) has parental responsibility for a child; or

(c) is a foster parent of a child,

does not act as a child minder for the purposes of this Part when looking after that child.

> **Subsection (4)** *This subsection ensures that commonplace arrangements, for example, where a child is cared for by his grandmother while his mother works, do not require registration. This would presumably be very cumbersome. Under (c) see s 71(14) for the definition of a foster parent.*

(5) Where a person is employed as a nanny for a child, she does not act as a child minder when looking after that child wholly or mainly in the home of the person so employing her.

(6) Where a person is so employed by two different employers, she does not act as a child minder when looking after any of the children concerned wholly or mainly in the home or either of her employers.

> **Subsection (6)** *This subsection exempts a "nanny-sharing" arrangement from the regulations applying to child minders.*

(7) A local authority may refuse to register an applicant for registration under subsection (1)(a) if they are satisfied that–

    (a) the applicant; or

    (b) any person looking after, or likely to be looking after, any children on any premises on which the applicant is, or is likely to be, child minding,

is not fit to look after children under the age of eight.

> **Subsection (7)** *This gives the local authority a discretion not to register a child minder if they are satisfied that the child minder, or any person likely to be looking after any children on the premises where the child minder is likely to be child minding, is not fit to look after children under 8.*

(8) A local authority may refuse to register an applicant for registration under subsection (1)(a) if they are satisfied that–

    (a) any person living, or likely to be living, at any premises on which the applicant is, or is likely to be, child minding; or

    (b) any person employed, or likely to be employed, on those premises,

is not fit to be in the proximity of children under the age of eight.

> **Subsection (8)** *This is a similar provision to subsection (7) above, which extends to unsuitable people who either live or work at, or are likely to live or work at the premises where the child minding is to take place.*

(9) A local authority may refuse to register an applicant for registration under subsection (1)(b) if they are satisfied that any person looking after, or likely to be looking after, any children on the premises to which the application relates is not fit to look after children under the age of eight.

(10) A local authority may refuse to register an applicant for registration under subsection (1)(b) if they are satisfied that–

    (a) any person living, or likely to be living, at the premises to which the application relates; or

    (b) any person employed, or likely to be employed, on those premises,

is not fit to be in the proximity of children under the age of eight.

(11) A local authority may refuse to register an applicant for registration under this section if they are satisfied–

    (a) in the case of an application under subsection (1)(a), that any premises on which the applicant is, or is likely to be, child minding; or

    (b) in the case of an application under subsection (1)(b), that the premises to which the application relates,

are not fit to be used for looking after children under the age of eight, whether because of their condition or the condition of any equipment used on the premises or for any reason connected with their situation, construction or size.

> **Subsection (11)** *This subsection permits the local authority to refuse to register where they consider that the premises or equipment on the premises is not fit to be used by a child under eight.*

(12) In this section–

'domestic premises' means any premises which are wholly or mainly used as a private dwelling;

'premises' includes any vehicle.

(13) For the purposes of this Part a person acts as a nanny for a child if she is employed to look after the child by–

(a) a parent of the child;

(b) a person who is not a parent of the child but who has parental responsibility for him; or

(c) a person who is a relative of the child and who has assumed responsibility for his care.

(14) For the purposes of this section, a person fosters a child if–

(a) he is a local authority foster parent in relation to the child;

(b) he is a foster parent with whom the child has been placed by a voluntary organisation; or

(c) he fosters the child privately.

(15) Any register kept under this section–

(a) shall be open to inspection by members of the public at all reasonable times; and

(b) may be kept by means of a computer.

(16) Schedule 9 shall have effect for the purpose of making further provision with respect to registration under this section including, in particular, further provision for exemption from the requirement to be registered and provision for disqualification.

72 – (1) Where a local authority register a person under section 71(1)(a), they shall impose such reasonable requirements on him as they consider appropriate in his case.

72 Requirements to be complied with by child minders

Subsection (1) This subsection imposes a duty on a local authority when registering a child minder to impose whatever reasonable requirements they consider appropriate in addition to the requirements set out in subsection (2) below.

(2) In imposing requirements on him, the authority shall–

(a) specify the maximum number of children, or the maximum number of children within specified age groups, whom he may look after when acting as a child minder;

(b) require him to secure that any premises on which he so looks after any child, and the equipment used in those premises, are adequately maintained and kept safe;

(c) require him to keep a record of the name and address of–

(i) any child so looked after by him on any premises within the authority's area;

(ii) any person who assists in looking after any such child; and

(iii) any person living, or likely at any time to be living, at those premises;

(d) require him to notify the authority in writing of any change in the persons mentioned in paragraph (c)(ii) and (iii).

Subsection (2) *The local authority is under a duty to impose the various requirements set out at (a) to (g).*

(3) The Secretary of State may by regulations make provision as to–

(a) requirements which must be imposed by local authorities under this section in prescribed circumstances;

(b) requirements of such descriptions as may be prescribed which must not be imposed by local authorities under this section.

(4) In determining the maximum number of children to be specified under subsection (2)(a), the authority shall take account of the number of other children who may at any time be on any premises on which the person concerned acts, or is likely to act, as a child minder.

Subsection (4) *The local authority is required when determining the maximum number of children that the child minder can look after, to take account of the number of other children who may be on the premises, for example, the child minder's own children.*

(5) Where, in addition to the requirements mentioned in subsection (2), a local authority impose other requirements, those other requirements must not be incompatible with any of the subsection (2) requirements.

(6) A local authority may at any time vary any requirement imposed under this section, impose any additional requirement or remove any requirement.

73 – (1) Where a local authority register a person under section 71(1)(b) they shall impose such reasonable requirements on him as they consider appropriate in his case.

73 Requirements to be complied with by persons providing day care for young children
Subsection (1) *This section imposes a duty on a local authority when registering a day carer to impose whatever reasonable requirements it considers appropriate in addition to the requirements set out in subsection (3) below.*

(2) Where a person is registered under section 71(1)(b) with respect to different premises within the area of the same authority, this section applies separately in relation to each registration.

> **Subsection (2)** *If a registered provider of day care operates from more than one set of premises, the local authority is required to look at each of the premises separately and impose requirements as appropriate to each.*

(3) In imposing requirements on him, the authority shall–

   (a) specify the maximum number of children, or the maximum number of children within specified age groups, who may be looked after on the premises;
   (b) require him to secure that the premises, and the equipment used in them, are adequately maintained and kept safe;
   (c) require him to notify the authority of any change in the facilities which he provides or in the period during which he provides them;
   (d) specify the number of persons required to assist in looking after children on the premises;
   (e) require him to keep a record of the name and address of–
       (i) any child looked after on the registered premises;
       (ii) any person who assists in looking after any such child; and
       (iii) any person who lives, or is likely at any time to be living, at those premises;
   (f) require him to notify the authority of any change in the persons mentioned in paragraph (e)(ii) and (iii).

> **Subsection (3)** *This subsection sets out the requirements which the local authority is obliged to impose.*

(4) The Secretary of State may by regulations make provision as to–

   (a) requirements which must be imposed by local authorities under this section in prescribed circumstances;
   (b) requirements of such descriptions as may be prescribed which must now be imposed by local authorities under this section.

> **Subsection (4)** *No such regulations have been made to date.*

(5) In subsection (3), references to children looked after are to children looked after in accordance with the provision of day care made by the registered person.

(6) In determining the maximum number of children to be specified under subsection (3)(a), the authority shall take account of the number of other children who may at any time be on the premises.

(7) Where, in addition to the requirements mentioned in subsection (3), a local authority impose other requirements, those other requirements must not be incompatible with any of the subsection (3) requirements.

(8) A local authority may at any time vary any requirement imposed under this section, impose any additional requirement or remove any requirement.

74 – (1) A local authority may at any time cancel the registration of any person under section 71(1)(a) if–

(a) it appears to them that the circumstances of the case are such that they would be justified in refusing to register that person as a child minder;

(b) the care provided by that person when looking after any child as a child minder is, in the opinion of the authority, seriously inadequate having regard to the needs of that child; or

(c) that person has–
  (i) contravened, or failed to comply with, any requirement imposed on him under section 72; or
  (ii) failed to pay any annual fee under paragraph 7 of Schedule 9 within the prescribed time.

> **74 Cancellation of Registration**
> *Subsection (1)* There is no clear definition of what constitutes "seriously inadequate". Arguably a higher standard of care is required of a child minder than of a natural parent because the same policy reasons for endeavouring to keep children with their natural parents do not apply to child minders.

(2) A local authority may at any time cancel the registration of any person under section 71(1)(b) with respect to particular premises if–

(a) it appears to them that the circumstances of the case are such that they would be justified in refusing to register that person with respect to those premises;

(b) the day care provided by that person on those premises is, in the opinion of the authority, seriously inadequate having regard to the needs of the children concerned; or

(c) that person has–
  (i) contravened, or failed to comply with, any requirement imposed on him under section 73; or

(ii) failed to pay any annual registration fee under paragraph 7 of Schedule 9 within the prescribed time.

(3) A local authority may at any time cancel all registrations of any person under section 71(1)(b) if it appears to them that the circumstances of the case are such that they would be justified in refusing to register that person with respect to any premises.

> **Subsection (3)** *This gives the local authority a discretion to cancel all of a day carer's registrations even where there are only grounds to cancel the registration in the case of one of the premises.*

(4) Where a requirement to carry out repairs or make alterations or additions has been imposed on a registered person under section 72 or 73, his registration shall not be cancelled on the ground that the premises are not fit to be used for looking after children if–

(a) the time set for complying with the requirements has not expired, and
(b) it is shown that the condition of the premises is due to the repairs not having been carried out or the alterations or additions not having been made.

(5) Any cancellation under this section must be in writing.

(6) In considering the needs of any child for the purposes of subsection (1)(b) or (2)(b), a local authority shall, in particular, have regard to the child's religious persuasion, racial origin and cultural and linguistic background.

75 – (1) If–

(a) a local authority apply to the court for an order–
    (i) cancelling a registered person's registration;
    (ii) varying any requirement imposed on a registered person under section 72 or 73; or
    (iii) removing a requirement or imposing an additional requirement on such a person; and
(b) it appears to the court that a child who is being, or may be, looked after by that person, or (as the case may be) in accordance with the provision for day care made by that person, is suffering, or is likely to suffer, significant harm,

the court may make the order.

> **75 Protection of children in an emergency**
> *Subsection (1) This enables a local authority to apply for a court order cancelling a person's registration as either a child minder or day carer where a child who is, or*

may be, looked after by the registered person is suffering or likely to suffer significant harm. The standard of proof required is on the balance of probabilities. The court to which the application can be made is the magistrates court. There is only power to transfer the case to another magistrates court and not upwards to the county court.

(2) Any such cancellation, variation, removal or imposition shall have effect from the date on which the order is made.

(3) An application under subsection (1) may be made ex parte and shall be supported by a written statement of the authority's reasons for making it.

Subsection (3) This enables a local authority to apply without notice to the registered person. It is not good practice to apply without notice unless the circumstances justify this, for example, if the giving of notice might put a child at risk. A hearing without notice would be followed, within a short period, by an on notice hearing.

(4) Where an order is made under this section, the authority shall serve on the registered person, as soon as is reasonably practicable after the making of the order–

    (a) notice of the order and of its terms; and

    (b) a copy of the statement of the authority's reasons which supported their application for the order.

(5) Where the court imposes or varies any requirement under subsection (1), the requirement, or the requirement as varied, shall be treated for all purposes, other than those of section 77, as if it had been imposed under section 72 or (as the case may be) 73 by the authority concerned.

76 – (1) Any person authorised to do so by a local authority may at any reasonable time enter–

    (a) any domestic premises within the authority's area on which child minding is at any time carried on; or

    (b) any premises within their area on which day care for children under the age of eight is at any time provided.

    (c)

(2) Where a local authority have reasonable cause to believe that a child is being looked after on any premises within their area in contravention of this Part, any person authorised to do so by the authority may enter those premises at any reasonable time.

76 Inspection

Subsection (2) *This subsection enables a local authority to send an authorised person to inspect any premises where it is believed that a child is being cared for in contravention of Part IX of the Act.*

(3) Any person entering premises under this section may inspect–

   (a) the premises;
   (b) any children being looked after on the premises;
   (c) the arrangements made for their welfare; and
   (d) any records relating to them which are kept as a result of this Part.

Subsection (3) *It should be noted that there is only power to inspect the children being looked after on the premises. If there was concern about any other child on the premises then a social worker could request permission to see the child and if this was refused could consider applying for an emergency protection order if the circumstances warranted this.*

(4) Every local authority shall exercise their power to inspect the premises mentioned in subsection (1) at least once every year.

Subsection (4) *This places an obligation on local authorities to inspect both child minding and day care facilities at least once a year.*

(5) Any person inspecting any records under this section–

   (a) shall be entitled at any reasonable time to have access to, and inspect and check the operation of, any computer and any associated apparatus or material which is, or has been, in use in connection with the records in question; and
   (b) may require–
      (i) the person by whom or on whose behalf the computer is or has been so used; or
      (ii) any person having charge of, or otherwise concerned with the operation of, the computer, apparatus or material,

   to afford him such reasonable assistance as he may require.

(6) A person exercising any power conferred by this section shall, if so required, produce some duly authenticated document showing his authority to do so.

(7) Any person who intentionally obstructs another in the exercise of any such power shall be guilty of an offence and liable on summary conviction to a fine not exceeding level 3 on the standard scale.

77 – (1) Not less than 14 days before–

(a) refusing an application for registration under section 71;
(b) cancelling any such registration;
(c) refusing consent under paragraph 2 of Schedule 9;
(d) imposing, removing or varying any requirement under section 72 or 73; or
(e) refusing to grant any application for the variation or removal of any such requirement,

the authority concerned shall send to the applicant, or (as the case may be) registered person, notice in writing of their intention to take the step in question ('the step').

(2) Every such notice shall–

(a) give the authority's reasons for proposing to take the step; and
(b) inform the person concerned of his rights under this section.

(3) Were the recipient of such a notice informs the authority in writing of his desire to object to the step being taken, the authority shall afford him an opportunity to do so.

(4) Any objection made under subsection (3) may be made in person or by a representative.

(5) If the authority, after giving the person concerned an opportunity to object to the step being taken, decide nevertheless to take it they shall send him written notice of their decision.

(6) A person aggrieved by the taking of any step mentioned in subsection (1) may appeal against it to the court.

(7) Where the court imposes or varies any requirement under subsection (8) or (9) the requirement, or the requirement as varied, shall be treated for all purposes (other than this section) as if it had been imposed by the authority concerned.

(8) Where the court allows an appeal against the refusal or cancellation of any registration under section 71 it may impose requirements under section 72 or (as the case may be) 73.

(9) Where the court allows an appeal against such a requirement it may, instead of cancelling the requirement, vary it.

(10) (applies to Scotland only)

(11) A step of a kind mentioned in subsection (1)(b) or (d) shall not take effect until

the expiry of the time within which an appeal may be brought under this section or, where such an appeal is brought, before its determination.

77 Appeals

This section provides a wide right of appeal against decisions in respect of not only registration of child minders and day carers, but also as to the imposition of requirements on them. The applicant child minder is first given the opportunity to object to the local authority's decision following which the local authority must reconsider the matter and again give written notice of their decision. The applicant then has a right of appeal to the family proceedings court. Under subsection (6) the court referred to is the family proceedings court. The appeal must be lodged within 21 days of the decision.

78 – (1) No person shall provide day care for children under the age of eight on any premises within the area of a local authority unless he is registered by the authority under section 71(1)(b) with respect to those premises.

78 Offences

Subsection (1) *This confirms that it is an offence to provide unregistered day care for children under 8. There is no requirement for an enforcement notice as for an unregistered child minder before a prosecution can be brought.*

(2) If any person contravenes subsection (1) without reasonable excuse, he shall be guilty of an offence.

(3) No person shall act as a child minder on domestic premises within the area of a local authority unless he is registered by the authority under section 71(1)(a).

(4) Where it appears to a local authority that a person has contravened subsection (3), they may serve a notice ('an enforcement notice') on him.

(5) An enforcement notice shall have effect for a period of one year beginning with the date on which it is served.

Subsection (5) *An enforcement notice lasts for 1 year. If an unregistered child minder takes on any child minding work within that period then they are liable for prosecution.*

(6) If a person with respect to whom an enforcement notice is in force contravenes subsection (3) without reasonable excuse, he shall be guilty of an offence.

(7) Subsection (6) applies whether or not the subsequent contravention occurs within the area of the authority who served the enforcement notice.

> **Subsection (7)** *This confirms that it is an offence to child mind after service of an enforcement notice even if the child minding takes place in the area of a local authority other than that which served the enforcement notice.*

(8) Any person who without reasonable excuse contravenes, or otherwise fails to comply with, any requirement imposed on him under sections 72 or 73 shall be guilty of an offence.

(9) If any person–

   (a) acts as a child minder on domestic premises at any time when he is disqualified by regulations made under paragraph 2 of Schedule 9; or
   (b) contravenes any of sub-paragraphs (3) to (5) of paragraph 2,

   he shall be guilty of an offence.

> **Subsection (9)** *The provisions of Schedule 9, paragraph 2, are designed to prevent unsuitable people from providing child care.*

(10) Where a person contravenes sub-paragraph (3) of paragraph 2 he shall not be guilty of an offence under this section if he proves that he did not know, and had no reasonable grounds for believing, that the person in question was living or employed in the household.

(11) Where a person contravenes sub-paragraph (5) of paragraph 2 he shall not be guilty of an offence under this section if he proves that he did not know, and had no reasonable grounds for believing, that the person whom he was employing was disqualified.

(12) A person guilty of an offence under this section shall be liable on summary conviction–

   (a) in the case of an offence under subsection (8), to a fine not exceeding level 4 on the standard scale;
   (b) in the case of an offence under subsection (9), to imprisonment for a term not exceeding six months, or to a fine not exceeding level 5 on the standard scale, or to both; and

(c) in the case of any other offence, to a fine not exceeding level 5 on the standard scale.

79 (applies to Scotland only)

PART XI

SECRETARY OF STATE'S SUPERVISORY FUNCTIONS AND RESPONSIBILITIES

80 – (1) The Secretary of State may cause to be inspected from time to time any–

(a) children's home;

(b) premises in which a child who is being looked after by a local authority is living;

(c) premises in which a child who is being accommodated by or on behalf of a local education authority or voluntary organisation is living;

(d) premises in which a child who is being accommodated by or on behalf of a [Health Authority, Special Health Authority] [or National Health Service trust] is living;

(e) premises in which a child is living with a person with whom he has been placed by an adoption agency;

(f) premises in which a child who is a protected child is, or will be, living;

(g) premises in which a privately fostered child, or child who is treated as a foster child by virtue of paragraph 9 of Schedule 8, is living or in which it is proposed that he will live;

(h) premises on which any person is acting as a child minder;

(i) premises with respect to which a person is registered under section 71(1)(b);

(j) residential care home, nursing home or mental nursing home required to be registered under the Registered Homes Act 1984 and used to accommodate children;

(k) premises which are provided by a local authority and in which any service is provided by that authority under Part III;

(l) independent school providing accommodation for any child.

(2) An inspection under this section shall be conducted by a person authorised to do so by the Secretary of State.

(3) An officer of a local authority shall not be authorised except with the consent of that authority.

(4) The Secretary of State may require any person of a kind mentioned in subsection (5) to furnish him with such information, or allow him to inspect such records (in whatever form they are held), relating to–

(a) any premises to which subsection (1) or, in relation to Scotland, subsection (1)(h) or (i) applies;

(b) any child who is living in any such premises;

(c) the discharge by the Secretary of State of any of his functions under this Act; or

(d) the discharge by any local authority of any of their functions under this Act,

as the Secretary of State may at any time direct.

Section 81

Subsection (4) Section 250(2) to(5) of the Local Government Act 1972 stipulate the following in relation to an inquiry.

"(2) the person holding the inquiry may by summons, require any person to attend or to produce any document relating to the matter in question, provided the expenses of his attendance are tendered to him, and he is not required to produce any document concerning the title of land, not owned by the local authority

(3) If a person summonsed as in (2) above fails to attend of produce the documentation they may be fined up to £100 or face 6 months imprisonment.

(4) The costs of the inquiry shall be paid by the local authority or such party to the inquiry as the Minister may direct.

(5) The Minister may make orders as to the costs of the parties at the enquiry and who should pay such costs."

(5) The persons are any–

    (a) local authority;

    (b) voluntary organisation;

    (c) person carrying on a children's home;

    (d) proprietor of an independent school;

    (e) person fostering any privately fostered child or providing accommodation for a child on behalf of a local authority, local education authority, [Health Authority, Special Health Authority][, National Health Service trust] or voluntary organisation;

    (f) local education authority providing accommodation for any child;

    (g) person employed in a teaching or administrative capacity at any educational establishment (whether or not maintained by a local education authority) at which a child is accommodated on behalf of a local authority or local education authority;

    (h) person who is the occupier of any premises in which any person acts as a child minder (within the meaning of Part X) or provides day care for young children (within the meaning of that Part);

    (i) person carrying on any home of a kind mentioned in subsection (1)(j).

(6) Any person inspecting any home or other premises under this section may–

(a) inspect the children there; and

(b) make such examination into the state and management of the home or premises and the treatment of the children there as he thinks fit.

(7) Any person authorised by the Secretary of State to exercise the power to inspect records conferred by subsection (4)–

(a) shall be entitled at any reasonable time to have access to, and inspect and check the operation of, any computer and any associated apparatus or material which is or has been in use in connection with the records in question; and

(b) may require–

(i) the person by whom or on whose behalf the computer is or has been so used; or

(ii) any person having charge of, or otherwise concerned with the operation of, the computer, apparatus or material,

to afford him such reasonable assistance as he may require.

(8) A person authorised to inspect any premises under this section shall have a right to enter the premises for that purpose, and for any purpose specified in subsection (4), at any reasonable time.

(9) Any person exercising that power shall, if so required, produce some duly authenticated document showing his authority to do so.

(10) Any person who intentionally obstructs another in the exercise of that power shall be guilty of an offence and liable on summary conviction to a fine not exceeding level 3 on the standard scale.

(11) The Secretary of State may by order provide for subsections (1), (4) and (6) not to apply in relation to such homes, or other premises, as may be specified in the order.

(12) Without prejudice to section 104, any such order may make different provision with respect to each of those subsections.

81 – (1) The Secretary of State may cause an inquiry to be held into any matter connected with–

(a) the functions of the social services committee of a local authority, in so far as those functions relate to children;

(b) the functions of an adoption agency;

(c) the functions of a voluntary organisation, in so far as those functions relate to children;

(d) a ... children's home or voluntary home;

(e) a residential care home, nursing home or mental nursing home, so far as it provides accommodation for children;

(f) a home provided [in accordance with arrangements made] by the Secretary of State under section 82(5);

(g) the detention of a child under section 53 of the Children and Young Persons Act 1933.

(2) Before an inquiry is begun, the Secretary of State may direct that it shall be held in private.

(3) Where no direction has been given, the person holding the inquiry may if he thinks fit hold it, or any part of it, in private.

(4) Subsections (2) to (5) of section 250 of the Local Government Act 1972 (powers in relation to local inquiries) shall apply in relation to an inquiry under this section as they apply in relation to a local inquiry under that section.

(5) In this section 'functions' includes powers and duties which a person has otherwise than by virtue of any enactment.

82 – (1) The Secretary of State may (with the consent of the Treasury) defray or contribute towards–

   (a) any fees or expenses incurred by any person undergoing approved child care training;
   (b) any fees charged, or expenses incurred, by any person providing approved child care training or preparing material for use in connection with such training; or
   (c) the cost of maintaining any person undergoing such training.

(2) The Secretary of State may make grants to local authorities in respect of expenditure incurred by them in providing secure accommodation in community homes other than assisted community homes.

Subsection (2) *For "secure accommodation" see section 25 above*

(3) Where–

   (a) a grant has been made under subsection (2) with respect to any secure accommodation; but
   (b) the grant is not used for the purpose for which it was made or the accommodation is not used as, or ceases to be used as, secure accommodation,

   the Secretary of State may (with the consent of the Treasury) require the authority concerned to repay the grant, in whole or in part.

(4) The Secretary of State may make grants to voluntary organisations towards–

   (a) expenditure incurred by them in connection with the establishment, maintenance or improvement of voluntary homes which, at the time when the expenditure was incurred–
       (i) were assisted community homes; or
       (ii) were designated as such; or
   (b) expenses incurred in respect of the borrowing of money to defray any such expenditure.

141

(5) The Secretary of State may arrange for the provision, equipment and maintenance of homes for the accommodation of children who are in need of particular facilities and services which–

(a) are or will be provided in those homes; and

(b) in the opinion of the Secretary of State, are unlikely to be readily available in community homes.

(6) In this Part–

'child care training' means training undergone by any person with a view to, or in the course of–

(a) his employment for the purposes of any of the functions mentioned in section 83(9) or in connection with the adoption of children or with the accommodation of children in a residential care home, nursing home or mental nursing home; or

(b) his employment by a voluntary organisation for similar purposes;

'approved child care training' means child care training which is approved by the Secretary of State; and

'secure accommodation' means accommodation provided for the purpose of restricting the liberty of children.

(7) Any grant made under this section shall be of such amount, and shall be subject to such conditions, as the Secretary of State may (with the consent of the Treasury) determine.

83 – (1) The Secretary of State may conduct, or assist other persons in conducting, research into any matter connected with–

(a) his functions, or the functions of local authorities, under the enactments mentioned in subsection (9);

(b) the adoption of children; or

(c) the accommodation of children in a residential care home, nursing home or mental nursing home.

(2) Any local authority may conduct, or assist other persons in conducting, research into any matter connected with–

(a) their functions under the enactments mentioned in subsection (9);

(b) the adoption of children; or

(c) the accommodation of children in a residential care home, nursing home or mental nursing home.

(3) Every local authority shall, at such times and in such form as the Secretary of State may direct, transmit to him such particulars as he may require with respect to–

(a) the performance by the local authority of all or any of their functions–

(i) under the enactments mentioned in subsection (9); or

(ii) in connection with the accommodation of children in a residential care home, nursing home or mental nursing home; and

(b) the children in relation to whom the authority have exercised those functions.

(4) Every voluntary organisation shall, at such times and in such form as the Secretary of State may direct, transmit to him such particulars as he may require with respect to children accommodated by them or on their behalf.

(5) The Secretary of State may direct the clerk of [-] each magistrates' court to which the direction is expressed to relate to transmit–

(a) to such person as may be specified in the direction; and
(b) at such times and in such form as he may direct,

such particulars as he may require with respect to proceedings of the court which relate to children.

(6) The Secretary of State shall in each year lay before Parliament a consolidated and classified abstract of the information transmitted to him under subsections (3) to (5).

(7) The Secretary of State may institute research designed to provide information on which requests for information under this section may be based.

(8) The Secretary of State shall keep under review the adequacy of the provision of child care training and for that purpose shall receive and consider any information from or representations made by–

(a) the Central Council for Education and Training in Social Work;
(b) such representatives of local authorities as appear to him to be appropriate; or
(c) such other persons or organisations as appear to him to be appropriate,

concerning the provision of such training.

(9) The enactments are–

(a) this Act;
(b) the Children and Young Persons Acts 1933 to 1969;
(c) section 116 of the Mental Health Act 1983 (so far as it relates to children looked after by local authorities);
(d) (applies to Scotland only)

84 – (1) If the Secretary of State is satisfied that any local authority has failed, without reasonable excuse, to comply with any of the duties imposed on them by or under this Act he may make an order declaring that authority to be in default with respect to that duty.

(2) An order under subsection (1) shall give the Secretary of State's reasons for making it.

(3) An order under subsection (1) may contain such directions for the purpose of ensuring that the duty is complied with, within such period as may be specified in the order, as appear to the Secretary of State to be necessary.

(4) Any such direction shall, on the application of the Secretary of State, be enforceable by mandamus.

> **Section 84**
> **Subsection (4)** *"Mandamus" is a command from the Court that a legal duty be performed. It is a remedy which can only be used in public law i.e. where public bodies such as a local authority are involved. If a mandamus is disobeyed it is a contempt of court and it is punishable by imprisonment or a fine.*

PART XII

MISCELLANEOUS AND GENERAL

Notification of children accommodated in certain establishments

85 – (1) Where a child is provided with accommodation by any [Health Authority, Special Health Authority] [National Health Service trust] or local education authority ('the accommodating authority')–

(a) for a consecutive period of at least three months; or
(b) with the intention, on the part of that authority, of accommodating him for such a period,

the accommodating authority shall notify the responsible authority.

(2) Where subsection (1) applies with respect to a child, the accommodating authority shall also notify the responsible authority when they cease to accommodate the child.

(3) In this section 'the responsible authority' means–

(a) the local authority appearing to the accommodating authority to be the authority within whose area the child was ordinarily resident immediately before being accommodated; or
(b) where it appears to the accommodating authority that a child was not ordinarily resident within the area of any local authority, the local authority within whose area the accommodation is situated.

(4) Where a local authority have been notified under this section, they shall–

(a) take such steps as are reasonably practicable to enable them to determine whether the child's welfare is adequately safeguarded and promoted while he is accommodated by the accommodating authority; and
(b) consider the extent to which (if at all) they should exercise any of their functions under this Act with respect to the child.

86 – (1) Where a child is provided with accommodation in any residential care home, nursing home or mental nursing home–

(a) for a consecutive period of at least three months; or

(b) with the intention, on the part of the person taking the decision to accommodate him, of accommodating him for such period,

the person carrying on the home shall notify the local authority within whose area the home is carried on.

(2) Where subsection (1) applies with respect to a child, the person carrying on the home shall also notify that authority when he ceases to accommodate the child in the home.

(3) Where a local authority have been notified under this section, they shall–

(a) take such steps as are reasonably practicable to enable them to determine whether the child's welfare is adequately safeguarded and promoted while he is accommodated in the home; and

(b) consider the extent to which (if at all) they should exercise any of their functions under this Act with respect to the child.

(4) If the person carrying on any home fails, without reasonable excuse, to comply with this section he shall be guilty of an offence.

(5) A person authorised by a local authority may enter any residential care home, nursing home or mental nursing home within the authority's area for the purpose of establishing whether the requirements of this section have been complied with.

(6) Any person who intentionally obstructs another in the exercise of the power of entry shall be guilty of an offence.

(7) Any person exercising the power of entry shall, if so required, produce some duly authenticated document showing his authority to do so.

(8) Any person committing an offence under this section shall be liable on summary conviction to a fine not exceeding level 3 on the standard scale.

Section 86 - Children in Mental/Nursing Homes

In circumstances where a child is accommodated by an Area Health Authority or a Local Education Authority home, responsibility for that accommodation would rest with the authority home concerned and not with the Local Authority, until such time as the Local Authority is requested to provide the child with accommodation.

Sections 87 and 87A - Independent Schools
Where a child is accommodated in an independent school within the area of a Local Authority, the Authority has the power through an authorised person to inspect school premises, the children attending the school and the records kept by the school. The Authority is under a duty to determine whether the welfare of such children is adequately safeguarded and promoted so far as is reasonably practicable.

87 – (1) It shall be the duty of–

(a) the proprietor of any independent school which provides accommodation for any child; and

(b) any person who is not the proprietor of such a school but who is responsible for conducting it,

to safeguard and promote the child's welfare.

(2) Subsection (1) does not apply in relation to a school which is a children's home or a residential care home [(other than a small home)].

(3) Where accommodation is provided for a child by an independent school within the area of a local authority, the authority shall take such steps as are reasonably practicable to enable them to determine whether the child's welfare is adequately safeguarded and promoted while he is accommodated by the school.

(4) Where a local authority are of the opinion that there has been a failure to comply with subsection (1) in relation to a child provided with accommodation by a school within their area, they shall notify the Secretary of State.

(5) Any person authorised by a local authority may, for the purpose of enabling the authority to discharge their duty under this section, enter at any reasonable time any independent school within their area which provides accommodation for any child.

(6) Any person entering an independent school in exercise of the power conferred by subsection (5) may carry out such inspection of premises, children and records as is prescribed by regulations made by the Secretary of State for the purposes of this section.

(7) Any person exercising that power shall, if asked to do so, produce some duly authenticated document showing his authority to do so.

(8) Any person authorised by the regulations to inspect records–

(a) shall be entitled at any reasonable time to have access to, and inspect and check the operation of, any computer and any associated apparatus or material which is or has been in use in connection with the records in question; and

(b) may require–

(i) the person by whom or on whose behalf the computer is or has been so used; or

(ii) any person having charge of, or otherwise concerned with the operation of, the computer, apparatus or material,

to afford him such assistance as he may reasonably require.

(9) Any person who intentionally obstructs another in the exercise of any power conferred by this section or the regulations shall be guilty of an offence and liable on summary conviction to a fine not exceeding level 3 on the standard scale.

(10) In this section 'proprietor' has the same meaning as in the [Education Act 1996].

87A – (1) The Secretary of State may appoint a person to be an inspector for the purposes of this section if–

(a) that person already acts as an inspector for other purposes in relation to independent schools to which section 87(1) applies, and

(b) the Secretary of State is satisfied that the person is an appropriate person to determine whether the welfare of children provided with accommodation by such schools is adequately safeguarded and promoted while they are accommodated by them.

(2) Where–

(a) the proprietor of an independent school to which section 87(1) applies enters into an agreement in writing with a person appointed under subsection (1),

(b) the agreement provides for the person so appointed to have in relation to the school the function of determining whether section 87(1) is being complied with, and

(c) the local authority in whose area the school is situated receive from the person with whom the proprietor of the school has entered into the agreement notice in writing that the agreement has come into effect,

the authority's duty under section 87(3) in relation to the school shall be suspended.

(3) Where a local authority's duty under section 87(3) in relation to any school is suspended under this section, it shall cease to be so suspended if the authority receive–

(a) a notice under subsection (4) relating to the person with whom the proprietor of the school entered into the relevant agreement, or

(b) a notice under subsection (5) relating to that agreement.

(4) The Secretary of State shall terminate a person's appointment under subsection (1) if–

(a) that person so requests, or

(b) the Secretary of State ceases, in relation to that person, to be satisfied that he is such a person as is mentioned in paragraph (b) of that subsection, and shall give notice of the termination of that person's appointment to every local authority.

(5) Where–

    (a) a local authority's duty under section 87(3) in relation to any school is suspended under this section, and

    (b) the relevant agreement ceases to have effect,

the person with whom the proprietor of the school entered into that agreement shall give to the authority notice in writing of the fact that it has ceased to have effect.

(6) In this section–

    (a) 'proprietor' has the same meaning as in [the Education Act 1996], and

    (b) references to the relevant agreement, in relation to the suspension of a local authority's duty under section 87(3) as regards any school, are to the agreement by virtue of which the authority's duty under that provision as regards that school is suspended.]

87B – (1) The Secretary of State may impose on a person appointed under section 87A(1) ('an authorised inspector') such requirements relating to, or in connection with, the carrying out under substitution agreements of the function mentioned in section 87A(2)(b) as the Secretary of State thinks fit.

(2) Where, in the course of carrying out under a substitution agreement the function mentioned in section 87A(2)(b), it appears to an authorised inspector that there has been a failure to comply with section 87(1) in the case of a child provided with accommodation by the school to which the agreement relates, the inspector shall give notice of that fact to the Secretary of State.

(3) Where, in the course of carrying out under a substitution agreement the function mentioned in section 87A(2)(b), it appears to an authorised inspector that a child provided with accommodation by the school to which the agreement relates is suffering, or is likely to suffer, significant harm, the inspector shall–

    (a) give notice of that fact to the local authority in whose area the school is situated, and

    (b) where the inspector is required to make inspection reports to the Secretary of State, supply that local authority with a copy of the latest inspection report to have been made by the inspector to the Secretary of State in relation to the school.

(4) In this section–

    (a) 'proprietor' has the same meaning as in [the Education Act 1996], and

    (b) references to substitution agreement are to an agreement between an authorised inspector and the proprietor of an independent school by virtue of which the local authority's duty in relation to the school under section 87(3) is suspended.]

Adoption

88 – (1) The Adoption Act 1976 shall have effect subject to the amendments made by Part I of Schedule 10.

(2) (applies to Scotland only)

Paternity tests

89 – In section 20 of the Family Law Reform Act 1969 (power of court to require use of tests to determine paternity), the following subsections shall be inserted after subsection (1)–

'(1A) Where–

(a) an application is made for a direction under this section; and
(b) the person whose paternity is in issue is under the age of eighteen when the application is made,

the application shall specify who is to carry out the tests.

(1B) In the case of a direction made on an application to which subsection (1A) applies the court shall–

(a) specify, as the person who is to carry out the tests, the person specified in the application; or
(b) where the court considers that it would be inappropriate to specify that person (whether because to specify him would be incompatible with any provision made by or under regulations made under section 22 of this Act or for any other reason), decline to give the direction applied for.'

Criminal care and supervision orders

90 – (1) The power of a court to make an order under subsection (2) of section 1 of the Children and Young Persons Act 1969 (care proceedings in [youth courts]) where it is of the opinion that the condition mentioned in paragraph (f) of that subsection ('the offence condition') is satisfied is hereby abolished.

(2) The powers of the court to make care orders–

(a) under section 7(7)(a) of the Children and Young Persons Act 1969 (alteration in treatment of young offenders etc); and
(b) under section 15(1) of that Act, on discharging a supervision order made under section 7(7)(b) of that Act,

are hereby abolished.

(3) The powers given by that Act to include requirements in supervision orders shall have effect subject to amendments made by Schedule 12.

Effect and duration of orders etc

91 – (1) The making of a residence order with respect to a child who is the subject of a care order discharges the care order.

(2) The making of a care order with respect to a child who is the subject of any section 8 order discharges that order.

(3) The making of a care order with respect to a child who is the subject of a supervision order discharges that other order.

(4) The making of a care order with respect to a child who is a ward of court brings that wardship to an end.

(5) The making of a care order with respect to a child who is the subject of a school attendance order made under [section 437 of the Education Act 1996] discharges the school attendance order.

(6) Where an emergency protection order is made with respect to a child who is in care, the care order shall have effect subject to the emergency protection order.

(7) Any order made under section 4(1) or 5(1) shall continue in force until the child reaches the age of eighteen, unless it is brought to an end earlier.

(8) Any–

(a) agreement under section 4; or
(b) appointment under section 5(3) or (4),

shall continue in force until the child reaches the age of eighteen, unless it is brought to an end earlier.

(9) An order under Schedule 1 has effect as specified in that Schedule.

(10) A section 8 order shall, if it would otherwise still be in force, cease to have effect when the child reaches the age of sixteen, unless it is to have effect beyond that age by virtue of section 9(6).

(11) Where a section 8 order has effect with respect to a child who has reached the age of sixteen, it shall, if it would otherwise still be in force, cease to have effect when he reaches the age of eighteen.

(12) Any care order, other than an interim care order, shall continue in force until the child reaches the age of eighteen, unless it is brought to an end earlier.

(13) Any order made under any other provision of this Act in relation to a child shall, if it would otherwise still be in force, cease to have effect when he reaches the age of eighteen.

(14) On disposing of any application for an order under this Act, the court may (whether or not it makes any other order in response to the application) order that no application for an order under this Act of any specified kind may be made with respect to the child concerned by any person named in the order without leave of the court.

Section 91

Subsection (14) This subsection is comparable to a "vexatious litigant" provision. The fundamental freedom of a parent or carer to raise issues affecting a child's welfare should not be interfered with unless the child's best interests require it and where it might be said that the application is oppressive. This section is draconian and should be used sparingly, although proof of repeated applications is not necessary if the child's welfare requires an order. The court may specify the period of time during which applications may not be made without the permission of the court. Once an order under this section is granted, the test for giving permission to make a further application within the stipulated time period is that the applicant has an arguable case rather than having a reasonable likelihood of success.

(15) Where an application ('the previous application') has been made for–

    (a) the discharge of a care order;

    (b) the discharge of a supervision order;

    (c) the discharge of an education supervision order;

    (d) the substitution of a supervision order for a care order; or

    (e) a child assessment order,

    no further application of a kind mentioned in paragraphs (a) to (e) may be made with respect to the child concerned, without leave of the court, unless the period between the disposal of the previous application and the making of the further application exceeds six months.

(16) Subsection (15) does not apply to applications made in relation to interim orders.

(17) Where–

    (a) a person has made an application for an order under section 34;

    (b) the application has been refused; and

    (c) a period of less than six months has elapsed since the refusal,

that person may not make a further application for such an order with respect to the same child, unless he has obtained the leave of the court.

Subsection (17) This subsection prevents a person who has applied for contact to a child in care [under s34] from making a further application within six months of refusal of that application. This applies to children subject to either full or interim care orders.

Jurisdiction and procedure etc

92 – (1) The name 'domestic proceedings', given to certain proceedings in magistrates' courts, is hereby changed to 'family proceedings' and the names 'domestic court' and 'domestic court panel' are hereby changed to 'family proceedings court' and 'family panel', respectively.

(2) Proceedings under this Act shall be treated as family proceedings in relation to magistrates' courts.

(3) Subsection (2) is subject to the provisions of section 65(1) and (2) of the Magistrates' Courts Act 1980 (proceedings which may be treated as not being family proceedings), as amended by this Act.

(4) A magistrates' court shall not be competent to entertain any application, or make any order, involving the administration or application of–

(a) any property belonging to or held in trust for a child; or
(b) the income of any such property.

(5) The powers of a magistrates' court under section 63(2) of the Act of 1980 to suspend or rescind orders shall not apply in relation to any order made under this Act.

(6) Part I of Schedule 11 makes provision, including provision for the Lord Chancellor to make orders, with respect to the jurisdiction of courts and justices of the peace in relation to–

(a) proceedings under this Act; and
(b) proceedings under certain other enactments.

(7) For the purposes of this Act 'the court' means the High Court, a county court or a magistrates' court.

(8) Subsection (7) is subject to the provision made by or under Part I of Schedule 11 and to any express provision as to the jurisdiction of any court made by any other provision of this Act.

(9) The Lord Chancellor may by order make provision for the principal registry of the Family Division of the High Court to be treated as if it were a county court for such purposes of this Act, or of any provision made under this Act, as may be specified in the order.

(10) Any order under subsection (9) may make such provision as the Lord Chancellor thinks expedient for the purpose of applying (with or without modifications) provisions which apply in relation to the procedure in county courts to the principal registry when it acts as if it were a county court.

(11) Part II of Schedule 11 makes amendments consequential on this section.

93 – (1) An authority having power to make rules of court may make such provision for giving effect to–

(a) this Act;

(b) the provisions of any statutory instrument made under this Act; or

(c) any amendment made by this Act in any other enactment,

as appears to that authority to be necessary or expedient.

(2) The rules may, in particular, make provision–

(a) with respect to the procedure to be followed in any relevant proceedings (including the manner in which any application is to be made or other proceedings commenced);

(b) as to the persons entitled to participate in any relevant proceedings, whether as parties to the proceedings or by being given the opportunity to make representations to the court;

(c) with respect to the documents and information to be furnished, and notices to be given, in connection with any relevant proceedings;

(d) applying (with or without modification) enactments which govern the procedure to be followed with respect to proceedings brought on a complaint made to a magistrates' court to relevant proceedings in such a court brought otherwise than on a complaint;

(e) with respect to preliminary hearings;

(f) for the service outside [England and Wales], in such circumstances and in such manner as may be prescribed, of any notice of proceedings in a magistrates' court;

(g) for the exercise by magistrates' courts, in such circumstances as may be prescribed, of such powers as may be prescribed (even though a party to the proceedings in question is [or resides] outside England and Wales);

(h) enabling the court, in such circumstances as may be prescribed, to proceed on any application even though the respondent has not been given notice of the proceedings;

(i) authorising a single justice to discharge the functions of a magistrates' court with respect to such relevant proceedings as may be prescribed;

(j) authorising a magistrates' court to order any of the parties to such relevant proceedings as may be prescribed, in such circumstances as may be prescribed, to pay the whole or part of the costs of all or any of the other parties.

(3) In subsection (2)–

'notice of proceedings' means a summons or such other notice of proceedings as is required; and 'given', in relation to a summons, means 'served';

'prescribed' means prescribed by the rules; and

'relevant proceedings' means any application made, or proceedings brought, under any of the provisions mentioned in paragraphs (a) to (c) of subsection (1) and any part of such proceedings.

(4) This section and any other power in this Act to make rules of court are not to be taken as in any way limiting any other power of the authority in question to make rules of court.

(5) When making any rules under this section an authority shall be subject to the same requirements as to consultation (if any) as apply when the authority makes rules under its general rule making power.

94 – (1) [Subject to any express provision to the contrary made by or under this Act, an] appeal shall lie to the High Court against–

(a) the making by a magistrates' court of any order under this Act; or
(b) any refusal by a magistrates' court to make such an order.

(2) Where a magistrates' court has power, in relation to any proceedings under this Act, to decline jurisdiction because it considers that the case can more conveniently be dealt with by another court, no appeal shall lie against any exercise by that magistrates' court of that power.

(3) Subsection (1) does not apply in relation to an interim order for periodical payments made under Schedule 1.

(4) On an appeal under this section, the High Court may make such orders as may be necessary to give effect to its determination of the appeal.

(5) Where an order is made under subsection (4) the High Court may also make such incidental or consequential orders as appear to it to be just.

(6) Where an appeal from a magistrates' court relates to an order for the making of periodical payments, the High Court may order that its determination of the appeal shall have effect from such date as it thinks fit to specify in the order.

(7) The date so specified must not be earlier than the earliest date allowed in accordance with rules of court made for the purposes of this section.

(8) Where, on an appeal under this section in respect of an order requiring a person to make periodical payments, the High Court reduces the amount of those payments or discharges the order–

(a) it may order the person entitled to the payments to pay to the person making them such sum in respect of payments already made as the High Court thinks fit; and
(b) if any arrears are due under the order for periodical payments, it may remit payment of the whole, or part, of those arrears.

(9) Any order of the High Court made on an appeal under this section (other than one directing that an application be re-heard by a magistrates' court) shall, for the purposes–

(a) of the enforcement of the order; and
(b) of any power to vary, revive or discharge orders,

be treated as if it were an order of the magistrates' court from which the appeal was brought and not an order of the High Court.

(10) The Lord Chancellor may by order make provision as to the circumstances in which appeals may be made against decisions taken by courts on questions arising

in connection with the transfer, or proposed transfer, of proceedings by virtue of any order under paragraph 2 of Schedule 11.

(11) Except to the extent provided for in any order made under subsection (10), no appeal may be made against any decision of a kind mentioned in that subsection.

95 – (1) In any proceedings in which a court is hearing an application for an order under Part IV or V, or is considering whether to make any such order, the court may order the child concerned to attend such stage or stages of the proceedings as may be specified in the order.

(2) The power conferred by subsection (1) shall be exercised in accordance with rules of court.

(3) Subsections (4) to (6) apply where–

(a) an order under subsection (1) has not been complied with; or
(b) the court has reasonable cause to believe that it will not be complied with.

(4) The court may make an order authorising a constable, or such person as may be specified in the order–

(a) to take charge of the child and to bring him to the court; and
(b) to enter and search any premises specified in the order if he has reasonable cause to believe that the child may be found on the premises.

(5) The court may order any person who is in a position to do so to bring the child to the court.

(6) Where the court has reason to believe that a person has information about the whereabouts of the child it may order him to disclose it to the court.

96 – (1) Subsection (2) applies where a child who is called as a witness in any civil proceedings does not, in the opinion of the court, understand the nature of an oath.

(2) The child's evidence may be heard by the court if, in its opinion–

(a) he understands that it is his duty to speak the truth; and
(b) he has sufficient understanding to justify his evidence being heard.

(3) The Lord Chancellor may by order make provision for the admissibility of evidence which would otherwise be inadmissible under any rule of law relating to hearsay.

(4) An order under subsection (3) may only be made with respect to–

(a) civil proceedings in general or such civil proceedings, or class of civil proceedings, as may be prescribed; and
(b) evidence in connection with the upbringing, maintenance or welfare of a child.

(5) An order under subsection (3)–

(a) may, in particular, provide for the admissibility of statements which are made orally or in a prescribed form or which are recorded by any prescribed method of recording;

(b) may make different provision for different purposes and in relation to different descriptions of court; and

(c) may make such amendments and repeals in any enactment relating to evidence (other than in this Act) as the Lord Chancellor considers necessary or expedient in consequence of the provision made by the order.

(6) Subsection (5)(b) is without prejudice to section 104(4).

(7) In this section–

['civil proceedings' means civil proceedings, before any tribunal, in relation to which the strict rules of evidence apply, whether as a matter of law or by agreement of the parties, and references to 'the court' shall be construed accordingly;] and

'prescribed' means prescribed by an order under subsection (3).

97 – (1) Rules made under section 144 of the Magistrates' Courts Act 1980 may make provision for a magistrates' court to sit in private in proceedings in which any powers under this Act may be exercised by the court with respect to any child.

(2) No person shall publish any material which is intended, or likely, to identify–

(a) any child as being involved in any proceedings before [the High Court, a county court or] a magistrates' court in which any power under this Act may be exercised by the court with respect to that or any other child; or

(b) an address or school as being that of a child involved in any such proceedings.

(3) In any proceedings for an offence under this section it shall be a defence for the accused to prove that he did not know, and had no reason to suspect, that the published material was intended, or likely, to identify the child.

(4) The court or the [Lord Chancellor] may, if satisfied that the welfare of the child requires it, by order dispense with the requirements of subsection (2) to such extent as may be specified in the order.

(5) For the purposes of this section–

'publish' includes–

(a) [include in a programme service (within the meaning of the Broadcasting Act 1990);] or

(b) cause to be published; and

'material' includes any picture or representation.

(6) Any person who contravenes this section shall be guilty of an offence and liable, on summary conviction, to a fine not exceeding level 4 on the standard scale.

(7) Subsection (1) is without prejudice to–

(a) the generality of the rule making power in section 144 of the Act of 1980; or

(b) any other power of a magistrates' court to sit in private.

(8) [Sections 69 (sittings of magistrates' courts for family proceedings) and 71

(newspaper reports of certain proceedings) of the Act of 1980] shall apply in relation to any proceedings [(before a magistrates' court)] to which this section applies subject to the provisions of this section.

98 – (1) In any proceedings in which a court is hearing an application for an order under Part IV or V, no person shall be excused from–

(a) giving evidence on any matter; or
(b) answering any question put to him in the course of his giving evidence,

on the ground that doing so might incriminate him or his spouse of an offence.

(2) A statement or admission made in such proceedings shall not be admissible in evidence against the person making it or his spouse in proceedings for an offence other than perjury.

99 – (1) The Legal Aid Act 1988 is amended as mentioned in subsections (2) to (4).

(2) In section 15 (availability of, and payment for, representation under provisions relating to civil legal aid), for the words 'and (3)' in subsection (1) there shall be substituted 'to (3B)'; and the following subsections shall be inserted after subsection (3)–

'(3A) Representation under this Part shall not be available–

(a) to any local authority; or
(b) to any other body which falls within a prescribed description,

for the purposes of any proceedings under the Children Act 1989.

(3B) Regardless of subsection (2) or (3), representation under this Part must be granted where a child who is brought before a court under section 25 of the 1989 Act (use of accommodation for restricting liberty) is not, but wishes to be, legally represented before the court.'

(3) In section 19(5) (scope of provisions about criminal legal aid), at the end of the definition of 'criminal proceedings' there shall be added 'and also includes proceedings under section 15 of the Children and Young Persons Act 1969 (variation and discharge of supervision orders) and section 16(8) of that Act (appeals in such proceedings)'.

(4) Sections 27, 28 and 30(1) and (2) (provisions about legal aid in care, and other, proceedings in relation to children) shall cease to have effect.

(5) The Lord Chancellor may by order make such further amendments in the Legal Aid Act 1988 as he considers necessary or expedient in consequence of any provision made by or under this Act. ...

100 – (1) Section 7 of the Family Law Reform Act 1969 (which gives the High Court power to place a ward of court in the care, or under the supervision, of a local authority) shall cease to have effect.

(2) No court shall exercise the High Court's inherent jurisdiction with respect to

children–

(a) so as to require a child to be placed in the care, or put under the supervision, of a local authority;

(b) so as to require a child to be accommodated by or on behalf of a local authority;

(c) so as to make a child who is the subject of a care order a ward of court; or

(d) for the purpose of conferring on any local authority power to determine any question which has arisen, or which may arise, in connection with any aspect of parental responsibility for a child.

(3) No application for any exercise of the court's inherent jurisdiction with respect to children may be made by a local authority unless the authority have obtained the leave of the court.

(4) The court may only grant leave if it is satisfied that–

(a) the result which the authority wish to achieve could not be achieved through the making of any order of a kind to which subsection (5) applies; and

(b) there is reasonable cause to believe that if the court's inherent jurisdiction is not exercised with respect to the child he is likely to suffer significant harm.

(5) This subsection applies to any order–

(a) made otherwise than in the exercise of the court's inherent jurisdiction; and

(b) which the local authority is entitled to apply for (assuming, in the case of any application which may only be made with leave, that leave is granted).

101 – (1) The Secretary of State may make regulations providing–

(a) for prescribed orders which–

   (i) are made by a court in Northern Ireland; and

   (ii) appear to the Secretary of State to correspond in their effect to orders which may be made under any provision of this Act,

   to have effect in prescribed circumstances, for prescribed purposes of this Act, as if they were orders of a prescribed kind made under this Act;

(b) for prescribed orders which–

   (i) are made by a court in England and Wales; and

   (ii) appear to the Secretary of State to correspond in their effect to orders which may be made under any provision in force in Northern Ireland,

   to have effect in prescribed circumstances, for prescribed purposes of the law of Northern Ireland, as if they were orders of a prescribed kind made in Northern Ireland.

(2) Regulations under subsection (1) may provide for the order concerned to cease to have effect for the purposes of the law of Northern Ireland, or (as the case may be) the law of England and Wales, if prescribed conditions are satisfied.

(3) The Secretary of State may make regulations providing for prescribed orders which–

(a) are made by a court in the Isle of Man or in any of the Channel Islands; and

(b) appear to the Secretary of State to correspond in their effect to orders which may be made under this Act,

to have effect in prescribed circumstances for prescribed purposes of this Act, as if they were orders of a prescribed kind made under this Act.

(4) Where a child who is in the care of a local authority is lawfully taken to live in Northern Ireland, the Isle of Man or in any of the Channel Islands, the care order in question shall cease to have effect if the conditions prescribed in regulations made by the Secretary of State are satisfied.

(5) Any regulations made under this section may–

(a) make such consequential amendments (including repeals) in–
   (i) section 25 of the Children and Young Persons Act 1969 (transfers between England and Wales and Northern Ireland); or
   (ii) section 26 (transfers between England and Wales and Channel Islands or Isle of Man) of that Act,

   as the Secretary of State considers necessary or expedient; and

(b) modify any provision of this Act, in its application (by virtue of the regulations) in relation to an order made otherwise than in England and Wales.

Search warrants

102 – (1) Where, on an application made by any person for a warrant under this section, it appears to the court–

(a) that a person attempting to exercise powers under any enactment mentioned in subsection (6) has been prevented from doing so by being refused entry to the premises concerned or refused access to the child concerned; or

(b) that any such person is likely to be so prevented from exercising any such powers,

it may issue a warrant authorising any constable to assist that person in the exercise of those powers, using reasonable force if necessary.

(2) Every warrant issued under this section shall be addressed to, and executed by, a constable who shall be accompanied by the person applying for the warrant if–

(a) that person so desires; and

(b) the court by whom the warrant is issued does not direct otherwise.

(3) A court granting an application for a warrant under this section may direct that the constable concerned may, in executing the warrant, be accompanied by a registered medical practitioner, registered nurse or registered health visitor if he so chooses.

(4) An application for a warrant under this section shall be made in the manner and form prescribed by rules of court.

(5) Where–

(a) an application for a warrant under this section relates to a particular child; and
(b) it is reasonably practicable to do so,

the application and any warrant granted on the application shall name the child; and where it does not name him it shall describe him as clearly as possible.

(6) The enactments are–

(a) sections 62, 64, 67, 76, 80, 86 and 87;
(b) paragraph 8(1)(b) and (2)(b) of Schedule 3;
(c) section 33 of the Adoption Act 1976 (duty of local authority to secure that protected children are visited from time to time).

General

103 – (1) This section applies where any offence under this Act is committed by a body corporate.

(2) If the offence is proved to have been committed with the consent or connivance of or to be attributable to any neglect on the part of any director, manager, secretary or other similar officer of the body corporate, or any person who was purporting to act in any such capacity, he (as well as the body corporate) shall be guilty of the offence and shall be liable to be proceeded against and punished accordingly.

104 – (1) Any power of the Lord Chancellor or the Secretary of State under this Act to make an order, regulations, or rules, except an order under section 54(2), 56(4)(a), 57(3), 84 or 97(4) or paragraph 1(1) of Schedule 4, shall be exercisable by statutory instrument.

(2) Any such statutory instrument, except one made under section 17(4), 107 or 108(2), shall be subject to annulment in pursuance of a resolution of either House of Parliament.

(3) An order under section 17(4) shall not be made unless a draft of it has been laid before, and approved by a resolution of, each House of Parliament.

(4) Any statutory instrument made under this Act may–

(a) make different provision for different cases;
(b) provide for exemptions from any of its provisions; and
(c) contain such incidental, supplemental and transitional provisions as the person making it considers expedient.

105 – (1) In this Act–

Section 105 gives definitions of words or phrases used throughout the Children Act or refers the reader to the relevant sections and Acts where those word are defined.

'adoption agency' means a body which may be referred to as an adoption agency by virtue of section 1 of the Adoption Act 1976;

'bank holiday' means a day which is a bank holiday under the Banking and Financial Dealings Act 1971;

'care order' has the meaning given by section 31(11) and also includes any order which by or under any enactment has the effect of, or is deemed to be, a care order for the purposes of this Act; and any reference to a child who is in the care of an authority is a reference to a child who is in their care by virtue of a care order;

'child' means, subject to paragraph 16 of Schedule 1, a person under the age of eighteen;

'child assessment order' has the meaning given by section 43(2);

'child minder' has the meaning given by section 71;

'child of the family', in relation to the parties to a marriage, means–

(a) a child of both of those parties;
(b) any other child, not being a child who is placed with those parties as foster parents by a local authority or voluntary organisation, who has been treated by both of those parties as a child of their family;

'children's home', has the same meaning as in section 63;

'community home' has the meaning given by section 53;

'contact order' has the meaning given by section 8(1);

'day care' has the same meaning as in section 18;

'disabled', in relation to a child, has the same meaning as in section 17(11);

...

'domestic premises' has the meaning given by section 71(12);

['dwelling-house' includes–

(a) any building or part of a building which is occupied as a dwelling;
(b) any caravan, house-boat or structure which is occupied as a dwelling;

and any yard, garage or outhouse belonging to it and occupied with it;]

'education supervision order' has the meaning given in section 36;

'emergency protection order' means an order under section 44;

'family assistance order' has the meaning given in section 16(2);

'family proceedings' has the meaning given by section 8(3);

'functions' includes powers and duties;

'guardian of a child' means a guardian (other than a guardian of the estate of a child) appointed in accordance with the provisions of section 5;

'harm' has the same meaning as in section 31(9) and the question of whether harm is significant shall be determined in accordance with section 31(10);

['Health Authority' means a Health Authority established under section 8 of the National Health Service Act 1977;]

'health service hospital' has the same meaning as in the National Health Service Act 1977;

'hospital' has the same meaning as in the Mental Health Act 1983, except that it does not include a special hospital within the meaning of that Act;

'ill-treatment' has the same meaning as in section 31(9);

['income-based jobseeker's allowance' has the same meaning as in the Jobseekers Act 1995;]

'independent school' has the same meaning as in [the Education Act 1996];

'local authority' means, in relation to England ..., the council of a county, a metropolitan district, a London Borough or the Common Council of the City of London[, in relation to Wales, the council of a county or a county borough] and, in relation to Scotland, a local authority within the meaning of section 1(2) of the Social Work (Scotland) Act 1968;

'local authority foster parent' has the same meaning as in section 23(3);

'local education authority' has the same meaning as in [the Education Act 1996];

'local housing authority' has the same meaning as in the Housing Act 1985;

'mental nursing home' has the same meaning as in the Registered Homes Act 1984;

'nursing home' has the same meaning as in the Act of 1984;

'parental responsibility' has the meaning given in section 3;

'parental responsibility agreement' has the meaning given in section 4(1);

'prescribed' means prescribed by regulations made under this Act;

'privately fostered child' and 'to foster a child privately' have the same meaning as in section 66;

'prohibited steps order' has the meaning given by section 8(1);

'protected child' has the same meaning as in Part III of the Adoption Act 1976;

'registered children's home' has the same meaning as in section 63;

'registered pupil' has the same meaning as in [the Education Act 1996];

'relative', in relation to a child, means a grandparent, brother, sister, uncle or aunt (whether of the full blood or half blood or by affinity) or step-parent;

'residence order' has the meaning given by section 8(1);

'residential care home' has the same meaning as in the Registered Homes Act 1984 [and 'small home' has the meaning given by section 1(4A) of that Act];

'responsible person', in relation to a child who is the subject of a supervision order, has the meaning given in paragraph 1 of Schedule 3;

'school' has the same meaning as in [the Education Act 1996] or, in relation to Scotland, in the Education (Scotland) Act 1980;

'service', in relation to any provision made under Part III, includes any facility;

'signed', in relation to any person, includes the making by that person of his mark;

'special educational needs' has the same meaning as in [the Education Act 1993];

['Special Health Authority' means a Special Health Authority established under section 11 of the National Health Service Act 1977;]

'specific issue order' has the meaning given by section 8(1);

'supervision order' has the meaning given by section 31(11);

'supervised child' and 'supervisor', in relation to a supervision order or an education supervision order, mean respectively the child who is (or is to be) under supervision and the person under whose supervision he is (or is to be) by virtue of the order;

'upbringing', in relation to any child, includes the care of the child but not his maintenance;

'voluntary home' has the meaning given by section 60;

'voluntary organisation' means a body (other than a public or local authority) whose activities are not carried on for profit.

(2) References in this Act to a child whose father and mother were, or (as the case may be) were not, married to each other at the time of his birth must be read with section 1 of the Family Law Reform Act 1987 (which extends the meaning of such references).

(3) References in this Act to–

(a) a person with whom a child lives, or is to live, as the result of a residence order; or

(b) a person in whose favour a residence order is in force,

shall be construed as references to the person named in the order as the person with whom the child is to live.

(4) References in this Act to a child who is looked after by a local authority have the same meaning as they have (by virtue of section 22) in Part III.

(5) References in this Act to accommodation provided by or on behalf of a local authority are references to accommodation so provided in the exercise of functions which stand referred to the social services committee of that or any other local authority under the Local Authority Social Services Act 1970.

(6) In determining the 'ordinary residence' of a child for any purpose of this Act, there shall be disregarded any period in which he lives in any place–

(a) which is a school or other institution;

(b) in accordance with the requirements of a supervision order under this Act or an order under section 7(7)(b) of the Children and Young Persons Act 1969; or

(c) while he is being provided with accommodation by or on behalf of a local authority.

(7) References in this Act to children who are in need shall be construed in accordance with section 17.

(8) Any notice or other document required under this Act to be served on any person may be served on him by being delivered personally to him, or being sent by post to him in a registered letter or by the recorded delivery service at his proper address.

(9) Any such notice or other document required to be served on a body corporate or a firm shall be duly served if it is served on the secretary or clerk of that body or a partner of that firm.

(10) For the purposes of this section, and of section 7 of the Interpretation Act 1978 in its application to this section, the proper address of a person–

(a) in the case of a secretary or clerk of a body corporate, shall be that of the registered or principal office of that body;

(b) in the case of a partner of a firm, shall be that of the principal office of the firm; and

(c) in any other case, shall be the last known address of the person to be served.

106 – (1) Any–

(a) grants made by the Secretary of State under this Act; and

(b) any other expenses incurred by the Secretary of State under this Act,

shall be payable out of money provided by Parliament.

(2) Any sums received by the Secretary of State under section 58, or by way of the repayment of any grant made under section 82(2) or (4) shall be paid into the Consolidated Fund.

107 Her Majesty may by Order in Council direct that any of the provisions of this Act shall extend to any of the Channel Islands with such exceptions and modifications as may be specified in the Order.

108 – (1) This Act may be cited as the Children Act 1989.

(2) Sections 89 and 96(3) to (7), and paragraph 35 of Schedule 12, shall come into force on the passing of this Act and paragraph 36 of Schedule 12 shall come into force at the end of the period of two months beginning with the day on which this Act is passed but otherwise this Act shall come into force on such date as may be appointed by order made by the Lord Chancellor or the Secretary of State, or by both acting jointly.

(3) Different dates may be appointed for different provisions of this Act and in relation to different cases.

(4) The minor amendments set out in Schedule 12 shall have effect.

(5) The consequential amendments set out in Schedule 13 shall have effect.

(6) The transitional provisions and savings set out in Schedule 14 shall have effect.

(7) The repeals set out in Schedule 15 shall have effect.

(8) An order under subsection (2) may make such transitional provisions or savings as appear to the person making the order to be necessary or expedient in connection with the provisions brought into force by the order, including–

(a) provisions adding to or modifying the provisions of Schedule 14; and
(b) such adaptations–
   (i) of the provisions brought into force by the order; and
   (ii) of any provisions of this Act then in force,

as appear to him necessary or expedient in consequence of the partial operation of this Act.

(9) The Lord Chancellor may by order make such amendments or repeals, in such enactments as may be specified in the order, as appear to him to be necessary or expedient in consequence of any provision of this Act.

(10) This Act shall, in its application to the Isles of Scilly, have effect subject to such exceptions, adaptations and modifications as the Secretary of State may by order prescribe.

(11) The following provisions of this Act extend to Scotland–

section 19;

section 25(8);

section 50(13);

Part X;

section 80(1)(h) and (i), (2) to (4), (5)(a), (b) and (h) and (6) to (12);

section 88;

section 104 (so far as necessary);

section 105 (so far as necessary);

subsections (1) to (3), (8) and (9) and this subsection;

in Schedule 2, paragraph 24;

in Schedule 12, paragraphs 1, 7 to 10, 18, 27, 30(a) and 41 to 44;

in Schedule 13, paragraphs 18 to 23, 32, 46, 47, 50, 57, 62, 63, 68(a) and (b) and 71;

in Schedule 14, paragraphs 1, 33 and 34;

in Schedule 15, the entries relating to–

(a) the Custody of Children Act 1891;
(b) the Nurseries and Child Minders Regulation Act 1948;
(c) section 53(3) of the Children and Young Persons Act 1963;
(d) section 60 of the Health Services and Public Health Act 1968;
(e) the Social Work (Scotland) Act 1968;
(f) the Adoption (Scotland) Act 1978;
(g) the Child Care Act 1980;
(h) the Foster Children (Scotland) Act 1984;
(i) the Child Abduction and Custody Act 1985; and
(j) the Family Law Act 1986.

(12) The following provisions of this Act extend to Northern Ireland–

section 50;

section 101(1)(b), (2) and (5)(a)(i);

subsections (1) to (3), (8) and (9) and this subsection;

in Schedule 2, paragraph 24;

in Schedule 12, paragraphs 7 to 10, 18 and 27;

in Schedule 13, paragraphs 21, 22, 46, 47, 57, 62, 63, 68(c) to (e) and 69 to 71;

in Schedule 14, paragraphs ... 28 to 30 and 38(a); and

in Schedule 15, the entries relating to the Guardianship of Minors Act 1971, the Children Act 1975, the Child Care Act 1980, and the Family Law Act 1986.

SCHEDULE 1

FINANCIAL PROVISION FOR CHILDREN

Orders for financial relief against parents

1 – (1) On an application made by a parent or guardian of a child, or by any person in whose favour a residence order is in force with respect to a child, the court may–

(a) in the case of an application to the High Court or a county court, make one or more of the orders mentioned in sub-paragraph (2);

(b) in the case of an application to a magistrates' court, make one or both of the orders mentioned in paragraphs (a) and (c) of that sub-paragraph.

Paragraph 1

Subparagraph(1) There are five types of financial order that a court may make against a parent, for the benefit of a child. It can order that a parent pay periodical payments, secured periodical payments, a lump sum or settle property on a child or transfer property for the benefit of a child. A magistrates court can only make an order for periodical payments or the payment of a lump sum. The High Court or County Court may make any of the orders.

All such payments can be made to the applicant for the benefit of the child, or to the child directly

The only people who can apply for these orders are parents, guardians or those in whose favour a residence order is in force. The categories cannot be extended.

(2) The orders referred to in sub-paragraph (1) are–

(a) an order requiring either or both parents of a child–
 (i) to make to the applicant for the benefit of the child; or
 (ii) to make to the child himself,

 such periodical payments, for such term, as may be specified in the order;

Subparagraph(2)(a) Periodical payments are for example monthly payments of a set amount. The "period" can be varied.

(b) an order requiring either or both parents of a child–
 (i) to secure to the applicant for the benefit of the child; or
 (ii) to secure to the child himself,

 such periodical payments, for such term, as may be so specified;

Subparagraph (2)(b) *The court can ensure that the periodical payments will be met by securing them against something i.e. a property or a fund of money.*

(c) an order requiring either or both parents of a child–
  (i) to pay to the applicant for the benefit of the child; or
  (ii) to pay to the child himself,

such lump sum as may be so specified;

Subparagraph(2)(c) *A lump sum of money means a single payment, as opposed to periodical payments*

(d) an order requiring a settlement to be made for the benefit of the child, and to the satisfaction of the court, of property–
  (i) to which either parent is entitled (either in possession or in reversion); and
  (ii) which is specified in the order;

Subparagraph (2)(d) *Under this subparagraph property can be settled for the benefit of a child.*

(e) an order requiring either or both parents of a child–
  (i) to transfer to the applicant, for the benefit of the child; or
  (ii) to transfer to the child himself,

such property to which the parent is, or the parents are, entitled (either in possession or in reversion) as may be specified in the order.

(3) The powers conferred by this paragraph may be exercised at any time.

(4) An order under sub-paragraph (2)(a) or (b) may be varied or discharged by a subsequent order made on the application of any person by or to whom payments were required to be made under the previous order.

(5) Where a court makes an order under this paragraph–

  (a) it may at any time make a further such order under sub-paragraph (2)(a), (b) or (c) with respect to the child concerned if he has not reached the age of eighteen;
  (b) it may not make more than one order under sub-paragraph (2)(d) or (e) against the same person in respect of the same child.

> **Subparagraph(5)** *The court may make multiple orders for periodical payments or lump sum payments, but it can only make one order for a settlement or transfer of property against a person.*

(6) On making, varying or discharging a residence order the court may exercise any of its powers under this Schedule even though no application has been made to it under this Schedule.

(7) Where a child is a ward of court, the court may exercise any of its powers under this Schedule even though no application has been made to it.

Orders for financial relief for persons over eighteen

2 – (1) If, on an application by a person who has reached the age of eighteen, it appears to the court–

    (a) that the applicant is, will be or (if an order were made under this paragraph) would be receiving instruction at an educational establishment or undergoing training for a trade, profession or vocation, whether or not while in gainful employment; or

    (b) that there are special circumstances which justify the making of an order under this paragraph,

the court may make one or both of the orders mentioned in sub-paragraph (2).

(2) The orders are–

    (a) an order requiring either or both of the applicant's parents to pay to the applicant such periodical payments, for such term, as may be specified in the order;

    (b) an order requiring either or both of the applicant's parents to pay to the applicant such lump sum as may be so specified.

(3) An application may not be made under this paragraph by any person if, immediately before he reached the age of sixteen, a periodical payments order was in force with respect to him.

(4) No order shall be made under this paragraph at a time when the parents of the applicant are living with each other in the same household.

(5) An order under sub-paragraph (2)(a) may be varied or discharged by a subsequent order made on the application of any person by or to whom payments were required to be made under the previous order.

(6) In sub-paragraph (3) 'periodical payments order' means an order made under–

    (a) this Schedule;

    (b) ...

(c) section 23 or 27 of the Matrimonial Causes Act 1973;

(d) Part I of the Domestic Proceedings and Magistrates' Courts Act 1978,
for the making or securing of periodical payments.

(7) The powers conferred by this paragraph shall be exercisable at any time.

(8) Where the court makes an order under this paragraph it may from time to time
while that order remains in force make a further such order.

> **Paragraph 2**
> *Once a child reaches the age of eighteen he may apply to the court for an order that
> his parents pay him a lump sum or periodical payments, if he is in education or
> training, and there are special circumstances. No order can be made if the parents
> continue to live together. If prior to reaching the age of 16 there was an order in force
> that periodical payments should be made for the benefit of the child, then no
> application may be made under this section.*

Duration of orders for financial relief

3 – (1) The term to be specified in an order for periodical payments made under
paragraph 1(2)(a) or (b) in favour of a child may begin with the date of the making
of an application for the order in question or any later date [or a date ascertained in
accordance with sub-paragraph (5) or (6)] but–

(a) shall not in the first instance extend beyond the child's seventeenth birthday
unless the court thinks it right in the circumstances of the case to specify a
later date; and

(b) shall not in any event extend beyond the child's eighteenth birthday.

> **Paragraph 3**
> **Subparagraph (1)** *An order for periodical payments shall not extend in usual
> circumstances beyond a child's 17th birthday, and subject to the exceptions in section
> 3(2) of this schedule it will never extend beyond a child's 18th birthday.*

(2) Paragraph (b) of sub-paragraph (1) shall not apply in the case of a child if it
appears to the court that–

(a) the child is, or will be (if an order were made without complying with that
paragraph) would be receiving instruction at an educational establishment or
undergoing training for a trade, profession or vocation, whether or not while in
gainful employment; or

(b) there are special circumstances which justify the making of an order without complying with that paragraph.

> **Subparagraph (2)** *An order will not come to an end on a child's 18th birthday if the child is continuing in education or training, and there are special circumstances which the court find justify the order being extended.*

(3) An order for periodical payments made under paragraph 1(2)(a) or 2(2)(a) shall, notwithstanding anything in the order, cease to have effect on the death of the person liable to make payments under the order.

(4) Where an order is made under paragraph 1(2)(a) or (b) requiring periodical payments to be made or secured to the parent of a child, the order shall cease to have effect if–

(a) any parent making or securing the payments; and
(b) any parent to whom the payments are made or secured,
    live together for a period of more than six months.

> **Subparagraph (4)** *Any such orders will end if the parents of the child live together for more than six months. This is because such orders are intended to be for the benefit of a child whose parents have separated.*

(5) Where–

(a) a maintenance assessment ('the current assessment') is in force with respect to a child; and

> **Subparagraph (5)(a)** *A maintenance assessment is an assessment made under the Child Support Act 1991*

(b) an application is made for an order under paragraph 1(2)(a) or (b) of this Schedule for periodical payments in favour of that child–
    (i) in accordance with section 8 of the Child Support Act 1991; and

> **Subparagraph (5)(b)(i)** *If the Child Support Act applies in a situation and a maintenance assessment will be made by the Child Support Agency, then the courts should not become involved in assessing maintenance payments. Section 8 of the Child Support Act does however provide for the courts to exercise powers under Schedule 1 of the Children Act 1989, and it sets out the circumstances in which that can happen. These circumstances are as follows :*
>
> *i) if there is a written agreement which makes provision for periodical payments by an absent parent of the child, and the order that the court makes is in the terms of that agreement, or;*
>
> *ii) if the court is satisfied that the circumstances of the case make it appropriate for the absent parent to make periodical payments to or for the benefit of the child, or;*
>
> *iii) if the child would be receiving education or training and the order is to meet the costs of that instruction or training, or;*
>
> *iv) if the child is disabled and the payments would be made to meet payments attributable to his disability.*

    (ii) before the end of the period of 6 months beginning with the making of the current assessment,the term to be specified in any such order made on that application may be expressed to begin on, or at any time after, the earliest permitted date.

(6) For the purposes of subsection (5) above, 'the earliest permitted date' is whichever is the later of–

    (a) the date 6 months before the application is made; or

    (b) the date on which the current assessment took effect or, where successive maintenance assessmentss have been continuously in force with respect to a child, on which the first of those assessments took effect.

(7) Where–

    (a) a maintenance assessment ceases to have effect or is cancelled by or under any provision of the Child Support Act 1991, and

    (b) an application is made, before the end of the period of 6 months beginning with the relevant date, for an order for periodical payments under paragraph 1(2)(a) or (b) in favour of a child with respect to whom that maintenance assessment was in force immediately before it ceased to have effect or was cancelled,

    the term to be specified in any such order, or in any interim order under paragraph 9, made on that application may begin with the date on which that maintenance assessment ceased to have effect or, as the case may be, the date with effect from which it was cancelled, or any later date.

(8) In sub-paragraph (7)(b)–

    (a) where the maintenance assessment ceased to have effect, the relevant date is the date on which it so ceased; and

    (b) where the maintenance assessment was cancelled, the relevant date is the later of–

       (i) the date on which the person who cancelled it did so, and

      (ii) the date from which the cancellation first had effect.

Matters to which court is to have regard in making orders for financial relief

4 – (1) In deciding whether to exercise its powers under paragraph 1 or 2, and if so in what manner, the court shall have regard to all the circumstances including–

    (a) the income, earning capacity, property and other financial resources which each person mentioned in sub-paragraph (4) has or is likely to have in the foreseeable future;

    (b) the financial needs, obligations and responsibilities which each person mentioned in sub-paragraph (4) has or is likely to have in the foreseeable future;

    (c) the financial needs of the child;

    (d) the income, earning capacity (if any), property and other financial resources of the child;

    (e) any physical or mental disability of the child;

    (f) the manner in which the child was being, or was expected to be, educated or trained.

(2) In deciding whether to exercise its powers under paragraph 1 against a person who is not the mother or father of the child, and if so in what manner, the court shall in addition have regard to–

    (a) whether that person had assumed responsibility for the maintenance of the child, and, if so, the extent to which and basis on which he assumed that responsibility and the length of the period during which he met that responsibility;

    (b) whether he did so knowing that the child was not his child;

    (c) the liability of any other person to maintain the child.

(3) Where the court makes an order under paragraph 1 against a person who is not the father of the child, it shall record in the order that the order is made on the basis that the person against whom the order is made is not the child's father.

(4) The persons mentioned in sub-paragraph (1) are–

    (a) in relation to a decision whether to exercise its powers under paragraph 1, any parent of the child;

    (b) in relation to a decision whether to exercise its powers under paragraph 2, the mother and father of the child;

    (c) the applicant for the order;

(d) any other person in whose favour the court proposes to make the order.

> **Paragraph 4**
> **Subparagraph (4)** *In subparagraphs (a) and (b) there is in fact a difference in meaning between the words, " any parent of the child" and, " the mother and father of the child". The word "parent" is to be interpreted more widely than the biological parents of a child. See Paragraph 16 of this Schedule for its extended meaning.*

Provisions relating to lump sums

5 – (1) Without prejudice to the generality of paragraph 1, an order under that paragraph for the payment of a lump sum may be made for the purpose of enabling any liabilities or expenses–

  (a) incurred in connection with the birth of the child or in maintaining the child; and

  (b) reasonably incurred before the making of the order,
   to be met.

(2) The amount of any lump sum required to be paid by an order made by a magistrates' court under paragraph 1 or 2 shall not exceed £1000 or such larger amount as the [Lord Chancellor] may from time to time by order fix for the purposes of this sub-paragraph.

(3) The power of the court under paragraph 1 or 2 to vary or discharge an order for the making or securing of periodical payments by a parent shall include power to make an order under that provision for the payment of a lump sum by that parent.

> **Paragraph 5**
> **Subparagraph (3)** *If a court makes an order varying or discharging an order for periodical payment it may make instead an order for the payment of a lump sum by the parent. In this paragraph the word "parent" is given the interpretation at paragraph 16.*

(4) The amount of any lump sum which a parent may be required to pay by virtue of sub-paragraph (3) shall not, in the case of an order made by a magistrates' court, exceed the maximum amount that may at the time of the making of the order be required to be paid under sub-paragraph (2), but a magistrates' court may make an order for the payment of a lump sum not exceeding that amount even though the parent was required to pay a lump sum by a previous order under this Act.

(5) An order made under paragraph 1 or 2 for the payment of a lump sum may provide for the payment of that sum by instalments.

(6) Where the court provides for the payment of a lump sum by instalments the court, on an application made either by the person liable to pay or the person entitled to receive that sum, shall have power to vary that order by varying–

   (a) the number of instalments payable;
   (b) the amount of any instalment payable;
   (c) the date on which any instalment becomes payable.

Variation etc of orders for periodical payments

6 – (1) In exercising its powers under paragraph 1 or 2 to vary or discharge an order for the making or securing of periodical payments the court shall have regard to all the circumstances of the case, including any change in any of the matters to which the court was required to have regard when making the order.

(2) The power of the court under paragraph 1 or 2 to vary an order for the making or securing of periodical payments shall include power to suspend any provision of the order temporarily and to revive any provision so suspended.

(3) Where on an application under paragraph 1 or 2 for the variation or discharge of an order for the making or securing of periodical payments the court varies the payments required to be made under that order, the court may provide that the payments as so varied shall be made from such date as the court may specify [except that, subject to sub-paragraph (9), the date shall not be] earlier than the date of the making of the application.

(4) An application for the variation of an order made under paragraph 1 for the making or securing of periodical payments to or for the benefit of a child may, if the child has reached the age of sixteen, be made by the child himself.

(5) Where an order for the making or securing of periodical payments made under paragraph 1 ceases to have effect on the date on which the child reaches the age of sixteen, or at any time after that date but before or on the date on which he reaches the age of eighteen, the child may apply to the court which made the order for an order for its revival.

(6) If on such an application it appears to the court that–

   (a) the child is, will be or (if an order were made under this sub-paragraph) would be receiving instruction at an educational establishment or undergoing training for a trade, profession or vocation, whether or not while in gainful employment; or
   (b) there are special circumstances which justify the making of an order under this paragraph,

the court shall have power by order to revive the order from such date as the court may specify, not being earlier than the date of the making of the application.

(7) Any order which is revived by an order under sub-paragraph (5) may be varied or discharged under that provision, on the application of any person by whom or to whom payments are required to be made under the revived order.

(8) An order for the making or securing of periodical payments made under paragraph 1 may be varied or discharged, after the death of either parent, on the application of a guardian of the child concerned.

(9) Where–

(a) an order under paragraph 1(2)(a) or (b) for the making or securing of periodical payments in favour of more than one child ('the order') is in force;

(b) the order requires payments specified in it to be made to or for the benefit of more than one child without apportioning those payments between them;

(c) a maintenance assessment ('the assessment') is made with respect to one or more, but not all, of the children with respect to whom those payments are to be made; and

(d) an application is made, before the end of the period of 6 months beginning with the date on which the assessment was made, for the variation or discharge of the order,

the court may, in exercise of its powers under paragraph 1 to vary or discharge the order, direct that the variation or discharge shall take effect from the date on which the assessment took effect or any later date.

Paragraph 6
Subparagraph (9) This subparagraph deals with the situation where an order has been made for a parent to make periodical payments in respect of more than one child, and subsequently an assessment for maintenance has been made against the parent in respect of one or more (but not all) of those children. On an application to vary or discharge the periodical payments order the court can order that it should be discharged not simply from the date of the application, but from the date of the assessment. This provision therefore assists against a parent being liable both for periodical payments and a maintenance assessment.

6A – (1) Subject to sub-paragraphs (7) and (8), the power of a magistrates' court–

(a) under paragraph 1 or 2 to vary an order for the making of periodical payments, or

(b) under paragraph 5(6) to vary an order for the payment of a lump sum by instalments,

shall include power, if the court is satisfied that payment has not been made in accordance with the order, to exercise one of its powers under paragraphs (a) to (d) of section 59(3) of the Magistrates' Courts Act 1980.

Paragraph 6A

Subparagraph (1) The powers under section 59(3) of the Magistrates Court Act 1980, referred to in this section are :

a) to order that money be paid direct from the debtor to the creditor

b) to order the payments be made to the clerk of a magistrates court

c) to order the payments be made by standing order or direct debit

d) to make an attachment of earnings order to secure the payment

(2) In any case where–
- (a) a magistrates' court has made an order under this Schedule for the making of periodical payments or for the payment of a lump sum by instalments, and
- (b) payments under the order are required to be made by any method of payment falling within section 59(6) of the Magistrates' Courts Act 1980 (standing order, etc),

any person entitled to make an application under this Schedule for the variation of the order (in this paragraph referred to as 'the applicant') may apply to the clerk to the justices for the petty sessions area for which the court is acting for the order to be varied as mentioned in sub-paragraph (3).

(3) Subject to sub-paragraph (5), where an application is made under sub-paragraph (2), the clerk, after giving written notice (by post or otherwise) of the application to any interested party and allowing that party, within the period of 14 days beginning with the date of the giving of that notice, an opportunity to make written representations, may vary the order to provide that payments under the order shall be made to the clerk [-].

(4) The clerk may proceed with an application under sub-paragraph (2) notwithstanding that any such interested party as is referred to in sub-paragraph (3) has not received written notice of the application.

(5) Where an application has been made under sub-paragraph (2), the clerk may, if he considers it inappropriate to exercise his power under sub-paragraph (3), refer the matter to the court which, subject to sub-paragraphs (7) and (8), may vary the order by exercising one of its powers under paragraphs (a) to (d) of section 59(3) of the Magistrates' Courts Act 1980.

(6) Subsection (4) of section 59 of the Magistrates' Courts Act 1980 (power of court to order that account be opened) shall apply for the purposes of sub-paragraphs (1) and (5) as it applies for the purposes of that section.

(7) Before varying the order by exercising one of its powers under paragraphs (a) to (d) of section 59(3) of the Magistrates' Courts Act 1980, the court shall have regard to any representations made by the parties to the application.

(8) If the court does not propose to exercise its power [under paragraph (c), (cc) or (d)] of subsection (3) of section 59 of the Magistrates' Courts Act 1980, the court shall, unless upon representations expressly made in that behalf by the applicant for the order it is satisfied that it is undesirable to do so, exercise its power under paragraph (b) of that subsection.

(9) None of the powers of the court, or of the clerk to the justices, conferred by this paragraph shall be exercisable in relation to an order under this Schedule for the making of periodical payments, or for the payment of a lump sum by instalments, which is not a qualifying maintenance order (within the meaning of section 59 of the Magistrates' Courts Act 1980).

> **Subparagraph (9)** *A maintenance order is a " qualifying maintenance order" within the meaning of s.59 of the Magistrates Court Act 1980 if at the time it was made the debtor was ordinarily resident in England and Wales.*

(11) In sub-paragraphs (3) and (4) 'interested party', in relation to an application made by the applicant under sub-paragraph (2), means a person who would be entitled to be a party to an application for the variation of the order made by the applicant under any other provision of this Schedule if such an application were made.]

Variation of orders for secured periodical payments after death of parent

7 – (1) Where the parent liable to make payments under a secured periodical payments order has died, the persons who may apply for the variation or discharge of the order shall include the personal representatives of the deceased parent.

(2) No application for the variation of the order shall, except with the permission of the court, be made after the end of the period of six months from the date on which representation in regard to the estate of that parent is first taken out.

(3) The personal representatives of a deceased person against whom a secured periodical payments order was made shall not be liable for having distributed any part of the estate of the deceased after the end of the period of six months referred to in sub-paragraph (2) on the ground that they ought to have taken into account the possibility that the court might permit an application for variation to be made after that period by the person entitled to payments under the order.

> **Paragraph 7**
> **Subparagraphs (2)(3)** *When a person who was making periodical payements dies, there is a limited period of six months from the date on which representation in regard to the estate of the deceased person was taken out, during which any claims*

> *for variation or discharge can be made to the court. The court may give permission for the six month period to be extended.*

(4) Sub-paragraph (3) shall not prejudice any power to recover any part of the estate so distributed arising by virtue of the variation of an order in accordance with this paragraph.

(5) Where an application to vary a secured periodical payments order is made after the death of the parent liable to make payments under the order, the circumstances to which the court is required to have regard under paragraph 6(1) shall include the changed circumstances resulting from the death of the parent.

(6) In considering for the purposes of sub-paragraph (2) the question when representation was first taken out, a grant limited to settled land or to trust property shall be left out of account and a grant limited to real estate or to personal estate shall be left out of account unless a grant limited to the remainder of the estate has previously been made or is made at the same time.

(6) In this paragraph 'secured periodical payments order' means an order for secured periodical payments under paragraph 1(2)(b).

Paragraph 8
If there is in existence a financial relief order in respect of a child, which has not been made under the Children Act 1989, and a residence order is then made in respect of the child, the court has the power under this Schedule to vary or revoke the financial relief order that is in existence.

Financial relief under other enactments

8 – (1) This paragraph applies where a residence order is made with respect to a child at a time when there is in force an order ('the financial relief order') made under any enactment other than this Act and requiring a person to contribute to the child's maintenance.

(2) Where this paragraph applies, the court may, on the application of–

(a) any person required by the financial relief order to contribute to the child's maintenance; or

(b) any person in whose favour a residence order with respect to the child is in force, make an order revoking the financial relief order, or varying it by altering the amount of any sum payable under that order or by substituting the applicant for the person to whom any such sum is otherwise payable under that order.

Interim Orders

9 – (1) Where an application is made under paragraph 1 or 2 the court may, at any time before it disposes of the application, make an interim order–

    (a) requiring either or both parents to make such periodical payments, at such times and for such term as the court thinks fit; and

    (b) giving any direction which the court thinks fit.

(2) An interim order made under this paragraph may provide for payments to be made from such date as the court may specify [except that, subject to paragraph 3(5) and (6), the date shall not be] earlier than the date of the making of the application under paragraph 1 or 2.

(3) An interim order made under this paragraph shall cease to have effect when the application is disposed of or, if earlier, on the date specified for the purposes of this paragraph in the interim order.

(4) An interim order in which a date has been specified for the purposes of sub-paragraph (3) may be varied by substituting a later date.

> **Paragraph 9**
> *This paragraph allows the court to make interim orders upon any application made under paragraph 1 or 2. All such interim orders will come to an end upon the making of a final order, if no date has been specified prior to that time on which the order should end.*

Alteration of maintenance agreements

10 – (1) In this paragraph and in paragraph 11 'maintenance agreement' means any agreement in writing made with respect to a child, whether before or after the commencement of this paragraph, which–

    (a) is or was made between the father and mother of the child; and

    (b) contains provision with respect to the making or securing of payments, or the disposition or use of any property, for the maintenance or education of the child,

and any such provisions are in this paragraph, and paragraph 11, referred to as 'financial arrangements'.

(2) Where a maintenance agreement is for the time being subsisting and each of the parties to the agreement is for the time being either domiciled or resident in England and Wales, then, either party may apply for an order under this paragraph.

(3) If the court to which the application is made is satisfied either–

(a) that, by reason of a change in the circumstances in the light of which any financial arrangements contained in the agreement were made (including a change foreseen by the parties when making the agreement), the agreement should be altered so as to make different financial arrangements; or

(b) that the agreement does not contain proper financial arrangements with respect to the child,

then that court may by order make such alterations in the agreement by varying or revoking any financial arrangements contained in it as may appear to it to be just having regard to all the circumstances.

(3) If the maintenance agreement is altered by an order under this paragraph, the agreement shall have effect thereafter as if the alteration had been made by agreement between the parties and for valuable consideration.

(5) Where a court decides to make an order under this paragraph altering the maintenance agreement–

(a) by inserting provision for the making or securing by one of the parties to the agreement of periodical payments for the maintenance of the child; or

(b) by increasing the rate of periodical payments required to be made or secured by one of the parties for the maintenance of the child,

then, in deciding the term for which under the agreement as altered by the order the payments or (as the case may be) the additional payments attributable to the increase are to be made or secured for the benefit of the child, the court shall apply the provisions of sub-paragraphs (1) and (2) of paragraph 3 as if the order were an order under paragraph 1(2)(a) or (b).

(6) A magistrates' court shall not entertain an application under sub-paragraph (2) unless both the parties to the agreement are resident in England and Wales and at least one of the parties is resident in the commission area ... for which the court is appointed, and shall not have power to make any order on such an application except–

(a) in a case where the agreement contains no provision for periodical payments by either of the parties, an order inserting provision for the making by one of the parties of periodical payments for the maintenance of the child;

(b) in a case where the agreement includes provision for the making by one of the parties of periodical payments, an order increasing or reducing the rate of, or terminating, any of those payments.

(7) For the avoidance of doubt it is hereby declared that nothing in this paragraph affects any power of a court before which any proceedings between the parties to a maintenance agreement are brought under any other enactment to make an order containing financial arrangements or any right of either party to apply for such an order in such proceedings.

Paragraph 10
This paragraph deals with the alteration of agreements which have been made between parties without the involvement of the courts

11 – (1) Where a maintenance agreement provides for the continuation, after the death of one of the parties, of payments for the maintenance of a child and that party dies domiciled in England and Wales, the surviving party or the personal representatives of the deceased party may apply to the High Court or a county court for an order under paragraph 10.

(2) If a maintenance agreement is altered by a court on an application under this paragraph, the agreement shall have effect thereafter as if the alteration had been made, immediately before the death, by agreement between the parties and for valuable consideration.

(3) An application under this paragraph shall not, except with leave of the High Court or a county court, be made after the end of the period of six months beginning with the day on which representation in regard to the estate of the deceased is first taken out.

(4) In considering for the purposes of sub-paragraph (3) the question when representation was first taken out, a grant limited to settled land or to trust property shall be left out of account and a grant limited to real estate or to personal estate shall be left out of account unless a grant limited to the remainder of the estate has previously been made or is made at the same time.

(5) A county court shall not entertain an application under this paragraph, or an application for leave to make an application under this paragraph, unless it would have jurisdiction to hear and determine proceedings for an order under section 2 of the Inheritance (Provision for Family and Dependants) Act 1975 in relation to the deceased's estate by virtue of section 25 of the County Courts Act 1984 (jurisdiction under the Act of 1975).

(6) The provisions of this paragraph shall not render the personal representatives of the deceased liable for having distributed any part of the estate of the deceased after the expiry of the period of six months referred to in sub-paragraph (3) on the ground that they ought to have taken into account the possibility that a court might grant leave for an application by virtue of this paragraph to be made by the surviving party after that period.

(7) Sub-paragraph (6) shall not prejudice any power to recover any part of the estate so distributed arising by virtue of the making of an order in pursuance of this paragraph.

> **Paragraph 11**
> *This paragraph deals with the continuation, and variation of such an agreement after the death of a party to it, where provision was made in the original agreement for payments to continue after the death of a party. Paragraph 11(3) sets out the time limits for such applications*

Enforcement of orders for maintenance

12 – (1) Any person for the time being under an obligation to make payments in pursuance of any order for the payment of money made by a magistrates' court under this Act shall give notice of any change of address to such person (if any) as may be specified in the order.

(2) Any person failing without reasonable excuse to give such a notice shall be guilty of an offence and liable on summary conviction to a fine not exceeding level 2 on the standard scale.

(3) An order for the payment of money made by a magistrates' court under this Act shall be enforceable as a magistrates' court maintenance order within the meaning of section 150(1) of the Magistrates' Courts Act 1980.

Direction for settlement of instrument by conveyancing counsel

13. Where the High Court or a county court decides to make an order under this Act for the securing of periodical payments or for the transfer or settlement of property, it may direct that the matter be referred to one of the conveyancing counsel of the court to settle a proper instrument to be executed by all necessary parties.

Financial provision for child resident in country outside England and Wales

14 – (1) Where one parent of a child lives in England and Wales and the child lives outside England and Wales with–

(a) another parent of his;
(b) a guardian of his; or
(c) a person in whose favour a residence order is in force with respect to the child,

the court shall have power, on an application made by any of the persons mentioned in paragraphs (a) to (c), to make one or both of the orders mentioned in paragraph 1(2)(a) and (b) against the parent living in England and Wales.

(2) Any reference in this Act to the powers of the court under paragraph 1(2) or to an order made under paragraph 1(2) shall include a reference to the powers which the court has by virtue of sub-paragraph (1) or (as the case may be) to an order made by virtue of sub-paragraph (1).

Paragraph 14
Even if a child lives outside of England and Wales (that being the area to which the Children Act 1989 applies), if a parent lives in England or Wales, the court may make orders for financial provision for the child, against the parent residing within the jurisdiction.

Local authority contribution to child's maintenance

15 – (1) Where a child lives, or is to live, with a person as the result of a residence order, a local authority may make contributions to that person towards the cost of the accommodation and maintenance of the child.

(2) Sub-paragraph (1) does not apply where the person with whom the child lives, or is to live, is a parent of the child or the husband or wife of a parent of the child.

Paragraph 15
This paragraph enables the local authority to assist with the financial maintenance of a child, when the child is living with someone who is not the child's parent or step-parent, for example a grandparent or unrelated adult.

Interpretation

16 – (1) In this Schedule 'child' includes, in any case where an application is made under paragraph 2 or 6 in relation to a person who has reached the age of eighteen, that person.

Paragraph 16
Subparagraph (1) In the Schedule, a reference to a "child" includes a person who has reached the age of 18, if the application is made under paragraph 2 or 6.

---

(2) In this Schedule except paragraphs 2 and 15, 'parent' includes any party to a marriage (whether or not subsisting) in relation to whom the child concerned is a

child of the family; and for this purpose any reference to either parent or both parents shall be construed as references to any parent of his and to all of his parents.

> **Subparagraph (2)** *In all paragraphs, except for paragraphs 2 and 15, a "parent" is not just the biological mother or father of a child, but any person to whom the child is a child of the family.*

(3) In this Schedule, 'maintenance assessment' has the same meaning as it has in the Child Support Act 1991 by virtue of section 54 of that Act as read with any regulations in force under that section.

> **Subparagraph (3)** *The definition of "maintenance assessment" as set out in the Child Support Act 1991 section 54 is as follows: "an assessment of maintenance made under this Act (the Child Support Act) and, except in prescribed circumstances, includes an interim maintenance assessment."*

SCHEDULE 2

> **Part I**
> **Provision of Services for Families**
> *This part deals generally with miscellaneous details surrounding the provision of services by the local authority. Paragraphs of particular note are;*
>
> *1. the requirement made of the local authority to identify those children in need in its area and to provide information about the services it provides,*
>
> *5. the power the local authority has to assist a person living within a child's household to find alternative accommodation, where that person is causing or is likely to cause the child to be ill treated,*
>
> *7. the obligation placed on the local authority to take steps to avoid where possible the need for court proceedings in respect of the children within its area,*
>
> *10. the obligation placed on the local authority to take steps to allow children in need in their area to live with their families or to have contact with their families, if that is in the child's best interests.*

Part II
Children looked after by Local Authorities
This part deals with specific aspects of the obligations and powers of the local authority in respect of children it is looking after. Of particular note:

15. which deals with the local authority's obligation to promote contact between a child it is looking after and the child's family and/or people connected with him or her, when it is consistent with the child's welfare. Note also that the local authority may refuse to inform a person of a child's whereabouts where the child is in the authority's care and the authority has reasonable cause to believe that giving the information would prejudice the child's welfare.

Part III
Contributions towards maintenance of children looked after by Local Authorities
This part deals in greater detail with the powers and procedures that the local authority should exercise to recover contributions from (financially eligible) parents or (when over the age of sixteen) from the child him or herself, towards the maintenance of the child when he or she is being looked after by the local authority.

PART I

PROVISION OF SERVICES FOR FAMILIES

Identification of children in need and provision of information

1 – (1) Every local authority shall take reasonable steps to identify the extent to which there are children in need within their area.

(2) Every local authority shall–

    (a) publish information–
        (i) about services provided by them under sections 17, 18, 20 and 24; and
        (ii) where they consider it appropriate, about the provision by others (including, in particular, voluntary organisations) of services which the local authority have power to provide under those sections; and
    (b) take such steps as are reasonably practicable to ensure that those who might benefit from the services receive the information relevant to them.

Children's services plans

IA – (1) Every local authority shall, on or before 31st March 1997–

    (a) review their provision of services under sections 17, 20, 21, 23 and 24; and
    (b) having regard to that review and to their most recent review under section 19, prepare and publish a plan for the provision of services under Part III.

(2) Every local authority–

(a) shall, from time to time review the plan prepared by them under sub-paragraph (1)(b) (as modified or last substituted under this sub-paragraph), and

(b) may, having regard to that review and to their most recent review under section 19, prepare and publish–

(i) modifications (or, as the case may be, further modifications) to the plan reviewed; or

(ii) a plan in substitution for that plan.

(3) In carrying out any review under this paragraph and in preparing any plan or modifications to a plan, a local authority shall consult–

(a) every health authority the whole or any part of whose area lies within the area of the local authority;

(b) every National Health Service trust which manages a hospital, establishment or facility (within the meaning of the National Health Service and Community Care Act 1990) in the authority's area;

(c) if the local authority is not itself a local education authority, every local education authority the whole or any part of whose area lies within the area of the local authority;

(d) any organisation which represents schools in the authority's area which are grant-maintained schools or grant-maintained special schools (within the meaning of the Education Act 1993);

(e) the governing body of every such school in the authority's area which is not so represented;

(f) such voluntary organisations as appear to the local authority–

(i) to represent the interests of persons who use or are likely to use services provided by the local authority under Part III; or

(ii) to provide services in the area of the local authority which, were they to be provided by the local authority, might be categorised as services provided under that Part;

(g) the chief constable of the police force for the area;

(h) the probation committee for the area;

(i) such other persons as appear to the local authority to be appropriate; and

(j) such other persons as the Secretary of State may direct.

(4) Every local authority shall, within 28 days of receiving a written request from the Secretary of State, submit to him a copy of–

(a) the plan prepared by them under sub-paragraph (1); or

(b) where that plan has been modified or substituted, the plan as modified or last substituted.

Maintenance of a register of disabled children

2 – (1) Every local authority shall open and maintain a register of disabled children within their area.

(2) The register may be kept by means of a computer.

Assessment of children's needs

3. Where it appears to a local authority that a child within their area is in need, the local authority may assess his needs for the purposes of this Act at the same time as any assessment of his needs is made under–

    (a) the Chronically Sick and Disabled Persons Act 1970;
    (b) [Part IV of the Education Act 1996];
    (c) the Disabled Persons (Services, Consultation and Representation) Act 1986; or
    (b) any other enactment.

Prevention of neglect and abuse

4 – (1) Every local authority shall take reasonable steps, through the provision of services under Part III of this Act, to prevent children within their area suffering ill-treatment or neglect.

(2) Where a local authority believe that a child who is at any time within their area–

    (a) is likely to suffer harm; but
    (b) lives or proposes to live in the area of another local authority they shall inform that other local authority.

(3) When informing that other local authority they shall specify–

    (a) the harm that they believe he is likely to suffer; and
    (b) (if they can) where the child lives or proposes to live.

Provision of accommodation in order to protect child

5 – (1) Where–

    (a) it appears to a local authority that a child who is living on particular premises is suffering, or is likely to suffer, ill treatment at the hands of another person who is living on those premises; and
    (b) that other person proposes to move from the premises,

    the local authority may assist that other person to obtain alternative accommodation.

(2) Assistance given under this paragraph may be in cash.

(3) Subsections (7) to (9) of section 17 shall apply in relation to assistance given under this paragraph as they apply in relation to assistance given under that section.

Provision for disabled children

6. Every local authority shall provide services designed–

    (a) to minimise the effect on disabled children within their area of their disabilities; and

(b) to give such children the opportunity to lead lives which are as normal as possible.

7   Provision to reduce need for care proceedings etc

Every local authority shall take reasonable steps designed–

(a) to reduce the need to bring–
    (i) proceedings for care or supervision orders with respect to children within their area;
    (ii) criminal proceedings against such children;
    (iii)   any family or other proceedings with respect to such children which might lead to them being placed in the authority's care; or
    (iv)proceedings under the inherent jurisdiction of the High Court with respect to children;
(b) to encourage children within their area not to commit criminal offences; and
(c) to avoid the need for children within their area to be placed in secure accommodation.

Provision for children living with their families

8.   Every local authority shall make such provision as they consider appropriate for the following services to be available with respect to children in need within their area while they are living with their families–

(a) advice, guidance and counselling;
(b) occupational, social, cultural or recreational activities;
(c) home help (which may include laundry facilities);
(d) facilities for, or assistance with, travelling to and from home for the purpose of taking advantage of any other service provided under this Act or of any similar service;
(d) assistance to enable the child concerned and his family to have a holiday.

Family centres

9 – (1) Every local authority shall provide such family centres as they consider appropriate in relation to children within their area.

(2) 'Family centre' means a centre at which any of the persons mentioned in sub-paragraph (3) may–

(a) attend for occupational, social, cultural or recreational activities;
(b) attend for advice, guidance or counselling; or
(c) be provided with accommodation while he is receiving advice, guidance or counselling.

(3) The persons are–

(a) a child;

(b) his parents;

(c) any person who is not a parent of his but who has parental responsibility for him;

(d) any other person who is looking after him.

Maintenance of the family home

10. Every local authority shall take such steps as are reasonably practicable, where any child within their area who is in need and whom they are not looking after is living apart from his family–

(a) to enable him to live with his family; or

(b) to promote contact between him and his family,

if, in their opinion, it is necessary to do so in order to safeguard or promote his welfare.

Duty to consider racial groups to which children in need belong

11. Every local authority shall, in making any arrangements–

(a) for the provision of day care within their area; or

(b) designed to encourage persons to act as local authority foster parents,

have regard to the different racial groups to which children within their area who are in need belong.

PART II

CHILDREN LOOKED AFTER BY LOCAL AUTHORITIES

Regulations as to placing of children with local authority foster parents

12. Regulations under section 23(2)(a) may, in particular, make provision–

(a) with regard to the welfare of children placed with local authority foster parents;

(b) as to the arrangements to be made by local authorities in connection with the health and education of such children;

(c) as to the records to be kept by local authorities;

(d) for securing that a child is not placed with a local authority foster parent unless that person is for the time being approved as a local authority foster parent by such local authority as may be prescribed;

(e) for securing that where possible the local authority foster parent with whom a child is to be placed is–

(i) of the same religious persuasion as the child; or

(ii) gives an undertaking that the child will be brought up in that religious persuasion;

(f) for securing that children placed with local authority foster parents, and the premises in which they are accommodated, will be supervised and inspected by a local authority and that the children will be removed from those premises if their welfare appears to require it;

(g) as to the circumstances in which local authorities may make arrangements for duties imposed on them by the regulations to be discharged, on their behalf.

Regulations as to arrangements under section 23(2)(f)

13. Regulations under section 23(2)(f) may, in particular, make provision as to–

(a) the persons to be notified of any proposed arrangements;
(b) the opportunities such persons are to have to make representations in relation to the arrangements proposed;
(c) the persons to be notified of any proposed changes in arrangements;
(d) the records to be kept by local authorities;
(e) the supervision by local authorities of any arrangements made.

Regulations as to conditions under which child in care is allowed to live with parent, etc

14. Regulations under section 23(5) may, in particular, impose requirements on a local authority as to–

(a) the making of any decision by a local authority to allow a child to live with any person falling within section 23(4) (including requirements as to those who must be consulted before the decision is made, and those who must be notified when it has been made);
(b) the supervision or medical examination of the child concerned;
(c) the removal of the child, in such circumstances as may be prescribed, from the care of the person with whom he has been allowed to live.
(d) the records to be kept by local authorities.

Promotion and maintenance of contact between child and family

15 – (1) Where a child is being looked after by a local authority, the local authority shall, unless it is not reasonably practicable or consistent with his welfare, endeavour to promote contact between the child and–

(a) his parents;
(b) any person who is not a parent of his but who has parental responsibility for him; and
(c) any relative, friend or other person connected with him.

(2) Where a child is being looked after by a local authority–

(a) the local authority shall take such steps as are reasonably practicable to secure that–
(i) his parents; and

(ii) any person who is not a parent of his but who has parental responsibility for him,

are kept informed of where he is being accommodated; and

(b) every such person shall secure that the local authority are kept informed of his or her address.

(3) Where a local authority ('the receiving authority') take over the provision of accommodation for a child from another local authority ('the transferring authority') under section 20(2)–

(a) the receiving authority shall (where reasonably practicable) inform–
(i) the child's parents; and
(ii) any person who is not a parent of his but who has parental responsibility for him;
(b) sub-paragraph (2)(a) shall apply to the transferring authority, as well as the receiving authority, until at least one such person has been informed of the change; and
(c) sub-paragraph (2)(b) shall not require any person to inform the receiving authority of his address until he has been so informed.

(4) Nothing in this paragraph requires a local authority to inform any person of the whereabouts of a child if–

(a) the child is in the care of the authority; and
(b) the local authority has reasonable cause to believe that informing the person would prejudice the child's welfare.

(2) Any person who fails (without reasonable excuse) to comply with sub-paragraph (2)(b) shall be guilty of an offence and liable on summary conviction to a fine not exceeding level 2 on the standard scale.

(3) It shall be a defence in any proceedings under sub-paragraph (5) to prove that the defendant was residing at the same address as another person who was the child's parent or had parental responsibility for the child and had reasonable cause to believe that the other person had informed the appropriate local authority that both of them were residing at that address.

Visits to or by children: expenses

16 – (1) This paragraph applies where–

(a) a child is being looked after by a local authority; and
(b) the conditions mentioned in sub-paragraph (3) are satisfied.

(2) The local authority may–

(a) make payments to–
(i) a parent of the child;

(ii) any person who is not a parent of his but who has parental responsibility for him; or

(iii) any relative, friend or other person connected with him,

in respect of travelling, subsistence or other expenses incurred by that person in visiting the child; or

(b) make payments to the child, or to any person on his behalf, in respect of travelling, subsistence or other expenses incurred by or on behalf of the child in his visiting–

(i) a parent of his;

(ii) any person who is not a parent of his but who has parental responsibility for him; or

(iii) any relative, friend or other person connected with him.

(3) The conditions are that–

(a) it appears to the local authority that the visit in question could not otherwise be made without undue financial hardship; and

(b) the circumstances warrant the making of the payments.

Appointment of visitor for child who is not being visited

17 – (1) Where it appears to a local authority in relation to any child that they are looking after that–

(a) communication between the child and–

(i) a parent of his, or

(ii) any person who is not a parent of his but who has parental responsibility for him,

has been infrequent; or

(b) he has not visited or been visited by (or lived with) any such person during the preceding twelve months,

and that it would be in the child's best interests for an independent person to be appointed to be his visitor for the purposes of this paragraph, they shall appoint such a visitor.

(2) A person so appointed shall–

(a) have the duty of visiting, advising and befriending the child; and

(b) be entitled to recover from the local authority who appointed him any reasonable expenses incurred by him for the purposes of his functions under this paragraph.

(3) A person's appointment as a visitor in pursuance of this paragraph shall be determined if–

(a) he gives notice in writing to the local authority who appointed him that he resigns the appointment; or

(b) the local authority give him notice in writing that they have terminated it.

(4) The determination of such an appointment shall not prejudice any duty under this paragraph to make a further appointment.

(5) Where a local authority propose to appoint a visitor for a child under this paragraph, the appointment shall not be made if–

(a) the child objects to it; and

(b) the local authority are satisfied that he has sufficient understanding to make an informed decision.

(6) Where a visitor has been appointed for a child under this paragraph, the local authority shall determine the appointment if–

(a) the child objects to its continuing; and

(b) the local authority are satisfied that he has sufficient understanding to make an informed decision.

(2) The Secretary of State may make regulations as to the circumstances in which a person appointed as a visitor under this paragraph is to be regarded as independent of the local authority appointing him.

Power to guarantee apprenticeship deeds etc

18 – (1) While a child is being looked after by a local authority, or is a person qualifying for advice and assistance, the local authority may undertake any obligation by way of guarantee under any deed of apprenticeship or articles of clerkship which he enters into.

(2) Where a local authority have undertaken any such obligation under any deed or articles they may at any time (whether or not they are still looking after the person concerned) undertake the like obligation under any supplemental deed or articles.

Arrangements to assist children to live abroad

19 – (1) A local authority may only arrange for, or assist in arranging for, any child in their care to live outside England and Wales with the approval of the court.

(2) A local authority may, with the approval of every person who has parental responsibility for the child arrange for, or assist in arranging for, any other child looked after by them to live outside England and Wales.

(3) The court shall not give its approval under sub-paragraph (1) unless it is satisfied that–

(a) living outside England and Wales would be in the child's best interests;

(b) suitable arrangements have been, or will be, made for his reception and welfare in the country in which he will live;

(c) the child has consented to living in that country; and

(c) every person who has parental responsibility for the child has consented to his living in that country.

(3) Where the court is satisfied that the child does not have sufficient understanding to give or withhold his consent, it may disregard sub-paragraph (3)(c) and give its approval if the child is to live in the country concerned with a parent, guardian, or other suitable person.

(5) Where a person whose consent is required by sub-paragraph (3)(d) fails to give his consent, the court may disregard that provision and give its approval if it is satisfied that that person–

(a) cannot be found;
(b) is incapable of consenting; or
(d) is withholding his consent unreasonably.

(7) Section 56 of the Adoption Act 1976 (which requires authority for the taking or sending abroad for adoption of a child who is a British subject) shall not apply in the case of any child who is to live outside England and Wales with the approval of the court given under this paragraph.

(8) Where a court decides to give its approval under this paragraph it may order that its decision is not to have effect during the appeal period.

(8) In sub-paragraph (7) 'the appeal period' means–

(a) where an appeal is made against the decision, the period between the making of the decision and the determination of the appeal; and
(b) otherwise, the period during which an appeal may be made against the decision.

Death of children being looked after by local authorities

20 – (1) If a child who is being looked after by a local authority dies, the authority–

(a) shall notify the Secretary of State;
(b) shall, so far as is reasonably practicable, notify the child's parents and every person who is not a parent of his but who has parental responsibility for him;
(c) may, with the consent (so far as it is reasonably practicable to obtain it) of every person who has parental responsibility for the child, arrange for the child's body to be buried or cremated; and
(c) may, if the conditions mentioned in sub-paragraph (2) are satisfied, make payments to any person who has parental responsibility for the child, or any relative, friend or other person connected with the child, in respect of travelling, subsistence or other expenses incurred by that person in attending the child's funeral.

(2) The conditions are that–

(a) it appears to the local authority that the person concerned could not otherwise attend the child's funeral without undue financial hardship; and
(b) that the circumstances warrant the making of the payments.

(4) Sub-paragraph (1) does not authorise cremation where it does not accord with the practice of the child's religious persuasion.

(5) Where a local authority have exercised their power under sub-paragraph (1)(c) with respect to a child who was under sixteen when he died, they may recover from any parent of the child any expenses incurred by them.

(6) Any sums so recoverable shall, without prejudice to any other method of recovery, be recoverable summarily as a civil debt.

(7) Nothing in this paragraph affects any enactment regulating or authorising the burial, cremation or anatomical examination of the body of a deceased person.

PART III

CONTRIBUTIONS TOWARDS MAINTENANCE OF CHILDREN LOOKED AFTER BY LOCAL AUTHORITIES

Liability to contribute

21 – (1) Where a local authority are looking after a child (other than in the cases mentioned in sub-paragraph (7)) they shall consider whether they should recover contributions towards the child's maintenance from any person liable to contribute ('a contributor').

(2) An local authority may only recover contributions from a contributor if they consider it reasonable to do so.

(3) The persons liable to contribute are–

(a) where the child is under sixteen, each of his parents;
(b) where he has reached the age of sixteen, the child himself.

(3) A parent is not liable to contribute during any period when he is in receipt of income support[, family credit or disability working allowance] under [Part VII of the Social Security Contributions and Benefits Act 1992] [or of an income-based jobseeker's allowance].

(4) A person is not liable to contribute towards the maintenance of a child in the care of a local authority in respect of any period during which the child is allowed by the local authority (under section 23(5)) to live with a parent of his.

(5) A contributor is not obliged to make any contribution towards a child's maintenance except as agreed or determined in accordance with this Part of this Schedule.

(7) The cases are where the child is looked after by a local authority under–

(a) section 21;
(b) an interim care order;

The Children Act 1989

(b) section 53 of the Children and Young Persons Act 1933.

Agreed contributions

22 – (1) Contributions towards a child's maintenance may only be recovered if the local authority have served a notice ('a contribution notice') on the contributor specifying–

(a) the weekly sum which they consider that he should contribute; and
(b) arrangements for payment.

(2) The contribution notice must be in writing and dated.

(3) Arrangements for payment shall, in particular, include–

(a) the date on which liability to contribute begins (which must not be earlier than the date of the notice);
(b) the date on which liability under the notice will end (if the child has not before that date ceased to be looked after by the authority); and
(c) the date on which the first payment is to be made.

(3) The local authority may specify in a contribution notice a weekly sum which is a standard contribution determined by them for all children looked after by them.

(5) The local authority may not specify in a contribution notice a weekly sum greater than that which they consider–

(a) they would normally be prepared to pay if they had placed a similar child with local authority foster parents; and
(b) it is reasonably practicable for the contributor to pay (having regard to his means).

(6) An local authority may at any time withdraw a contribution notice (without prejudice to their power to serve another).

(7) Where the local authority and the contributor agree–

(a) the sum which the contributor is to contribute; and
(b) arrangements for payment,

(whether as specified in the contribution notice or otherwise) and the contributor notifies the local authority in writing that he so agrees, the local authority may recover summarily as a civil debt any contribution which is overdue and unpaid.

(3) A contributor may, by serving a notice in writing on the authority, withdraw his agreement in relation to any period of liability falling after the date of service of the notice.

(4) Sub-paragraph (7) is without prejudice to any other method of recovery.

197

Contribution orders

23 – (1) Where a contributor has been served with a contribution notice and has–

    (a) failed to reach any agreement with the local authority as mentioned in paragraph 22(7) within the period of one month beginning with the day on which the contribution notice was served; or

    (b) served a notice under paragraph 22(8) withdrawing his agreement,

the local authority may apply to the court for an order under this paragraph.

(2) On such an application the court may make an order ('a contribution order') requiring the contributor to contribute a weekly sum towards the child's maintenance in accordance with arrangements for payment specified by the court.

(3) A contribution order–

    (a) shall not specify a weekly sum greater than that specified in the contribution notice; and

    (b) shall be made with due regard to the contributor's means.

(4) A contribution order shall not–

    (a) take effect before the date specified in the contribution notice; or

    (b) have effect while the contributor is not liable to contribute (by virtue of paragraph 21); or

    (c) remain in force after the child has ceased to be looked after by the local authority who obtained the order.

(4) An local authority may not apply to the court under sub-paragraph (1) in relation to a contribution notice which they have withdrawn.

(6) Where–

    (a) a contribution order is in force;

    (b) the local authority serve another contribution notice; and

    (c) the contributor and the local authority reach an agreement under paragraph 22(7) in respect of that other contribution notice,

the effect of the agreement shall be to discharge the order from the date on which it is agreed that the agreement shall take effect.

(7) Where an agreement is reached under sub-paragraph (6) the local authority shall notify the court–

    (a) of the agreement; and

    (b) of the date on which it took effect.

(9) A contribution order may be varied or revoked on the application of the contributor or the authority.

(9) In proceedings for the variation of a contribution order, the local authority shall specify–

(a) the weekly sum which, having regard to paragraph 22, they propose that the contributor should contribute under the order as varied; and

(b) the proposed arrangements for payment.

(10) Where a contribution order is varied, the order–

(a) shall not specify a weekly sum greater than that specified by the local authority in the proceedings for variation; and

(b) shall be made with due regard to the contributor's means.

(10) An appeal shall lie in accordance with rules of court from any order made under this paragraph.

Enforcement of contribution orders etc

24 – (1) A contribution order made by a magistrates' court shall be enforceable as a magistrates' court maintenance order (within the meaning of section 150(1) of the Magistrates' Courts Act 1980).

(2) Where a contributor has agreed, or has been ordered, to make contributions to a local authority, any other local authority within whose area the contributor is for the time being living may–

(a) at the request of the local authority who served the contribution notice; and

(b) subject to agreement as to any sum to be deducted in respect of services rendered,

collect from the contributor any contributions due on behalf of the local authority who served the notice.

(3) In sub-paragraph (2) the reference to any other local authority includes a reference to–

(a) a local authority within the meaning of section 1(2) of the Social Work (Scotland) Act 1968; and

(b) a Health and Social Services Board established under Article 16 of the Health and Personal Social Services (Northern Ireland) Order 1972.

(4) The power to collect sums under sub-paragraph (2) includes the power to–

(a) receive and give a discharge for any contributions due; and

(b) (if necessary) enforce payment of any contributions,

even though those contributions may have fallen due at a time when the contributor was living elsewhere.

(5) Any contributions collected under sub-paragraph (2) shall be paid (subject to any agreed deduction) to the local authority who served the contribution notice.

(6) In any proceedings under this paragraph, a document which purports to be–

(a) a copy of an order made by a court under or by virtue of paragraph 23; and

(b) certified as a true copy by the clerk of [-] the court,

shall be evidence of the order.

(7) In any proceedings under this paragraph, a certificate which–

(a) purports to be signed by the clerk or some other duly authorised officer of the local authority who obtained the contribution order; and

(b) states that any sum due to the local authority under the order is overdue and unpaid,

shall be evidence that the sum is overdue and unpaid.

Regulations

25. The Secretary of State may make regulations–

(a) as to the considerations which a local authority must take into account in deciding–
   (i) whether it is reasonable to recover contributions; and
   (ii) what the arrangements for payment should be;
(b) as to the procedures they must follow in reaching agreements with–
   (i) contributors (under paragraph 22 and 23); and
   (ii) any other local authority (under paragraph 23).

SCHEDULE 3

SUPERVISION ORDERS

Part 1

This gives the supervisor (usually a local authority social worker) power to give directions to the supervised child to live at a certain place for a specified period and to engage in specified activities. This may, for example, include attending at a day centre aimed at helping the child with certain problems. It should be noted that there is no power for the court to impose directions on the local authority in this context. The responsible person (usually the child's parent or parents) may, with his consent, be required to take reasonable steps to ensure that the child lives where directed or takes part in the specified activities. There are no methods for enforcing compliance by the responsible person. The sanction is that the local authority can apply to the court if a requirement in the supervision order is breached and may ask the court to replace the supervision order with a care order. Subsections 4 and 5 state that a supervision order may include a requirement that the child submit to psychiatric or medical examination or treatment: before making such requirements the court must be satisfied, on the evidence of a registered medical practitioner that they are appropriate. A court should not include a requirement that a child should submit to examination or treatment unless satisfied both that where the child has sufficient understanding he consents to the requirement, and that satisfactory arrangements have or can be made for the examination or treatment.

Part II

A supervision order lasts for a maximum of 1 year, but can be extended at the end of this period for such period as the court considers appropriate up to a maximum of 3 years from the date of the original order. At the end of this period, if the local authority still consider that a supervision order is required, they have to establish that the threshold criteria are met (see s.31 of the Act). It should be noted that the threshold criteria do not need to be established to obtain an extension of the original supervision order and that the test on such an application is the child's welfare.

A local authority can only be designated as a supervisor if the authority agree, or the child concerned lives in their area. This is a different test to that used to designate a local authority for a care order.

Part III

Unlike supervision orders, education supervision orders can be extended for as long as is required, up to the period when the child ceases to be of compulsory school age. An individual extension can not exceed the period of 3 years.

The making of a care order brings to an end any education supervision order, presumably as under a care order the local authority acquires parental responsibility for the child.

On discharging an education supervision order the court has power to direct the local authority to investigate the child's circumstances. This is a useful power where the court is concerned about a child's welfare and where care proceedings might be warranted.

PART I

GENERAL

Meaning of 'responsible person'

1. In this Schedule, 'the responsible person', in relation to a supervised child, means–

    (a) any person who has parental responsibility for the child; and
    (b) any other person with whom the child is living.

Power of supervisor to give directions to supervised child

2 – (1) A supervision order may require the supervised child to comply with any directions given from time to time by the supervisor which require him to do all or any of the following things–

    (a) to live at a place or places specified in the directions for a period or periods so specified;

    (b) to present himself to a person or persons specified in the directions at a place or places and on a day or days so specified;

    (c) to participate in activities specified in the directions on a day or days so specified.

(2) It shall be for the supervisor to decide whether, and to what extent, he exercises his power to give directions and to decide the form of any directions which he gives.

(3) Sub-paragraph (1) does not confer on a supervisor power to give directions in respect of any medical or psychiatric examination or treatment (which are matters dealt with in paragraphs 4 and 5).

Imposition of obligations on responsible person

3 – (1) With the consent of any responsible person, a supervision order may include a requirement–

    (a) that he take all reasonable steps to ensure that the supervised child complies with any direction given by the supervisor under paragraph 2;

    (b) that he take all reasonable steps to ensure that the supervised child complies with any requirement included in the order under paragraph 4 or 5;

    (d) that he comply with any directions given by the supervisor requiring him to attend at a place specified in the directions for the purpose of taking part in activities so specified.

(2) A direction given under sub-paragraph (1)(c) may specify the time at which the responsible person is to attend and whether or not the supervised child is required to attend with him.

(3) A supervision order may require any person who is a responsible person in relation to the supervised child to keep the supervisor informed of his address, if it differs from the child's.

Psychiatric and medical examinations

4 – (1) A supervision order may require the supervised child–

    (a) to submit to a medical or psychiatric examination; or

    (b) to submit to any such examination from time to time as directed by the supervisor.

(2) Any such examination shall be required to be conducted–

    (a) by, or under the direction of, such registered medical practitioner as may be specified in the order;

    (b) at a place specified in the order and at which the supervised child is to attend as a non resident patient; or

    (c) at–

(i) a health service hospital; or

(ii) in the case of a psychiatric examination, a hospital or mental nursing home,

at which the supervised child is, or is to attend as, a resident patient.

(3) A requirement of a kind mentioned in sub-paragraph (2)(c) shall not be included unless the court is satisfied, on the evidence of a registered medical practitioner, that–

(a) the child may be suffering from a physical or mental condition that requires, and may be susceptible to, treatment; and

(b) a period as a resident patient is necessary if the examination is to be carried out properly.

(4) No court shall include a requirement under this paragraph in a supervision order unless it is satisfied that–

(a) where the child has sufficient understanding to make an informed decision, he consents to its inclusion; and

(b) satisfactory arrangements have been, or can be, made for the examination.

Psychiatric and medical treatment

5 – (1) Where a court which proposes to make or vary a supervision order is satisfied, on the evidence of a registered medical practitioner approved for the purposes of section 12 of the Mental Health Act 1983, that the mental condition of the supervised child–

(a) is such as requires, and may be susceptible to, treatment; but

(b) is not such as to warrant his detention in pursuance of a hospital order under Part III of that Act,

the court may include in the order a requirement that the supervised child shall, for a period specified in the order, submit to such treatment as is so specified.

(2) The treatment specified in accordance with sub-paragraph (1) must be–

(a) by, or under the direction of, such registered medical practitioner as may be specified in the order;

(b) as a non-resident patient at such a place as may be so specified; or

(c) as a resident patient in a hospital or mental nursing home.

(4) Where a court which proposes to make or vary a supervision order is satisfied, on the evidence of a registered medical practitioner, that the physical condition of the supervised child is such as requires, and may be susceptible to, treatment, the court may include in the order a requirement that the supervised child shall, for a period specified in the order, submit to such treatment as is so specified.

(4) The treatment specified in accordance with sub-paragraph (3) must be–

(a) by, or under the direction of, such registered medical practitioner as may be specified in the order;

(b) as a non-resident patient at such place as may be so specified; or

(d) as a resident patient in a health service hospital.

(5) No court shall include a requirement under this paragraph in a supervision order unless it is satisfied–

(a) where the child has sufficient understanding to make an informed decision, that he consents to its inclusion; and

(b) that satisfactory arrangements have been, or can be, made for the treatment.

(6) If a medical practitioner by whom or under whose direction a supervised person is being treated in pursuance of a requirement included in a supervision order by virtue of this paragraph is unwilling to continue to treat or direct the treatment of the supervised child or is of the opinion that–

(a) the treatment should be continued beyond the period specified in the order;

(b) the supervised child needs different treatment;

(c) he is not susceptible to treatment; or

(d) he does not require further treatment,

the practitioner shall make a report in writing to that effect to the supervisor.

(6) On receiving a report under this paragraph the supervisor shall refer it to the court, and on such a reference the court may make an order cancelling or varying the requirement.

PART II

MISCELLANEOUS

Life of supervision order

6 – (1) Subject to sub-paragraph (2) and section 91, a supervision order shall cease to have effect at the end of the period of one year beginning with the date on which it was made.

(2) A supervision order shall also cease to have effect if an event mentioned in section 25(1)(a) or (b) of the Child Abduction and Custody Act 1985 (termination of existing orders) occurs with respect to the child.

(3) Where the supervisor applies to the court to extend, or further extend, a supervision order the court may extend the order for such period as it may specify.

(4) A supervision order may not be extended so as to run beyond the end of the period of three years beginning with the date on which it was made.

Limited life of directions

7   ...

Information to be given to supervisor etc

8 – (1) A supervision order may require the supervised child–

(a) to keep the supervisor informed of any change in his address; and
(b) to allow the supervisor to visit him at the place where he is living.

(2) The responsible person in relation to any child with respect to whom a supervision order is made shall–

(a) if asked by the supervisor, inform him of the child's address (if it is known to him); and
(b) if he is living with the child, allow the supervisor reasonable contact with the child.

Selection of supervisor

9 – (1) A supervision order shall not designate a local authority as the supervisor unless–

(a) the local authority agree; or
(b) the supervised child lives or will live within their area.

(2) A court shall not place a child under the supervision of a probation officer unless–

(a) the appropriate authority so request; and
(b) a probation officer is already exercising or has exercised, in relation to another member of the household to which the child belongs, duties imposed on probation officers [by section 14, or by rules under section 25(2)(c), of the Probation Service Act 1993].

(4) In sub-paragraph (2) 'the appropriate authority' means the local authority appearing to the court to be the authority in whose area the supervised child lives or will live.

(5) Where a supervision order places a person under the supervision of a probation officer, the officer shall be selected in accordance with arrangements made by the probation committee for the area in question.

(6) If the selected probation officer is unable to carry out his duties, or dies, another probation officer shall be selected in the same manner.

Effect of supervision order on earlier orders

10. he making of a supervision order with respect to any child brings to an end any earlier care or supervision order which–

(a) was made with respect to that child; and
(b) would otherwise continue in force.

Local authority functions and expenditure

11 – (1) The Secretary of State may make regulations with respect to the exercise by a local authority of their functions where a child has been placed under their supervision by a supervision order.

(2) Where a supervision order requires compliance with directions given by virtue of this section, any expenditure incurred by the supervisor for the purposes of the directions shall be defrayed by the local authority designated in the order.

PART III

EDUCATION SUPERVISION ORDERS

Effect of orders

12 – (1) Where an education supervision order is in force with respect to a child, it shall be the duty of the supervisor–

  (a) to advise, assist and befriend, and give directions to–
    (i) the supervised child; and
    (ii) his parents;
        in such a way as will, in the opinion of the supervisor, secure that he is properly educated;
  (b) where any such directions given to–
    (i) the supervised child; or
    (ii) a parent of his,
        have not been complied with, to consider what further steps to take in the exercise of the supervisor's powers under this Act.

(2) Before giving any directions under sub-paragraph (1) the supervisor shall, so far as is reasonably practicable, ascertain the wishes and feelings of–

  (a) the child; and
  (b) his parents;

including, in particular, their wishes as to the place at which the child should be educated.

(3) When settling the terms of any such directions, the supervisor shall give due consideration–

  (a) having regard to the child's age and understanding, to such wishes and feelings of his as the supervisor has been able to ascertain; and
  (b) to such wishes and feelings of the child's parents as he has been able to ascertain.

(4) Directions may be given under this paragraph at any time while the education supervision order is in force.

13 – (1) Where an education supervision order is in force with respect to a child, the duties of the child's parents under [sections 7 and 444 of the Education Act 1996 (duties to secure education of children and] to secure regular attendance of registered pupils) shall be superseded by their duty to comply with any directions in force under the education supervision order.

(2) Where an education supervision order is made with respect to a child–

  (a) any school attendance order–
    (i) made under [section 437 of the Education Act 1996] with respect to the child; and
    (ii) in force immediately before the making of the education supervision order, shall cease to have effect; and
  (b) while the education supervision order remains in force, the following provisions shall not apply with respect to the child–
    (i) [section 437] of that Act (school attendance orders);
    (ii) [section 9 of that Act] (pupils to be educated in accordance with wishes of their parents)';
    (iii) [sections 411 and 423 of that Act] (parental preference and appeals against admission decisions);
  (c) a supervision order made with respect to the child in criminal proceedings, while the education supervision order is in force, may not include an education requirement of the kind which could otherwise be included under section 12C of the Children and Young Persons Act 1969;
  (c) any education requirement of a kind mentioned in paragraph (c), which was in force with respect to the child immediately before the making of the education supervision order, shall cease to have effect.

Effect where child also subject to supervision order

14 – (1) This paragraph applies where an education supervision order and a supervision order, or order under section 7(7)(b) of the Children and Young Persons Act 1969, are in force at the same time with respect to the same child.

(2) Any failure to comply with a direction given by the supervisor under the education supervision order shall be disregarded if it would not have been reasonably practicable to comply with it without failing to comply with a direction given under the other order.

Duration of orders

15 – (1) An education supervision order shall have effect for a period of one year, beginning with the date on which it is made.

(2) An education supervision order shall not expire if, before it would otherwise have expired, the court has (on the application of the local authority in whose favour the order was made) extended the period during which it is in force.

(3) Such an application may not be made earlier than three months before the date on which the order would otherwise expire.

(4) The period during which an education supervision order is in force may be extended under sub-paragraph (2) on more than one occasion.

(5) No one extension may be for a period of more than three years.

(6) An education supervision order shall cease to have effect on–

(a) the child's ceasing to be of compulsory school age; or
(b) the making of a care order with respect to the child;

and sub-paragraphs (1) to (4) are subject to this sub-paragraph.

Information to be given to supervisor etc

16 – (1) An education supervision order may require the child–

(a) to keep the supervisor informed of any change in his address; and
(b) to allow the supervisor to visit him at the place where he is living.

(2) A person who is the parent of a child with respect to whom an education supervision order has been made shall–

(a) if asked by the supervisor, inform him of the child's address (if it is known to him); and
(b) if he is living with the child, allow the supervisor reasonable contact with the child.

Discharge of orders

17 – (1) The court may discharge any education supervision order on the application of–

(a) the child concerned;
(b) a parent of his; or
(c) the local education authority concerned.

(2) On discharging an education supervision order, the court may direct the local authority within whose area the child lives, or will live, to investigate the circumstances of the child.

Offences

18 – (1) If a parent of a child with respect to whom an education supervision order is in force persistently fails to comply with a direction given under the order he shall be guilty of an offence.

(2) It shall be a defence for any person charged with such an offence to prove that–

(a) he took all reasonable steps to ensure that the direction was complied with;
(b) the direction was unreasonable; or

(c) he had complied with–

    (i) a requirement included in a supervision order made with respect to the child; or

    (ii) directions given under such a requirement,

and that it was not reasonably practicable to comply both with the direction and with the requirement or directions mentioned in this paragraph.

(3) A person guilty of an offence under this paragraph shall be liable on summary conviction to a fine not exceeding level 3 on the standard scale.

Persistent failure of child to comply with directions

19 – (1) Where a child with respect to whom an education supervision order is in force persistently fails to comply with any direction given under the order, the local education authority concerned shall notify the appropriate local authority.

(2) Where a local authority have been notified under sub-paragraph (1) they shall investigate the circumstances of the child.

(3) In this paragraph 'the appropriate local authority' has the same meaning as in section 36.

Miscellaneous

20. The Secretary of State may by regulations make provision modifying, or displacing, the provisions of any enactment about education in relation to any child with respect to whom an education supervision order is in force to such extent as appears to the Secretary of State to be necessary or expedient in consequence of the provision made by this Act with respect to such orders.

Interpretation

21. In this part of this Schedule 'parent' has the same meaning as in [the Education Act 1996].

SCHEDULE 4

MANAGEMENT AND CONDUCT OF COMMUNITY HOMES

Section 53(6)
Management and Conduct of Community Homes
This schedule deals in greater detail with the management of community homes, making clearer the differing roles of the voluntary organisation and the local authority in the conduct of controlled and assisted community homes.

PART I

INSTRUMENTS OF MANAGEMENT

Instruments of management for controlled and assisted community homes

1 – (1) The Secretary of State may by order make an instrument of management providing for the constitution of a body of managers for any ... home which is designated as a controlled or assisted community home.

(2) Sub-paragraph (3) applies where two or more ... homes are designated as controlled community homes or as assisted community homes.

(3) If–

    (a) those homes are, or are to be, provided by the same voluntary organisation; and

    (b) the same local authority is to be represented on the body of managers for those homes,

a single instrument of management may be made by the Secretary of State under this paragraph constituting one body of managers for those homes or for any two or more of them.

(3) The number of persons who, in accordance with an instrument of management, constitute the body of managers for a ... home shall be such number (which must be a multiple of three) as may be specified in the instrument.

(5) The instrument shall provide that the local authority specified in the instrument shall appoint–

    (a) in the case of a ... home which is designated as a controlled community home, two-thirds of the managers; and

    (b) in the case of a ... home which is designated as an assisted community home, one-third of them.

(6) An instrument of management shall provide that the foundation managers shall be appointed, in such manner and by such persons as may be specified in the instrument–

    (a) so as to represent the interests of the voluntary organisation by which the home is, or is to be, provided; and

    (b) for the purpose of securing that–

        (i) so far as is practicable, the character of the home ... will be preserved; and

        (ii) subject to paragraph 2(3), the terms of any trust deed relating to the home are observed.

(6) An instrument of management shall come into force on such date as it may specify.

(7) If an instrument of management is in force in relation to a ... home the home shall be (and be known as) a controlled community home or an assisted community home, according to its designation.

(9) In this paragraph–

'foundation managers', in relation to a ... home, means those of the managers of the home who are not appointed by a local authority in accordance with sub-paragraph (5); and

'designated' means designated in accordance with section 53.

2 – (1) An instrument of management shall contain such provisions as the Secretary of State considers appropriate.

(2) Nothing in the instrument of management shall affect the purposes for which the premises comprising the home are held.

(3) Without prejudice to the generality of sub-paragraph (1), an instrument of management may contain provisions–

  (a) specifying the nature and purpose of the home (or each of the homes) to which it relates;

  (b) requiring a specified number or proportion of the places in that home (or those homes) to be made available to local authorities and to any other body specified in the instrument; and

  (c) relating to the management of that home (or those homes) and the charging of fees with respect to–

    (i) children placed there; or

    (ii) places made available to any local authority or other body.

(3) Subject to sub-paragraphs (1) and (2), in the event of any inconsistency between the provisions of any trust deed and an instrument of management, the instrument of management shall prevail over the provisions of the trust deed in so far as they relate to the home concerned.

(4) After consultation with the voluntary organisation concerned and with the local authority specified in its instrument of management, the Secretary of State may by order vary or revoke any provisions of the instrument.

PART II

MANAGEMENT OF CONTROLLED AND ASSISTED COMMUNITY HOMES

3 – (1) The management, equipment and maintenance of a controlled community home shall be the responsibility of the local authority specified in its instrument of management.

(2) The management, equipment and maintenance of an assisted community home shall be the responsibility of the voluntary organisation by which the home is provided.

(3) In this paragraph–

'home' means a controlled community home or (as the case may be) assisted community home; and 'the managers', in relation to a home, means the managers constituted by its instrument of management; and

'the responsible body', in relation to a home, means the local authority or (as the case may be) voluntary organisation responsible for its management, equipment and maintenance.

(3) The functions of a home's responsible body shall be exercised through the managers[, except in so far as, under section 53(3B), any of the accommodation is to be managed by another person].

(4) Anything done, liability incurred or property acquired by a home's managers shall be done, incurred or acquired by them as agents of the responsible body[; and similarly, to the extent that a contract so provides, as respects anything done, liability incurred or property acquired by a person by whom, under section 53(3B), any of the accommodation is to be managed].

(6) In so far as any matter is reserved for the decision of a home's responsible body by–

    (a) sub-paragraph (8);
    (b) the instrument of management;
    (c) the service by the body on the managers, or any of them, of a notice reserving any matter, that matter shall be dealt with by the body and not by the managers.

(8) In dealing with any matter so reserved, the responsible body shall have regard to any representations made to the body by the managers.

(9) The employment of persons at a home shall be a matter reserved for the decision of the responsible body.

(10) Where the instrument of management of a controlled community home so provides, the responsible body may enter into arrangements with the voluntary organisation by which that home is provided whereby, in accordance with such terms as may be agreed between them and the voluntary organisation, persons who are not in the employment of the responsible body shall undertake duties at that home.

(10) Subject to sub-paragraph (11)–

    (a) where the responsible body for an assisted community home proposes to engage any person to work at that home or to terminate without notice the employment of any person at that home, it shall consult the local authority specified in the instrument of management and, if that authority so direct, the responsible body shall not carry out its proposal without their consent; and
    (b) that local authority may, after consultation with the responsible body, require that body to terminate the employment of any person at that home.

(11) Paragraphs (a) and (b) of sub-paragraph (10) shall not apply–

    (a) in such cases or circumstances as may be specified by notice in writing given by the local authority to the responsible body; and

(b) in relation to the employment of any persons or class of persons specified in the home's instrument of management.

(11) The accounting year of the managers of a home shall be such as may be specified by the responsible body.

(12) Before such date in each accounting year as may be so specified, the managers of a home shall submit to the responsible body estimates, in such form as the body may require, of expenditure and receipts in respect of the next accounting year.

(14) Any expenses incurred by the managers of a home with the approval of the responsible body shall be defrayed by that body.

(15) The managers of a home shall keep–

(a) proper accounts with respect to the home; and
(b) proper records in relation to the accounts.

(16) Where an instrument of management relates to more than one home, one set of accounts and records may be kept in respect of all the homes to which it relates.

PART III

REGULATIONS

4 – (1) The Secretary of State may make regulations–

(a) as to the placing of children in community homes;
(b) as to the conduct of such homes; and
(c) for securing the welfare of children in such homes.

(2) The regulations may, in particular–

(a) prescribe standards to which the premises used for such homes are to conform;
(b) impose requirements as to the accommodation, staff and equipment to be provided in such homes, and as to the arrangements to be made for protecting the health of children in such homes;
(c) provide for the control and discipline of children in such homes;
(d) impose requirements as to the keeping of records and giving of notices in respect of children in such homes;
(e) impose requirements as to the facilities which are to be provided for giving religious instruction to children in such homes;
(f) authorise the Secretary of State to give and revoke directions requiring–
   (i) the local authority by whom a home is provided or who are specified in the instrument of management for a controlled community home, or
   (ii) the voluntary organisation by which an assisted community home is provided,
to accommodate in the home a child looked after by a local authority for whom no places are made available in that home or to take such action in relation to a child accommodated in the home as may be specified in the directions;

213

(g) provide for consultation with the Secretary of State as to applicants for appointment to the charge of a home;

(h) empower the Secretary of State to prohibit the appointment of any particular applicant in the cases (if any) in which the regulations dispense with such consultation by reason that the person to be appointed possesses such qualifications as may be prescribed;

(i) require the approval of the Secretary of State for the provision and use of accommodation for the purpose of restricting the liberty of children in such homes and impose other requirements (in addition to those imposed by section 25) as to the placing of a child in accommodation provided for that purpose, including a requirement to obtain the permission of any local authority who are looking after the child;

(j) provide that, to such extent as may be provided for in the regulations, the Secretary of State may direct that any provision of regulations under this paragraph which is specified in the direction and makes any such provision as is referred to in paragraph (a) or (b) shall not apply in relation to a particular home or the premises used for it, and may provide for the variation or revocation of any such direction by the Secretary of State.

(3) Without prejudice to the power to make regulations under this paragraph conferring functions on–

(a) the local authority or voluntary organisation by which a community home is provided; or

(b) the managers of a controlled or assisted community home,

regulations under this paragraph may confer functions in relation to a controlled or assisted community home on the local authority named in the instrument of management for the home.

SCHEDULE 5

Section 60(4)
Voluntary Homes and Voluntary Organisations
This schedule deals mainly with the procedure surrounding registration of voluntary homes and the obligation on the person in charge of a voluntary home to send particulars of the home each year to the Secretary of State. Once registered, the Secretary of State can at any time cancel the registration where the conduct of the home is unsatisfactory (paragraph 1(4)). For the procedures by which a person in charge of a voluntary home may question the Secretary of State's decision to cancel registration, see paragraphs 3 and 5.

VOLUNTARY HOMES AND VOLUNTARY ORGANISATIONS

PART I

REGISTRATION OF VOLUNTARY HOMES

GENERAL

1 – (1) An application for registration under this paragraph shall–

    (a) be made by the persons intending to carry on the home to which the application relates; and

    (b) be made in such manner, and be accompanied by such particulars, as the Secretary of State may prescribe.

(2) On an application duly made under sub-paragraph (1) the Secretary of State may–

    (a) grant or refuse the application, as he thinks fit; or

    (b) grant the application subject to such conditions as he considers appropriate.

(3) The Secretary of State may from time to time–

    (a) vary any condition for the time being in force with respect to a voluntary home by virtue of this paragraph; or

    (b) impose an additional condition,

either on the application of the person carrying on the home or without such an application.

(4) Where at any time it appears to the Secretary of State that the conduct of any voluntary home–

    (a) is not in accordance with regulations made under paragraph 7; or

    (b) is otherwise unsatisfactory,

he may cancel the registration of the home and remove it from the register.

(5) Any person who, without reasonable excuse, carries on a voluntary home in contravention of–

    (a) section 60; or

    (b) a condition to which the registration of the home is for the time being subject by virtue of this Part,

shall be guilty of an offence.

(6) Any person guilty of such an offence shall be liable on summary conviction to a fine not exceeding–

    (a) level 5 on the standard scale, if his offence is under sub-paragraph (5)(a); or

    (b) level 4, if it is under sub-paragraph (5)(b).

(7) Where the Secretary of State registers a home under this paragraph, or cancels the registration of a home, he shall notify the local authority within whose area the home is situated.

Procedure

2 – (1) Where–

(a) a person applies for registration of a voluntary home; and
(b) the Secretary of State proposes to grant his application,

the Secretary of State shall give him written notice of his proposal and of the conditions subject to which he proposes to grant the application.

(2) The Secretary of State need not give notice if he proposes to grant the application subject only to conditions which–

(a) the applicant specified in the application; or
(b) the Secretary of State and the applicant have subsequently agreed.

(4) Where the Secretary of State proposes to refuse such an application he shall give notice of his proposal to the applicant.

(4) The Secretary of State shall give any person carrying on a voluntary home notice of a proposal to–

(a) cancel the registration of the home;
(b) vary any condition for the time being in force with respect to the home by virtue of paragraph 1; or
(c) impose any additional condition.

(3) A notice under this paragraph shall give the Secretary of State's reasons for his proposal.

Right to make representations

3 – (1) A notice under paragraph 2 shall state that within 14 days of service of the notice any person on whom it is served may (in writing) require the Secretary of State to give him an opportunity to make representations to the Secretary of State concerning the matter.

(2) Where a notice has been served under paragraph 2, the Secretary of State shall not determine the matter until either–

(a) any person on whom the notice was served has made representations to him concerning the matter; or
(b) the period during which any such person could have required the Secretary of State to give him an opportunity to make representations has elapsed without the Secretary of State being required to give such an opportunity; or
(c) the conditions specified in sub-paragraph (3) are satisfied.

(3) The conditions are that–

(a) a person on whom the notice was served has required the Secretary of State to give him an opportunity to make representations to the Secretary of State;
(b) the Secretary of State has allowed him a reasonable period to make his

representations; and

(d) he has failed to make them within that period.

(5) The representations may be made, at the option of the person making them, either in writing or orally.

(6) If he informs the Secretary of State that he desires to make oral representations, the Secretary of State shall give him an opportunity of appearing before, and of being heard by, a person appointed by the Secretary of State.

Decision of Secretary of State

4 – (1) If the Secretary of State decides to adopt the proposal, he shall serve notice in writing of his decision on any person on whom he was required to serve notice of his proposal.

(2) A notice under this paragraph shall be accompanied by a notice explaining the right of appeal conferred by paragraph 5.

(3) A decision of the Secretary of State, other than a decision to grant an application for registration subject only to such conditions as are mentioned in paragraph 2(2) or to refuse an application for registration, shall not take effect–

(a) if no appeal is brought, until the end of the period of 28 days referred to in paragraph 5(3); and

(b) if an appeal is brought, until it is determined or abandoned.

Appeals

5 – (1) An appeal against a decision of the Secretary of State under Part VII shall lie to a Registered Homes Tribunal.

(2) An appeal shall be brought by notice in writing given to the Secretary of State.

(3) No appeal may be brought by a person more than 28 days after service on him of notice of the decision.

(4) On an appeal, the Tribunal may confirm the Secretary of State's decision or direct that it shall not have effect.

(5) A Tribunal shall also have power on an appeal to–

(a) vary any condition for the time being in force by virtue of Part VII with respect to the home to which the appeal relates;

(b) direct that any such condition shall cease to have effect; or

(c) direct that any such condition as it thinks fit shall have effect with respect to the home.

Notification of particulars with respect to voluntary homes

6 – (1) It shall be the duty of the person in charge of any voluntary home established after the commencement of this Act to send to the Secretary of State within three

months from the establishment of the home such particulars with respect to the home as the Secretary of State may prescribe.

(2) It shall be the duty of the person in charge of any voluntary home (whether established before or after the commencement of this Act) to send to the Secretary of State such particulars with respect to the home as may be prescribed.

(3) The particulars must be sent–

    (a) in the case of a home established before the commencement of this Act, in every year, or

    (b) in the case of a home established after the commencement of this Act, in every year subsequent to the year in which particulars are sent under sub-paragraph (1),

by such date as the Secretary of State may prescribe.

(4) Where the Secretary of State by regulations varies the particulars which are to be sent to him under sub-paragraph (1) or (2) by the person in charge of a voluntary home–

    (a) that person shall send to the Secretary of State the prescribed particulars within three months from the date of the making of the regulations;

    (b) where any such home was established before, but not more than three months before, the making of the regulations, compliance with paragraph (a) shall be sufficient compliance with the requirement of sub-paragraph (1) to send the prescribed particulars within three months from the establishment of the home;

    (d) in the year in which the particulars are varied, compliance with paragraph (a) by the person in charge of any voluntary home shall be sufficient compliance with the requirement of sub-paragraph (2) to send the prescribed particulars before the prescribed date in that year.

(2) If the person in charge of a voluntary home fails, without reasonable excuse, to comply with any of the requirements of this paragraph he shall be guilty of an offence.

(3) Any person guilty of such an offence shall be liable on summary conviction to a fine not exceeding level 2 on the standard scale.

PART II

REGULATIONS AS TO VOLUNTARY HOMES

Regulations as to conduct of voluntary homes

7 – (1) The Secretary of State may make regulations–

    (a) as to the placing of children in voluntary homes;

    (b) as to the conduct of such homes; and

    (c) for securing the welfare of children in such homes.

(2) The regulations may, in particular–

    (a) prescribe standards to which the premises used for such homes are to conform;

    (b) impose requirements as to the accommodation, staff and equipment to be provided in such homes, and as to the arrangements to be made for protecting the health of children in such homes;

    (c) provide for the control and discipline of children in such homes;

    (d) require the furnishing to the Secretary of State of information as to the facilities provided for–

        (i) the parents of children in the homes; and

        (ii) persons who are not parents of such children but who have parental responsibility for them; and

        (iii) other persons connected with such children,

          to visit and communicate with the children;

    (e) authorise the Secretary of State to limit the number of children who may be accommodated in any particular voluntary home;

    (f) ...

    [(ff) require the approval of the Secretary of State for the provision and use of accommodation for the purpose of restricting the liberty of children in such homes and impose other requirements (in addition to those imposed by section 25 as to the placing of a child in accommodation provided for that purpose, including a requirement to obtain the permission of any local authority who are looking after the child;]

    (g) impose requirements as to the keeping of records and giving of notices with respect to children in such homes;

    (h) impose requirements as to the facilities which are to be provided for giving religious instruction to children in such homes;

    (g) require notice to be given to the Secretary of State of any change of the person carrying on or in charge of a voluntary home or of the premises used by such a home.

(2) The regulations may provide that a contravention of, or failure to comply with, any specified provision of the regulations without reasonable excuse shall be an offence against the regulations.

(3) Any person guilty of such an offence shall be liable to a fine not exceeding level 4 on the standard scale.

Disqualification

8. The Secretary of State may by regulation make provision with respect to the disqualification of persons in relation to voluntary homes of a kind similar to that made in relation to children's homes by section 65.

SCHEDULE 6

REGISTERED CHILDREN'S HOMES

Section 63(11)
Registered Children's Homes
This schedule deals with the procedures surrounding registration of children's homes. Note that the application in this case is made to the local authority in which the home is situated, and not the Secretary of State, as with voluntary homes. Note also that the local authority has a duty to review registration and inspect the children's homes within its area on an annual basis, and has power to cancel a registration if it considers it necessary. There is also a prohibition (paragraph 9) on further application for registration of home for six months after an application has been refused or a registration of the home has been cancelled.

PART I

REGISTRATION

Application for registration

1 – (1) An application for the registration of a children's home shall be made–

(a) by the person carrying on, or intending to carry on, the home; and
(b) to the local authority for the area in which the home is, or is to be, situated.

(2) The application shall be made in the prescribed manner and shall be accompanied by–

(a) such particulars as may be prescribed; and
(b) such reasonable fee as the local authority may determine.

(2) In this Schedule 'prescribed' means prescribed by regulations made by the Secretary of State.

(4) If a local authority are satisfied that a children's home with respect to which an application has been made in accordance with this Schedule complies or (as the case may be) will comply–

(a) with such requirements as may be prescribed, and
(b) with such other requirements (if any) as appear to them to be appropriate,

they shall grant the application, either unconditionally or subject to conditions imposed under paragraph 2.

(4) Before deciding whether or not to grant an application a local authority shall comply with any prescribed requirements.

(5) Regulations made for the purposes of sub-paragraph (5) may, in particular, make provision as to the inspection of the home in question.

(6) Where an application is granted, the local authority shall notify the applicant that the home has been registered under this Act as from such date as may be specified in the notice.

(7) If the local authority are not satisfied as mentioned in sub-paragraph (4), they shall refuse the application.

(8) For the purposes of this Act, an application which has not been granted or refused within the period of twelve months beginning with the date when it is served on the local authority shall be deemed to have been refused by them, and the applicant shall be deemed to have been notified of their refusal at the end of that period.

(9) Where a school to which section 63(1) applies is registered it shall not cease to be a registered children's home by reason only of a subsequent change in the number of children for whom it provides accommodation.

Conditions imposed on registration

2 – (1) A local authority may grant an application for registration subject to such conditions relating to the conduct of the home as they think fit.

(2) A local authority may from time to time–

   (a) vary any condition for the time being in force with respect to a home by virtue of this paragraph; or
   (b) impose an additional condition,

either on the application of the person carrying on the home or without such an application.

(4) If any condition imposed or varied under this paragraph is not complied with, the person carrying on the home shall, if he has no reasonable excuse, be guilty of an offence and liable on summary conviction to a fine not exceeding level 4 on the standard scale.

Annual review of registration

3 – (1) In this [Schedule] 'the responsible authority', in relation to a registered children's home means the local authority who registered it.

(2) The responsible authority for a registered children's home shall, at the end of the period of twelve months beginning with the date of registration, and annually thereafter, review its registration for the purpose of determining whether the registration should continue in force or be cancelled under paragraph 4(3).

(3) If on any such annual review the responsible authority are satisfied that the home is being carried on in accordance with the relevant requirements they shall

determine that, subject to sub-paragraph (4), the registration should continue in force.

(4) The responsible authority shall give to the person carrying on the home notice of their determination under sub-paragraph (3) and the notice shall require him to pay to the local authority with respect to the review such reasonable fee as the local authority may determine.

(5) It shall be a condition of the home's continued registration that the fee is so paid before the expiry of the period of twenty-eight days beginning with the date on which the notice is received by the person carrying on the home.

(6) In this Schedule 'the relevant requirements' means any requirements of Part VIII and of any regulations made under paragraph 10, and any conditions imposed under paragraph 2.

Cancellation of registration

4 – (1) The person carrying on a registered children's home may at any time make an application, in such manner and including such particulars as may be prescribed, for the cancellation by the responsible authority of the registration of the home.

(2) If the local authority are satisfied, in the case of a school registered by virtue of section 63(6), that it is no longer a school to which that provision applies, the local authority shall give to the person carrying on the home notice that the registration of the home has been cancelled as from the date of the notice.

(3) If on any annual review under paragraph 3, or at any other time, it appears to the responsible authority that a registered home is being carried on otherwise than in accordance with the relevant requirements, they may determine that the registration of the home should be cancelled.

(4) The responsible authority may at any time determine that the registration of a home should be cancelled on the ground–

(a) that the person carrying on the home has been convicted of an offence under this Part or any regulations made under paragraph 10; or
(b) that any other person has been convicted of such an offence in relation to the home.

Procedure

5 – (1) Where–

(a) a person applies for the registration of a children's home; and
(b) the local authority propose to grant his application,

they shall give him written notice of their proposal and of the conditions (if any) subject to which they propose to grant his application.

(2) The local authority need not give notice if they propose to grant the application

subject only to conditions which–

(a) the applicant specified in the application; or

(b) the local authority and the applicant have subsequently agreed.

(4) The local authority shall give an applicant notice of a proposal to refuse his application.

(4) The local authority shall give any person carrying on a registered children's home notice of a proposal–

(a) to cancel the registration;

(b) to vary any condition for the time being in force with respect to the home by virtue of Part VIII; or

(c) to impose any additional condition.

(5) A notice under this paragraph shall give the local authority's reasons for their proposal.

Right to make representations

6 – (1) A notice under paragraph 5 shall state that within 14 days of service of the notice any person on whom it is served may in writing require the local authority to give him an opportunity to make representations to them concerning the matter.

(2) Where a notice has been served under paragraph 5, the local authority shall not determine the matter until–

(a) any person on whom the notice was served has made representations to them concerning the matter;

(b) the period during which any such person could have required the local authority to give him an opportunity to make representations has elapsed without their being required to give such an opportunity; or

(c) the conditions specified in sub-paragraph (3) below are satisfied.

(3) The conditions are–

(a) that a person on whom the notice was served has required the local authority to give him an opportunity to make representations to them concerning the matter;

(b) that the local authority have allowed him a reasonable period to make his representations; and

(c) that he has failed to make them within that period.

(2) The representations may be made, at the option of the person making them, either in writing or orally.

(6) If he informs the local authority that he desires to make oral representations, the local authority shall give him an opportunity of appearing before and of being heard by a committee or sub-committee of theirs.

Decision of local authority

7 – (1) If the local authority decide to adopt a proposal of theirs to grant an application, they shall serve notice in writing of their decision on any person on whom they were required to serve notice of their proposal.

(2) A notice under this paragraph shall be accompanied by an explanation of the right of appeal conferred by paragraph 8.

(3) A decision of a local authority, other than a decision to grant an application for registration subject only to such conditions as are mentioned in paragraph 5(2) or to refuse an application for registration, shall not take effect–

(a) if no appeal is brought, until the end of the period of 28 days referred to in paragraph 8(3); and
(b) if an appeal is brought, until it is determined or abandoned.

Appeals

8 – (1) An appeal against a decision of a local authority under Part VIII shall lie to a Registered Homes Tribunal.

(2) An appeal shall be brought by notice in writing given to the local authority.

(3) No appeal shall be brought by a person more than 28 days after service on him of notice of the decision.

(4) On an appeal the Tribunal may confirm the local authority's decision or direct that it shall not have effect.

(5) A Tribunal shall also have power on an appeal–

(a) to vary any condition in force with respect to the home to which the appeal relates by virtue of paragraph 2;
(b) to direct that any such condition shall cease to have effect; or
(c) to direct that any such condition as it thinks fit shall have effect with respect to the home.

(2) A local authority shall comply with any direction given by a Tribunal under this paragraph.

Prohibition on further applications

9 – (1) Where an application for the registration of a home is refused, no further application may be made within the period of six months beginning with the date when the applicant is notified of the refusal.

(2) Sub-paragraph (1) shall have effect, where an appeal against the refusal of an application is determined or abandoned, as if the reference to the date when the applicant is notified of the refusal were a reference to the date on which the appeal is determined or abandoned.

(3) Where the registration of a home is cancelled, no application for the registration of the home shall be made within the period of six months beginning with the date of cancellation.

(4) Sub-paragraph (3) shall have effect, where an appeal against the cancellation of the registration of a home is determined or abandoned, as if the reference to the date of cancellation were a reference to the date on which the appeal is determined or abandoned.

PART II

REGULATIONS

10 – (1) The Secretary of State may make regulations–

(a) as to the placing of children in registered children's homes;
(b) as to the conduct of such homes; and
(d) for securing the welfare of the children in such homes.

(2) The regulations may in particular–

(a) prescribe standards to which the premises used for such homes are to conform;
(b) impose requirements as to the accommodation, staff and equipment to be provided in such homes;
(c) impose requirements as to the arrangements to be made for protecting the health of children in such homes;
(d) provide for the control and discipline of children in such homes;
(e) require the furnishing to the responsible authority of information as to the facilities provided for–
  (i) the parents of children in such homes;
  (ii) persons who are not parents of such children but who have parental responsibility for them; and
  (iii) other persons connected with such children,
    to visit and communicate with the children.
(f) impose requirements as to the keeping of records and giving of notices with respect to children in such homes;
(g) impose requirements as to the facilities which are to be provided for giving religious instruction to children in such homes;
(h) make provision as to the carrying out of annual reviews under paragraph 3;
(i) authorise the responsible authority to limit the number of children who may be accommodated in any particular registered home;
(j) ...
[(jj) require the approval of the Secretary of State for the provision and use of accommodation for the purpose of restricting the liberty of children in such homes and impose other requirements (in addition to those imposed by section 25) as to the placing of a child in accommodation provided for that purpose, including a requirement to obtain the permission of any local authority who are looking after the child;]

(k) require notice to be given to the responsible authority of any change of the person carrying on or in charge of a registered home or of the premises used by such a home;

(j) make provision similar to that made by regulations under section 26.

(2) The regulations may provide that a contravention of or failure to comply with any specified provision of the regulations, without reasonable excuse, shall be an offence against the regulations.

(3) Any person guilty of such an offence shall be liable on summary conviction to a fine not exceeding level 4 on the standard scale.

SCHEDULE 7

FOSTER PARENTS: LIMITS ON NUMBER OF FOSTER CHILDREN

Schedule 7
Foster Parents: Limits on number of foster children
The usual limit is three children but in appropriate circumstances the limit may be exceeded. The exemption in the case of children who are siblings recognises the general view that, for their emotional well-being, siblings should be kept together. The effect of exceeding the limit, or going beyond the terms on which an exemption is granted, is that the fosterer will be treated as though he or she is carrying on a children's home which has the consequence that the foster parent will be committing an offence by running an unregistered children's home.

Interpretation

1. For the purposes of this Schedule, a person fosters a child if–

    (a) he is a local authority foster parent in relation to the child;
    (b) he is a foster parent with whom the child has been placed by a voluntary organisation; or
    (d) he fosters the child privately.

The usual fostering limit

2. Subject to what follows, a person may not foster more than three children ('the usual fostering limit').

Siblings

3. A person may exceed the usual fostering limit if the children concerned are all siblings with respect to each other.

Exemption by local authority

4 – (1) A person may exceed the usual fostering limit if he is exempted from it by the local authority within whose area he lives.

(2) In considering whether to exempt a person, a local authority shall have regard, in particular, to–

(a) the number of children whom the person proposes to foster;
(b) the arrangements which the person proposes for the care and accommodation of the fostered children;
(c) the intended and likely relationship between the person and the fostered children;
(d) the period of time for which he proposes to foster the children; and
(e) whether the welfare of the fostered children (and of any other children who are or will be living in the accommodation) will be safeguarded and promoted.

(3) Where a local authority exempt a person, they shall inform him by notice in writing–

(a) that he is so exempted;
(b) of the children, described by name, whom he may foster; and
(c) of any condition to which the exemption is subject.

(4) A local authority may at any time by notice in writing–

(a) vary or cancel an exemption; or
(b) impose, vary or cancel a condition to which the exemption is subject,

and, in considering whether to do so, they shall have regard in particular to the considerations mentioned in sub-paragraph (2).

(5) The Secretary of State may make regulations amplifying or modifying the provisions of this paragraph in order to provide for cases where children need to be placed with foster parents as a matter of urgency.

Effect of exceeding fostering limit

5 – (1) A person shall cease to be treated as fostering and shall be treated as carrying on a children's home if–

(a) he exceeds the usual fostering limit; or
(b) where he is exempted under paragraph 4,–
    (i) he fosters any child not named in the exemption; and
    (ii) in so doing, he exceeds the usual fostering limit.

(2) Sub-paragraph (1) does not apply if the children concerned are all siblings in respect of each other.

Complaints etc

6 – (1) Every local authority shall establish a procedure for considering any representations (including any complaint) made to them about the discharge of their functions under paragraph 4 by a person exempted or seeking to be exempted under that paragraph.

(2) In carrying out any consideration of representations under sub-paragraph (1), a local authority shall comply with any regulations made by the Secretary of State for the purposes of this paragraph.

SCHEDULE 8

PRIVATELY FOSTERED CHILDREN

Schedule 8
Privately Fostered Children
This schedule creates various exemptions from the definition of a privately fostered child set out in s 66 of the Act which are largely self explanatory. The right of appeal against a decision of the local authority in respect of the arrangements for privately fostering a child is to the magistrates court under Children (Allocation of Proceedings) Order 1991 art 3.

Exemptions

1. A child is not a privately fostered child while he is being looked after by a local authority.

2 – (1) A child is not a privately fostered child while he is in the care of any person–

(a) in premises in which any–
   (i) parent of his;
   (ii) person who is not a parent of his but who has parental responsibility for him; or
   (iii) person who is a relative of his and who has assumed responsibility for his care,
   is for the time being living;
(b) in any children's home;
(c) in accommodation provided by or on behalf of any voluntary organisation;
(d) in any school in which he is receiving full-time education;
(e) in any health service hospital;
(f) in any residential care home [(other than a small home)], nursing home or mental nursing home; or

(f) in any home or institution not specified in this paragraph but provided, equipped and maintained by the Secretary of State.

(2) Sub-paragraph (1)(b) to (g) does not apply where the person caring for the child is doing so in his personal capacity and not in the course of carrying out his duties in relation to the establishment mentioned in the paragraph in question.

3. A child is not a privately fostered child while he is in the care of any person in compliance with–

   (a) an order under section 7(7)(b) of the Children and Young Persons Act 1969; or
   (b) a supervision requirement within the meaning of [Part II of the Children (Scotland) Act 1995].

4. A child is not a privately fostered child while he is liable to be detained, or subject to guardianship, under the Mental Health Act 1983.

5. A child is not a privately fostered child while–

   (a) he is placed in the care of a person who proposes to adopt him under arrangements made by an adoption agency within the meaning of–
      (i) section 1 of the Adoption Act 1976;
      (ii) section 1 of the Adoption (Scotland) Act 1978; or
      (iii) Article 3 of the Adoption (Northern Ireland) Order 1987; or
   (b) he is a protected child.

Power of local authority to impose requirements

6 – (1) Where a person is fostering any child privately, or proposes to foster any child privately, the appropriate local authority may impose on him requirements as to–

   (a) the number, age and sex of the children who may be privately fostered by him;
   (b) the standard of the accommodation and equipment to be provided for them;
   (c) the arrangements to be made with respect to their health and safety; and
   (d) particular arrangements which must be made with respect to the provision of care for them,

   and it shall be his duty to comply with any such requirement before the end of such period as the local authority may specify unless, in the case of a proposal, the proposal is not carried out.

(2) A requirement may be limited to a particular child, or class of child.

(3) A requirement (other than one imposed under sub-paragraph (1)(a)) may be limited by the local authority so as to apply only when the number of children fostered by the person exceeds a specified number.

(4) A requirement shall be imposed by notice in writing addressed to the person on whom it is imposed and informing him of–

   (a) the reason for imposing the requirement;
   (b) his right under paragraph 8 to appeal against it; and

(c) the time within which he may do so.

(2) A local authority may at any time vary any requirement, impose any additional requirement or remove any requirement.

(6) In this Schedule–

(a) 'the appropriate local authority' means–
  (i) the local authority within whose area the child is being fostered; or
  (ii) in the case of a proposal to foster a child, the local authority within whose area it is proposed that he will be fostered; and
(b) 'requirement', in relation to any person, means a requirement imposed on him under this paragraph.

Regulations requiring notification of fostering etc

7 – (1) The Secretary of State may by regulations make provision as to–

(a) the circumstances in which notification is required to be given in connection with children who are, have been or are proposed to be fostered privately; and
(b) the manner and form in which such notification is to be given.

(2) The regulations may, in particular–

(a) require any person who is, or proposes to be, involved (whether or not directly) in arranging for a child to be fostered privately to notify the appropriate authority;
(b) require any person who is–
  (i) a parent of a child; or
  (ii) a person who is not a parent of his but who has parental responsibility for a child,
  and who knows that it is proposed that the child should be fostered privately, to notify the appropriate authority;
(c) require any parent of a privately fostered child, or person who is not a parent of such a child but who has parental responsibility for him, to notify the appropriate authority of any change in his address;
(d) require any person who proposes to foster a child privately, to notify the appropriate authority of his proposal;
(e) require any person who is fostering a child privately, or proposes to do so, to notify the appropriate authority of–
  (i) any offence of which he has been convicted;
  (ii) any disqualification imposed on him under section 68; or
  (iii) any prohibition imposed on him under section 69;
(f) require any person who is fostering a child privately, to notify the appropriate authority of any change in his address;
(g) require any person who is fostering a child privately to notify the appropriate authority in writing of any person who begins, or ceases, to be part of his household;

(b) require any person who has been fostering a child privately, but has ceased to do so, to notify the appropriate authority (indicating, where the child has died, that that is the reason).

Appeals

8 – (1) A person aggrieved by–

(a) a requirement imposed under paragraph 6;
(b) a refusal of consent under section 68;
(c) a prohibition imposed under section 69;
(d) a refusal to cancel such a prohibition;
(e) a refusal to make an exemption under paragraph 4 of Schedule 7;
(f) a condition imposed in such an exemption; or
(g) a variation or cancellation of such an exemption,

may appeal to the court.

(2) The appeal must be made within fourteen days from the date on which the person appealing is notified of the requirement, refusal, prohibition, condition, variation or cancellation.

(3) Where the appeal is against–

(a) a requirement imposed under paragraph 6;
(b) a condition of an exemption imposed under paragraph 4 of Schedule 7; or
(c) a variation or cancellation of such an exemption,

the requirement, condition, variation or cancellation shall not have effect while the appeal is pending.

(4) Where it allows an appeal against a requirement or prohibition, the court may, instead of cancelling the requirement or prohibition–

(a) vary the requirement, or allow more time for compliance with it; or
(b) if an absolute prohibition has been imposed, substitute for it a prohibition on using the premises after such time as the court may specify unless such specified requirements as the local authority had power to impose under paragraph 6 are complied with.

(5) Any requirement or prohibition specified or substituted by a court under this paragraph shall be deemed for the purposes of Part IX (other than this paragraph) to have been imposed by the local authority under paragraph 6 or (as the case may be) section 69.

(6) Where it allows an appeal against a refusal to make an exemption, a condition imposed in such an exemption or a variation or cancellation of such an exemption, the court may–

(a) make an exemption;
(b) impose a condition; or

(c) vary the exemption.

(7) Any exemption made or varied under sub-paragraph (6), or any condition imposed under that sub-paragraph, shall be deemed for the purposes of Schedule 7 (but not for the purposes of this paragraph) to have been made, varied or imposed under that Schedule.

(8) Nothing in sub-paragraph (1)(e) to (g) confers any right of appeal on–

(a) a person who is, or would be if exempted under Schedule 7, a local authority foster parent; or

(b) a person who is, or would be if so exempted, a person with whom a child is placed by a voluntary organisation.

Extension of Part IX to certain school children during holidays

9 – (1) Where a child under sixteen who is a pupil at a school which is not maintained by a local education authority lives at the school during school holidays for a period of more than two weeks, Part IX shall apply in relation to the child as if–

(a) while living at the school, he were a privately fostered child; and

(b) paragraphs 2(1)(d) and 6 were omitted.

(2) Sub-paragraph (3) applies to any person who proposes to care for and accommodate one or more children at a school in circumstances in which some or all of them will be treated as private foster children by virtue of this paragraph.

(3) That person shall, not less than two weeks before the first of those children is treated as a private foster child by virtue of this paragraph during the holiday in question, give written notice of his proposal to the local authority within whose area the child is ordinarily resident ('the appropriate authority'), stating the estimated number of the children.

(4) A local authority may exempt any person from the duty of giving notice under sub-paragraph (3).

(5) Any such exemption may be granted for a special period or indefinitely and may be revoked at any time by notice in writing given to the person exempted.

(6) Where a child who is treated as a private foster child by virtue of this paragraph dies, the person caring for him at the school shall, not later than 48 hours after the death, give written notice of it–

(a) to the appropriate local authority; and

(b) where reasonably practicable, to each parent of the child and to every person who is not a parent of his but who has parental responsibility for him.

(2) Where a child who is treated as a foster child by virtue of this paragraph ceases for any other reason to be such a child, the person caring for him at the school shall give written notice of the fact to the appropriate local authority.

Prohibition of advertisements relating to fostering

10. No advertisement indicating that a person will undertake, or will arrange for, a child to be privately fostered shall be published, unless it states that person's name and address.

Avoidance of insurances on lives of privately fostered children

11. A person who fosters a child privately and for reward shall be deemed for the purposes of the Life Assurance Act 1774 to have no interest in the life of the child.

SCHEDULE 9

CHILD MINDING AND DAY CARE FOR YOUNG CHILDREN

SCHEDULE 9
Child Minding and Day Care for Young Children
This schedule deals with the registration and disqualification of child minders and persons providing day care for children. It also provides for exemption from the obligations imposed by s 71 of the Act in respect of certain schools and other establishments that are subject to other forms of control. The provisions of this schedule are largely self-explanatory.

Applications for registration

1 – (1) An application for registration under section 71 shall be of no effect unless it contains–

  (a) a statement with respect to the applicant which complies with the requirements of regulations made for the purposes of this paragraph by the Secretary of State; and

  (b) a statement with respect to any person assisting or likely to be assisting in looking after children on the premises in question, or living or likely to be living there, which complies with the requirements of such regulations.

(2) Where a person provides, or proposes to provide, day care for children under the age of eight on different premises situated within the area of the same local authority, he shall make a separate application with respect to each of those premises.

(3) An application under section 71 shall be accompanied by such fee as may be prescribed.

(4) On receipt of an application for registration under section 71 from any person who is acting, or proposes to act, in any way which requires him to be registered under that section, a local authority shall register him if the application is properly made and they are not otherwise entitled to refuse to do so.

Disqualification from registration

2 – (1) A person may not be registered under section 71 if he is disqualified by regulations made by the Secretary of State for the purposes of this paragraph [unless

(a) he has disclosed the fact to the appropriate local authority; and
(b) obtained their written consent.

(2) The regulations may, in particular, provide for a person to be disqualified where–

(a) an order of a prescribed kind has been made at any time with respect to him;
(b) an order of a prescribed kind has been made at any time with respect to any child who has been in his care;
(c) a requirement of a prescribed kind has been imposed at any time with respect to such a child, under or by virtue of any enactment;
(d) he has at any time been refused registration under Part X or any other prescribed enactment or had any such registration cancelled;
(e) he has been convicted of any offence of a prescribed kind, or has been placed on probation or discharged absolutely or conditionally for any such offence;
(f) he has at any time been disqualified from fostering a child privately;
(g) a prohibition has been imposed on him at any time under section [69], section 10 of the Foster Children (Scotland) Act 1984 or any other prescribed enactment;
(h) his rights and powers with respect to a child have at any time been vested in a prescribed authority under a prescribed enactment.

(3) A person who lives–

(a) in the same household as a person who is himself disqualified by the regulations; or
(b) in a household at which any such person is employed,

shall be disqualified unless he has disclosed the fact to the appropriate local authority and obtained their written consent.

(4) A person who is disqualified shall not provide day care, or be concerned in the management of, or have any financial interest in, any provision of day care unless he has–

(a) disclosed the fact to the appropriate local authority; and
(b) obtained their written consent.

(5) No person shall employ, in connection with the provision of day care, a person who is disqualified, unless he has–

(a) disclosed to the appropriate local authority the fact that that person is so disqualified; and

(b) obtained their written consent.

(2) In this paragraph 'enactment' means any enactment having effect, at any time, in any part of the United Kingdom.

Exemption of certain schools

3 – (1) Section 71 does not apply in relation to any child looked after in any–

(a) school maintained or assisted by a local education authority;

(b) school under the management of an education authority;

(c) school in respect of which payments are made by the Secretary of State under [section 485 of the Education Act 1996];

(d) independent school;

(e) grant-aided school;

(f) grant maintained school; ...

(g) self-governing school;

(b) play centre maintained or assisted by a local education authority under [section 508 of that Act], or by an education authority under section 6 of the Education (Scotland) Act 1980.

(2) The exemption provided by sub-paragraph (1) only applies where the child concerned is being looked after in accordance with provision for day care made by–

(a) the person carrying on the establishment in question as part of the establishment's activities; or

(b) a person employed to work at that establishment and authorised to make that provision as part of the establishment's activities.

(3) In sub-paragraph (1)–

'assisted' and 'maintained' have the same meanings as in [the Education Act 1996]; [-]

'grant maintained' has the same meaning as in [that Act]; and ...

'grant-aided school', 'self-governing school' and (in relation to Scotland) 'independent school' have the same meaning as in the Education (Scotland) Act 1980.

Exemption for other establishments

4 – (1) Section 71(1)(b) does not apply in relation to any child looked after in–

(a) a registered children's home;

(b) a voluntary home;

(c) a community home;

(d) a residential care home, nursing home or mental nursing home required to be registered under the Registered Homes Act 1984;

(e) a health service hospital;

(f) a home provided, equipped and maintained by the Secretary of State; or

(f) an establishment which is required to be registered under section 61 of the Social Work (Scotland) Act 1968.

(2) The exemption provided by sub-paragraph (1) only applies where the child concerned is being looked after in accordance with provision for day care made by–

(a) the department, authority or other person carrying on the establishment in question as part of the establishment's activities; or

(b) a person employed to work at that establishment and authorised to make that provision as part of the establishment's activities.

(2) In this paragraph 'health service hospital' includes a health service hospital within the meaning of the National Health Service (Scotland) Act 1978.

Exemption for occasional facilities

5 – (1) Where day care for children under the age of eight is provided in particular premises on less than six days in any year, that provision shall be disregarded for the purposes of section 71 if the person making it has notified the appropriate local authority in writing before the first occasion on which the premises concerned are so used in that year.

(2) In sub-paragraph (1) 'year' means the year beginning with the day on which the day care in question is (after the commencement of this paragraph) first provided in the premises concerned and any subsequent year.

Certificates of registration

6 – (1) Where a local authority register a person under section 71 they shall issue him with a certificate of registration.

(2) The certificate shall specify–

(a) the registered person's name and address;

(b) in a case falling within section 71(1)(b), the address or situation of the premises concerned; and

(c) any requirements imposed under section 72 or 73.

(3) Where, due to a change of circumstances, any part of the certificate requires to be amended, the authority shall issue an amended certificate.

(4) Where the authority are satisfied that the certificate has been lost or destroyed, they shall issue a copy, on payment by the registered person of such fee as may be prescribed.

Fees for annual inspection of premises

7 – (1) Where–

(a) a person is registered under section 71; and

(b) the local authority concerned make an annual inspection of the premises in question under section 76,

they shall serve on that person a notice informing him that the inspection is to be carried out and requiring him to pay to them such fee as may be prescribed.

(2) It shall be a condition of the continued registration of that person under section 71 that the fee is so paid before the expiry of the period of twenty-eight days beginning with the date on which the inspection is carried out.

Co-operation between authorities

8 – (1) Where it appears to a local authority that any local education authority or, in Scotland, education authority could, by taking any specified action, help in the exercise of any of their functions under Part X, they may request the help of that local education authority, or education authority, specifying the action in question.

(2) An authority whose help is so requested shall comply with the request if it is compatible with their own statutory or other duties and obligations and does not unduly prejudice the discharge of any of their functions.

SCHEDULE 10

ADOPTION ACT

Schedule 10
This schedule deals with the amendments which the Children Act 1989 made to the Adoption Act 1976, and the Amendments of Adoption (Scotland) Act 1978.

PART I

Amendments of Adoption Act 1976 (c. 36)

1. In section 2 (local authorities' social services) for the words from "relating to" to the end there shall be substituted-

(a) under the Children Act 1989, relating to family assistance orders, local authority support for children and families, care and supervision and emergency protection of children, community homes, voluntary homes and organisations, registered children's homes, private arrangements for fostering children, child minding and day care for young children and children accommodated by health authorities and local education authorities or in residential care, nursing or mental nursing homes or in independent schools; and

(b) under the National Health Service Act 1977, relating to the provision of care for expectant and nursing mothers

2. In section 11 (restrictions on arranging adoptions and placing of children) for subsection (2) there shall be substituted-

(2) An adoption society which is-

(a) approved as respects Scotland under section 3 of the Adoption (Scotland) Act 1978; or

(b) registered as respects Northern Ireland under Article 4 of the Adoption (Northern Ireland) Order 1987,

but which is not approved under section 3 of this Act, shall not act as an adoption society in England and Wales except to the extent that the society considers it necessary to do so in the interests of a person mentioned in section 1 of the Act of 1978 or Article 3 of the Order of 1987.

3. – (1) In section 12 (adoption orders), in subsection (1) for the words "vesting the parental rights and duties relating to a child in" there shall be substituted "giving parental responsibility for a child to".

(2) In subsection (2) of that section for the words "the parental rights and duties so far as they relate" there shall be substituted "parental responsibility so far as it relates".

(3) In subsection (3) of that section for paragraph (a) there shall be substituted-

(a) the parental responsibility which any person has for the child immediately before the making of the order;

(aa) any order under the Children Act 1989

and in paragraph (b) for the words from "for any period" to the end there shall be substituted "or upbringing for any period after the making of the order."

4. For section 14(1) (adoption by married couple) there shall be substituted-

"(1) An adoption order shall not be made on the application of more than one person except in the circumstances specified in subsections (1A) and (1B).

(1A) An adoption order may be made on the application of a married couple where both the husband and the wife have attained the age of 21 years.

(1B) An adoption order may be made on the application of a married couple where-

(a) the husband or the wife-
  (i) is the father or mother of the child; and
  (ii) has attained the age of 18 years:

and

(b) his or her spouse has attained the age of 21 years.

"5. – (1) In section 16 (parental agreement), in subsection (1) for the words from "in England" to "Scotland)" there shall be substituted-

> (i) in England and Wales, under section 18;
> (ii) in Scotland, under section 18 of the Adoption (Scotland) Act 1978; or
> (iii) in Northern Ireland, under Article 17(1) or 18(1) of the Adoption (Northern Ireland) Order 1987.

(2) In subsection (2)(c) of that section for the words "the parental duties in relation to" there shall be substituted "his parental responsibility for".

6. – (1) In section 18 (freeing child for adoption), after subsection (2) there shall be inserted-

"(2A) For the purposes of subsection (2) a child is in the care of an adoption agency if the adoption agency is a local authority and he is in their care.

(2) In subsection (5) of that section, for the words from "the parental rights" to "vest in" there shall be substituted "parental responsibility for the child is given to", and for the words "and (3)" there shall be substituted "to (4)".

(3) For subsections (7) and (8) of that section there shall be substituted-

(7) Before making an order under this section in the case of a child whose father does not have parental responsibility for him, the court shall satisfy itself in relation to any person claiming to be the father that-

> (a) he has no intention of applying for-
> > (i) an order under section 4(1) of the Children Act 1989, or
> > (ii) a residence order under section 10 of that Act, or
> (b) if he did make any such application, it would be likely to be refused.

(8) Subsections (5) and (7) of section 12 apply in relation to the making of an order under this section as they apply in relation to the making of an order under that section.

7. In section 19(2) (progress reports to former parents) for the words "in which the parental rights and duties were vested" there shall be substituted "to which parental responsibility was given".

8. – (1) In section 20 (revocation of section 18 order), in subsections (1) and (2) for the words "the parental rights and duties", in both places where they occur, there shall be substituted "parental responsibility".

(2) For subsection (3) of that section there shall be substituted-

(3) The revocation of an order under section 18 ("a section 18 order") operates-

> (a) to extinguish the parental responsibility given to the adoption agency under the section 18 order;

(b) to give parental responsibility for the child to-
- (i) the child's mother; and
- (ii) where the child's father and mother were married to each other at the time of his birth, the father; and

(c) to revive-
- (i) any parental responsibility agreement,
- (ii) any order under section 4(1) of the Children Act 1989, and
- (iii) any appointment of a guardian in respect of the child (whether made by a court or otherwise),

extinguished by the making of the section 18 order.

(3A) Subject to subsection (3)(c), the revocation does not-

(a) operate to revive-
- (i) any order under the Children Act 1989, or
- (ii) any duty referred to in section 12(3)(b),

extinguished by the making of the section 18 order; or

(b) affect any person's parental responsibility so far as it relates to the period between the making of the section 18 order and the date of revocation of that order.

9. For section 21 (transfer of parental rights and duties between adoption agencies) there shall be substituted-

21. – (1) On an application to which this section applies, an authorised court may vary an order under section 18 so as to give parental responsibility for the child to another adoption agency ("the substitute agency") in place of the agency for the time being having parental responsibility for the child under the order ("the existing agency").

(2) This section applies to any application made jointly by-

(a) the existing agency; and
(b) the would-be substitute agency.

(3) Where an order under section 18 is varied under this section, section 19 shall apply as if the substitute agency had been given responsibility for the child on the making of the order.

10. – (1) In section 22 (notification to local authority of adoption application), after subsection (1) there shall be inserted the following subsections-

(1A) An application for such an adoption order shall not be made unless the person wishing to make the application has, within the period of two years preceding the making of the application, given notice as mentioned in subsection (1).

(1B) In subsections (1) and (1A) the references to the area in which the applicant or person has his home are references to the area in which he has his home at the time of giving the notice.

(2) In subsection (4) of that section for the word "receives" there shall be substituted "receive" and for the words "in the care of" there shall be substituted "looked after by".

11. In section 25(1) (interim orders) for the words "vesting the legal custody of the child in" there shall be substituted "giving parental responsibility for the child to".

12. In-

    (a) section 27(1) and (2) (restrictions on removal where adoption agreed or application made under section 18); and

    (b) section 28(1) and (2) (restrictions on removal where applicant has provided home for 5 years),

for the words "actual custody", in each place where they occur, there shall be substituted "home".

13. After section 27(2) there shall be inserted-

(2A) For the purposes of subsection (2) a child is in the care of an adoption agency if the adoption agency is a local authority and he is in their care.

14. – (1) After section 28(2) there shall be inserted-

(2A) The reference in subsections (1) and (2) to any enactment does not include a reference to section 20(8) of the Children Act 1989".

(2) For subsection (3) of that section there shall be substituted-

"(3)In any case where subsection (1) or (2) applies and-

    (a) the child was being looked after by a local authority before he began to have his home with the applicant or, as the case may be, the prospective adopter, and

    (b) the child is still being looked after by a local authority,

the authority which are looking after the child shall not remove him from the home of the applicant or the prospective adopter except in accordance with section 30 or 31 or with the leave of a court.

"(3) In subsection (5) of that section-

    (a) for the word "receives" there shall be substituted "receive"; and

    (b) for the words "in the care of another local authority or of a voluntary organisation" there shall be substituted "looked after by another local authority".

15. In section 29 (return of child taken away in breach of section 27 or 28) for subsections (1) and (2) there shall be substituted-

"(1) An authorised court may, on the application of a person from whose home a child has been removed in breach of-

    (a) section 27 or 28,

    (b) section 27 or 28 of the Adoption (Scotland) Act 1978, or

(c) Article 28 or 29 of the Adoption (Northern Ireland) Order 1987,

order the person who has so removed the child to return the child to the applicant.

(2) An authorised court may, on the application of a person who has reasonable grounds for believing that another person is intending to remove a child from his home in breach of-

(a) section 27 or 28,
(b) section 27 or 28 of the Adoption (Scotland) Act 1978, or
(c) Article 28 or 29 of the Adoption (Northern Ireland) Order 1987,

by order direct that other person not to remove the child from the applicant's home in breach of any of those provisions.

16. – (1) In section 30 (return of children placed for adoption by adoption agencies), in subsection (1) there shall be substituted-

(a) for the words "delivered into the actual custody of" the words "placed with";
(b) in paragraph (a) for the words "retain the actual custody of the child" the words "give the child a home"; and
(c) in paragraph (b) for the words "actual custody" the word "home".

(2) In subsection (3) of that section for the words "in his actual custody" there shall be substituted "with him".

17. – (1) In section 31 (application of section 30 where child not placed for adoption), in subsection (1) for the words from "child", where it first occurs, to "except" there shall be substituted

"child-

(a) who is (when the notice is given) being looked after by a local authority; but
(b) who was placed with that person otherwise than in pursuance of such arrangements as are mentioned in section 30(1),

that section shall apply as if the child had been placed in pursuance of such arrangements".

(2) In subsection (2) of that section for the words "for the time being in the care of" there shall be substituted "(when the notice is given) being looked after by".

(3) In subsection (3) of that section-

(a) for the words "remains in the actual custody of" there shall be substituted "has his home with"; and
(b) for the words "section 45 of the Child Care Act 1980" there shall be substituted "Part III of Schedule 2 to the Children Act 1989".

(4) At the end of that section there shall be added-

"(4) Nothing in this section affects the right of any person who has parental responsibility for a child to remove him under section 20(8) of the Children Act 1989".

18. – (1) In section 32 (meaning of "protected child"), in subsection (2) for the words "section 37 of the Adoption Act 1958" there shall be substituted-

"(a) section 32 of the Adoption (Scotland) Act 1978; or
(b) Article 33 of the Adoption (Northern Ireland) Order 1987.

"(2)   In subsection (3) of that section for paragraph (a) there shall be substituted-

"(a) he is in the care of any person-
(i) in any community home, voluntary home or registered children's home;
(ii) in any school in which he is receiving full-time education;
(iii)in any health service hospital";
and at the end of that subsection there shall be added-
"(d) he is in the care of any person in any home or institution not specified in this subsection but provided, equipped and maintained by the Secretary of State.

"(3) After that subsection there shall be inserted-

"(3A) In subsection (3)

"community home",

"voluntary home",

"registered children's home",

"school" and

"health service hospital" have the same meaning as in the Children Act 1989.

(4) For subsection (4) of that section there shall be substituted-

(4) A protected child ceases to be a protected child-

(a) on the grant or refusal of the application for an adoption order;
(b) on the notification to the local authority for the area where the child has his home that the application for an adoption order has been withdrawn;
(c) in a case where no application is made for an adoption order, on the expiry of the period of two years from the giving of the notice;
(d) on the making of a residence order, a care order or a supervision order under the Children Act 1989 in respect of the child;
(e) on the appointment of a guardian for him under that Act;
(f) on his attaining the age of 18 years; or
(g) on his marriage,

whichever first occurs.

(5) In subsection (4)(d) the references to a care order and a supervision order do not include references to an interim care order or interim supervision order.

19. – (1) In section 35 (notices and information to be given to local authorities), in subsection (1) for the words "who has a protected child in his actual custody" there shall be substituted "with whom a protected child has his home".

(2) In subsection (2) of that section for the words "in whose actual custody he was" there shall be substituted "with whom he had his home".

20. – (1) In section 51 (disclosure of birth records of adopted children), in subsection (1) for the words "subsections (4) and (6)" there shall be substituted "what follows".

(2) For subsections (3) to (7) of that section there shall be substituted-

(3) Before supplying any information to an applicant under subsection (1), the Registrar General shall inform the applicant that counselling services are available to him-

    (a) if he is in England and Wales-
        (i) at the General Register Office;
        (ii) from the local authority in whose area he is living;
        (iii)where the adoption order relating to him was made in England and Wales, from the local authority in whose area the court which made the order sat; or
        (iv)from any other local authority;
    (b) if he is in Scotland-
        (i) from the regional or islands council in whose area he is living;
        (ii) where the adoption order relating to him was made in Scotland, from the council in whose area the court which made the order sat; or
        (iii)from any other regional or islands council;
    (c) if he is in Northern Ireland-
        (i) from the Board in whose area he is living;
        (ii) where the adoption order relating to him was made in Northern Ireland, from the Board in whose area the court which made the order sat; or
        (iii)from any other Board;
    (d) if he is in the United Kingdom and his adoption was arranged by an adoption society-
        (i) approved under section 3,
        (ii) approved under section 3 of the Adoption (Scotland) Act 1978,
        (iii)registered under Article 4 of the Adoption (Northern Ireland) Order 1987,

    from that society.

(4) Where an adopted person who is in England and Wales-

    (a) applies for information under -
        (i) subsection (1), or
        (ii) Article 54 of the Adoption (Northern Ireland) Order 1987, or
    (b) is supplied with information under section 45 of the Adoption (Scotland) Act 1978,

it shall be the duty of the persons and bodies mentioned in subsection (5) to provide counselling for him if asked by him to do so.

(5) The persons and bodies are-

(a) the Registrar General;

(b) any local authority falling within subsection (3)(a)(ii) to (iv);

(c) any adoption society falling within subsection (3)(d) in so far as it is acting as an adoption society in England and Wales.

(6) If the applicant chooses to receive counselling from a person or body falling within subsection (3), the Registrar General shall send to the person or body the information to which the applicant is entitled under subsection (1).

(7) Where a person-

(a) was adopted before 12th November 1975, and

(b) applies for information under subsection (1),

the Registrar General shall not supply the information to him unless he has attended an interview with a counsellor arranged by a person or body from whom counselling services are available as mentioned in subsection (3).

(8) Where the Registrar General is prevented by subsection (7) from supplying information to a person who is not living in the United Kingdom, he may supply the information to any body which-

(a) the Registrar General is satisfied is suitable to provide counselling to that person, and

(b) has notified the Registrar General that it is prepared to provide such counselling.

(9) In this section-

"a Board" means a Health and Social Services Board established under Article 16 of the Health and Personal Social Services (Northern Ireland) Order 1972; and

"prescribed" means prescribed by regulations made by the Registrar General.

21. After section 51 there shall be inserted-

51A. – (1) The Registrar General shall maintain at the General Register Office a register to be called the Adoption Contact Register.

(2) The register shall be in two parts-

(a) Part I: Adopted Persons; and

(b) Part II: Relatives.

(3) The Registrar General shall, on payment of such fee as may be prescribed, enter in Part I of the register the name and address of any adopted person who fulfils the conditions in subsection (4) and who gives notice that he wishes to contact any relative of his.

(4) The conditions are that-

(a) a record of the adopted person's birth is kept by the Registrar General; and

(b) the adopted person has attained the age of 18 years and-
  (i) has been supplied by the Registrar General with information under section 51; or
  (ii) has satisfied the Registrar General that he has such information as is necessary to enable him to obtain a certified copy of the record of his birth.

(5) The Registrar General shall, on payment of such fee as may be prescribed, enter in Part II of the register the name and address of any person who fulfils the conditions in subsection (6) and who gives notice that he wishes to contact an adopted person.

(6) The conditions are that-

(a) a record of the adopted person's birth is kept by the Registrar General; and
(b) the person giving notice under subsection (5) has attained the age of 18 years and has satisfied the Registrar General that-
  (i) he is a relative of the adopted person; and
  (ii) he has such information as is necessary to enable him to obtain a certified copy of the record of the adopted person's birth.

(7) The Registrar General shall, on receiving notice from any person named in an entry in the register that he wishes the entry to be cancelled, cancel the entry.

(8) Any notice given under this section must be in such form as may be determined by the Registrar General.

(9) The Registrar General shall transmit to an adopted person whose name is entered in Part I of the register the name and address of any relative in respect of whom there is an entry in Part II of the register.

(10) Any entry cancelled under subsection (7) ceases from the time of cancellation to be an entry for the purposes of subsection (9).

(11) The register shall not be open to public inspection or search and the Registrar General shall not supply any person with information entered in the register (whether in an uncancelled or a cancelled entry) except in accordance with this section.

(12) The register may be kept by means of a computer.

(13) In this section-

(a) "relative" means any person (other than an adoptive relative) who is related to the adopted person by blood (including half-blood) or marriage;
(b) "address" includes any address at or through which the person concerned may be contacted; and
(c) "prescribed" means prescribed by the Secretary of State.

22. – (1) In section 55 (adoption of children abroad), in subsection (1) after the word "Scotland" there shall be inserted "or Northern Ireland" and for the words "vesting in him the parental rights and duties relating to the child" there shall be

substituted "giving him parental responsibility for the child".

(2) In subsection (3) of that section for the words "word "(Scotland)"" there shall be substituted "words "(Scotland)" or "(Northern Ireland)"."

23. – (1) In section 56 (restriction on removal of children for adoption outside Great Britain),-

    (a) in subsections (1) and (3) for the words "transferring the actual custody of a child to", in both places where they occur, there shall be substituted "placing a child with"; and

    (b) in subsection (3)(a) for the words "in the actual custody of" there shall be substituted "with".

(2) In subsection (1) of that section-

    (a) for the words from "or under" to "abroad)" there shall be substituted "section 49 of the Adoption (Scotland) Act 1978 or Article 57 of the Adoption (Northern Ireland) Order 1987"; and

    (b) for the words "British Islands" there shall be substituted "United Kingdom, the Channel Islands and the Isle of Man".

24. – (1) In section 57 (prohibition on certain payments) in subsection (1)(c), for the words "transfer by that person of the actual custody of a child" there shall be substituted "handing over of a child by that person".

(2) In subsection (3A)(b) of that section, for the words "in the actual custody of" there shall be substituted "with".

25. After section 57 there shall be inserted-

A.

(1) The Secretary of State may make regulations for the purpose of enabling adoption agencies to pay allowances to persons who have adopted, or intend to adopt, children in pursuance of arrangements made by the agencies.

(2) Section 57(1) shall not apply to any payment made by an adoption agency in accordance with the regulations.

(3) The regulations may, in particular, make provision as to-

    (a) the procedure to be followed by any agency in determining whether a person should be paid an allowance;

    (b) the circumstances in which an allowance may be paid;

    (c) the factors to be taken into account in determining the amount of an allowance;

    (d) the procedure for review, variation and termination of allowances; and

    (e) the information about allowances to be supplied by any agency to any person who is intending to adopt a child.

(4) Any scheme approved under section 57(4) shall be revoked as from the coming

into force of this section.

(5) Section 57(1) shall not apply in relation to any payment made-

(a) in accordance with a scheme revoked under subsection (4) or section 57(5)(b); and

(b) to a person to whom such payments were made before the revocation of the scheme.

(6) Subsection (5) shall not apply where any person to whom any payments may lawfully be made by virtue of subsection (5) agrees to receive (instead of such payments) payments complying with regulations made under this section.

26. – (1) In section 59 (effect of determination and orders made in Scotland and overseas in adoption proceedings), in subsection (1) for the words "Great Britain" there shall be substituted "the United Kingdom".

(2) For subsection (2) of that section there shall be substituted-

(2) Subsections (2) to (4) of section 12 shall apply in relation to an order freeing a child for adoption (other than an order under section 18) as if it were an adoption order; and, on the revocation in Scotland or Northern Ireland of an order freeing a child for adoption, subsections (3) and (3A) of section 20 shall apply as if the order had been revoked under that section.

27. In section 60 (evidence of adoption in Scotland and Northern Ireland), in paragraph (a) for the words "section 22(2) of the Adoption Act 1958" there shall be substituted "section 45(2) of the Adoption (Scotland) Act 1978" and in paragraph (b) for the words from "section 23(4)" to "in force" there shall be substituted "Article 63(1) of the Adoption (Northern Ireland) Order 1987".

28. In section 62(5)(b) (courts), for the words from "section 8" to "child)" there shall be substituted-

"(i) section 12 or 18 of the Adoption (Scotland) Act 1978; or
(ii) Article 12, 17 or 18 of the Adoption (Northern Ireland) Order 1987".

29. After section 65 (guardians ad litem and reporting officers) there shall be inserted-

"65A. - (1) The Secretary of State may by regulations provide for the establishment of panels of persons from whom guardians ad litem and reporting officers appointed under rules made under section 65 must be selected.

(2) The regulations may, in particular, make provision-

(a) as to the constitution, administration and procedures of panels;

(b) requiring two or more specified local authorities to make arrangements for the joint management of a panel;

(c) for the defrayment by local authorities of expenses incurred by members of panels;

(d) for the payment by local authorities of fees and allowances for members of panels;

(e) as to the qualifications for membership of a panel;

(f) as to the training to be given to members of panels;

(g) as to the co-operation required of specified local authorities in the provision of panels in specified areas; and

(h) for monitoring the work of guardians ad litem and reporting officers.

(3) Rules of court may make provision as to the assistance which any guardian ad litem or reporting officer may be required by the court to give to it.

"**30.**– (1) Section 72(1) (interpretation) shall be amended as follows.

(2) In the definition of "adoption agency" for the words from "section 1" to the end there shall be substituted

"-(a) section 1 of the Adoption (Scotland) Act 1978; and

(b) Article 3 of the Adoption (Northern Ireland) Order 1987.

"(3) For the definition of "adoption order" there shall be substituted-

"adoption order"-

(a) means an order under section 12(1); and

(b) in sections 12(3) and (4), 18 to 20, 27, 28 and 30 to 32 and in the definition of "British adoption order" in this subsection includes an order under section 12 of the Adoption (Scotland) Act 1978 and Article 12 of the Adoption (Northern Ireland) Order 1987 (adoption orders in Scotland and Northern Ireland respectively); and

(c) in sections 27, 28 and 30 to 32 includes an order under section 55, section 49 of the Adoption (Scotland) Act 1978 and Article 57 of the Adoption (Northern Ireland) Order 1987 (orders in relation to children being adopted abroad).

(4) For the definition of "British adoption order" there shall be substituted-

"British adoption order" means-

(a) an adoption order as defined in this subsection, and

(b) an order under any provision for the adoption of a child effected under the law of any British territory outside the United Kingdom.

(5) For the definition of "guardian" there shall be substituted-

"guardian" has the same meaning as in the Children Act 1989.

"(6) In the definition of "order freeing a child for adoption" for the words from "section 27(2)" to the end there shall be substituted

"sections 27(2) and 59 includes an order under-

(a) section 18 of the Adoption (Scotland) Act 1978; and

(b) Article 17 or 18 of the Adoption (Northern Ireland) Order 1987".

(7) After the definition of "overseas adoption" there shall be inserted-

"parent" means, in relation to a child, any parent who has parental responsibility for the child under the Children Act 1989;

"parental responsibility" and

"parental responsibility agreement" have the same meaning as in the Children Act 1989.

(8) After the definition of "United Kingdom national" there shall be inserted-

"upbringing" has the same meaning as in the Children Act 1989.

(9) For section 72(1A) there shall be substituted the following subsections-

"(1A) In this Act, in determining with what person, or where, a child has his home, any absence of the child at a hospital or boarding school and any other temporary absence shall be disregarded.

(1B) In this Act, references to a child who is in the care of or looked after by a local authority have the same meaning as in the Children Act 1989.

31. For section 74(3) and (4) (extent) there shall be substituted-

"(3) This Act extends to England and Wales only.

PART II

AMENDMENTS OF ADOPTION (SCOTLAND) ACT 1978 (C. 28)

32. In section 11 (restrictions on arranging of adoptions and placing of children) for subsection (2) there shall be substituted-

"(2) An adoption society which is-

(a) approved as respects England and Wales under section 3 of the Adoption Act 1976; or
(b) registered as respects Northern Ireland under Article 4 of the Adoption (Northern Ireland) Order 1987,

but which is not approved under section 3 of this Act, shall not act as an adoption society in Scotland except to the extent that the society considers it necessary to do so in the interests of a person mentioned in section 1 of that Act or, as the case may be, Article 3 of that Order.

"**33.** For section 14(1) (adoption by married couple) there shall be substituted-

"(1) Subject to section 53(1) of the Children Act 1975 (which provides for the making of a custody order instead of an adoption order in certain cases), an adoption order shall not be made on the application of more than one person except in the circumstances specified in subsections (1A) and (1B).

(1A) An adoption order may be made on the application of a married couple where both the husband and the wife have attained the age of 21 years.

(1B) An adoption order may be made on the application of a married couple where-

(a) the husband or the wife-
   (i) is the father or mother of the child; and
   (ii) has attained the age of 18 years; and
(b) his or her spouse has attained the age of 21 years.

"34 In section 16(1)(a) (parental agreement) for the words from "in England" to "revoked", in the second place where it occurs, there shall be substituted-

   (i) in Scotland under section 18;
   (ii) in England and Wales under section 18 of the Adoption Act 1976; or
   (iii) in Northern Ireland under Article 17(1) or 18(1) of the Adoption (Northern Ireland) Order 1987,
      and not revoked

35. In section 18(5) (effect of order freeing child for adoption) for the words "and (3)" there shall be substituted "to (4)".

36. In section 20(3)(c) (revocation of section 18 order) the words "section 12(3)(b) of the Adoption Act 1976 or of" shall cease to have effect.

37. For section 21 (transfer of parental rights and duties between adoption agencies) there shall be substituted-

"21. – (1) On an application to which this section applies an authorised court may vary an order under section 18 so as to transfer the parental rights and duties relating to the child from the adoption agency in which they are vested under the order ("the existing agency") to another adoption agency ("the substitute agency").

(2) This section applies to any application made jointly by the existing agency and the would-be substitute agency.

(3) Where an order under section 18 is varied under this section, section 19 shall apply as if the parental rights and duties relating to the child had vested in the substitute agency on the making of the order.

38. In section 22(4) (notification to local authority of adoption application) for the word "receives" there shall be substituted "receive".

39. In section 29 (return of child taken away in breach of section 27 or 28) after the word "1976" in each place where it occurs there shall be inserted "or Article 28 or 29 of the Adoption (Northern Ireland) Order 1987".

40. In section 32 (meaning of "protected child"), at the end of subsection (2) there shall be added "or Article 33 of the Adoption (Northern Ireland) Order 1987".

41. In section 45 (adopted children register)-

(a) for the words from
   "or an approved" in subsection (5) to the end of subsection (6) there shall be substituted-
   "Board or adoption society falling within subsection (6) which is providing counselling for that adopted person.

(6) Where the Registrar General for Scotland furnishes an adopted person with information under subsection (5), he shall advise that person that counselling services are available-

(a) if the person is in Scotland-
    (i) from the local authority in whose area he is living;
    (ii) where the adoption order relating to him was made in Scotland, from the local authority in whose area the court which made the order sat; or
    (iii) from any other local authority in Scotland;
(b) if the person is in England and Wales-
    (i) from the local authority in whose area he is living;
    (ii) where the adoption order relating to him was made in England and Wales, from the local authority in whose area the court which made the order sat; or
    (iii) from any other local authority in England and Wales;
(c) if the person is in Northern Ireland-
    (i) from the Board in whose area he is living;
    (ii) where the adoption order relating to him was made in Northern Ireland, from the Board in whose area the court which made the order sat; or
    (iii) from any other Board;
(d) if the person is in the United Kingdom and his adoption was arranged by an adoption society-
    (i) approved under section 3;
    (ii) approved under section 3 of the Adoption Act 1976; or
    (iii) registered under Article 4 of the Adoption (Northern Ireland) Order 1987,

from that society.

(6A) Where an adopted person who is in Scotland-

(a) is furnished with information under subsection (5); or
(b) applies for information under-
    (i) section 51(1) of the Adoption Act 1976; or
    (ii) Article 54 of the Adoption (Northern Ireland) Order 1987,

any body mentioned in subsection (6B) to which the adopted person applies for counselling shall have a duty to provide counselling for him.

(6B) The bodies referred to in subsection (6A) are-

(a) any local authority falling within subsection (6)(a); and
(b) any adoption society falling within subsection (6)(d) so far as it is acting as an adoption society in Scotland.";
(b) in subsection (7)-
    (i) for the word "under" there shall be substituted "from a local authority, Board or adoption society falling within";
    (ii) for the words "or adoption society which is providing that counselling" there shall be substituted ", Board or adoption society"; and

(iii) after the word
"authority" where it second occurs there shall be inserted ", Board"; and
(c) after subsection (9) there shall be inserted the following subsection-

(10) In this section-

"Board" means a Health and Social Services Board established under Article 16 of the Health and Personal Social Services (Northern Ireland) Order 1972; and

"local authority", in relation to England and Wales, means the council of a county (other than a metropolitan county), a metropolitan district, a London borough or the Common Council of the City of London.

"42. In section 49 (adoption of children abroad)-

(a) in subsection (1) after the word "Scotland" there shall be inserted "or Northern Ireland"; and
(b) in subsection (3) for the words "word "England"" there shall be substituted "words "(England)" or "(Northern Ireland)" ".

43. In section 50(1) (restriction on removal of children for adoption outside Great Britain) after the word "1976" there shall be inserted "or Article 57 of the Adoption (Northern Ireland) Order 1987".

44. In section 53(1) (effect of determination and orders made in England and Wales and overseas in adoption proceedings)-

(a) in subsection (1) for the words "Great Britain" there shall be substituted "the United Kingdom"; and
(b) for subsection (2) there shall be substituted-

(2) Subsections (2) to (4) of section 12 shall apply in relation to an order freeing a child for adoption (other than an order under section 18) as if it were an adoption order; and on the revocation in England and Wales or Northern Ireland of an order freeing a child for adoption subsection (3) of section 20 shall apply as if the order had been revoked under that section.

"45. In section 54(b) (evidence of adoption in Northern Ireland) for the words from "section 23(4)" to "in force" there shall be substituted "Article 63(1) of the Adoption (Northern Ireland) Order 1987".

46. In section 65(1) (interpretation)-

(a) in the definition of "adoption agency", at the end there shall be added "and an adoption agency within the meaning of Article 3 of the Adoption (Northern Ireland) Order 1987 (adoption agencies in Northern Ireland)";
(b) for the definition of "adoption order" there shall be substituted-
""adoption order"-
(a) means an order under section 12(1); and
(b) in sections 12(3) and (4), 18 to 20, 27, 28 and 30 to 32 and in the definition of "British adoption order" in this subsection includes an order under section 12 of

the Adoption Act 1976 and Article 12 of the Adoption (Northern Ireland) Order 1987 (adoption orders in England and Wales and Northern Ireland respectively); and

(c) in sections 27, 28 and 30 to 32 includes an order under section 49, section 55 of the Adoption Act 1976 and Article 57 of the Adoption (Northern Ireland) Order 1987 (orders in relation to children being adopted abroad);

(c) for the definition of "British adoption order" there shall be substituted- "British adoption order" means-

(a) an adoption order as defined in this subsection; and

(b) an order under any provision for the adoption of a child effected under the law of any British territory outside the United Kingdom;";

(d) in the definition of "order freeing a child for adoption" for the words from "section 27(2)" to the end there shall be substituted

"sections 27(2) and 53 includes an order under-

(a) section 18 of the Adoption Act 1976; and

(b) Article 17 or 18 of the Adoption (Northern Ireland) Order 1987;

SCHEDULE 11

JURISDICTION

> **Schedule 11**
> *This schedule provides the Lord Chancellor with powers to make provisions regarding where proceedings should commence and when proceedings should be transferred to another court. It also deals with the amendments to other legislation which must be made as a consequence of the coming into force of Section 92 of the Children Act 1989.*

PART I

GENERAL

Commencement of proceedings

1 – (1) The Lord Chancellor may by order specify proceedings under this Act or the Adoption Act 1976 which may only be commenced in–

(a) a specified level of court;

(b) a court which falls within a specified class of court; or

(d) a particular court determined in accordance with, or specified in, the order.

(2) The Lord Chancellor may by order specify circumstances in which specified proceedings under this Act or the Adoption Act 1976 (which might otherwise be

commenced elsewhere) may only be commenced in–

(a) a specified level of court;

(b) a court which falls within a specified class of court; or

(b) a particular court determined in accordance with, or specified in, the order.

(2A) Sub-paragraphs (1) and (2) shall also apply in relation to proceedings–

(a) under section 27 of the Child Support Act 1991 (reference to court for declaration of parentage); or

(b) which are to be dealt with in accordance with an order made under section 45 of that Act (jurisdiction of courts in certain proceedings under that Act).

(3) The Lord Chancellor may by order make provision by virtue of which, where specified proceedings with respect to a child under–

(a) this Act;

(b) the Adoption Act 1976;

[(bb) section 20 (appeals) or 27 (reference to court for declaration of parentage) of the Child Support Act 1991;] or

(c) the High Court's inherent jurisdiction with respect to children,

have been commenced in or transferred to any court (whether or not by virtue of an order under this Schedule), any other specified family proceedings which may affect, or are otherwise connected with, the child may, in specified circumstances, only be commenced in that court.

(2) A class of court specified in an order under this Schedule may be described by reference to a description of proceedings and may include different levels of court.

Transfer of proceedings

2 – (1) The Lord Chancellor may by order provide that in specified circumstances the whole, or any specified part of, specified proceedings to which this paragraph applies shall be transferred to–

(a) a specified level of court;

(b) a court which falls within a specified class of court; or

(b) a particular court determined in accordance with, or specified in, the order.

(2) Any order under this paragraph may provide for the transfer to be made at any stage, or specified stage, of the proceedings and whether or not the proceedings, or any part of them, have already been transferred.

(3) The proceedings to which this paragraph applies are–

(a) any proceedings under this Act;

(b) any proceedings under the Adoption Act 1976;

(bb) section 20 (appeals) or 27 (reference to court for declaration of parentage) of the Child Support Act 1991;

(c) any other proceedings which–

    (i) are family proceedings for the purposes of this Act, other than proceedings under the inherent jurisdiction of the High Court; and

    (ii) may affect, or are otherwise connected with, the child concerned.

(4) Proceedings to which this paragraph applies by virtue of sub-paragraph (3)(c) may only be transferred in accordance with the provisions of an order made under this paragraph for the purpose of consolidating them with proceedings under–

    (a) this Act;

    (b) the Adoption Act 1976; or

    (b) the High Court's inherent jurisdiction with respect to children.

(2) An order under this paragraph may make such provision as the Lord Chancellor thinks appropriate for excluding proceedings to which this paragraph applies from the operation of any enactment which would otherwise govern the transfer of those proceedings, or any part of them.

Hearings by single justice

3 – (1) In such circumstances as the Lord Chancellor may by order specify–

    (a) the jurisdiction of a magistrates' court to make an emergency protection order;

    (b) any specified question with respect to the transfer of specified proceedings to or from a magistrates' court in accordance with the provisions of an order under paragraph 2,

may be exercised by a single justice.

(2) Any provision made under this paragraph shall be without prejudice to any other enactment or rule of law relating to the functions which may be performed by a single justice of the peace.

General

4 – (1) For the purposes of this Schedule–

    (a) the commencement of proceedings under this Act includes the making of any application under this Act in the course of proceedings (whether or not those proceedings are proceedings under this Act); and

    (b) there are three levels of court, that is to say the High Court, any county court and any magistrates' court.

(2) In this Schedule 'specified' means specified by an order made under this Schedule.

(3) Any order under paragraph 1 may make provision as to the effect of commencing proceedings in contravention of any of the provisions of the order.

(4) An order under paragraph 2 may make provision as to the effect of a failure to comply with any of the provisions of the order.

(5) An order under this Schedule may–

    (a) make such consequential, incidental or transitional provision as the Lord

Chancellor considers expedient, including provision amending any other enactment so far as it concerns the jurisdiction of any court or justice of the peace;

(b) make provision for treating proceedings which are–

    (i) in part proceedings of a kind mentioned in paragraph (a) or (b) of paragraph 2(3); and

    (ii) in part proceedings of a kind mentioned in paragraph (c) of paragraph 2(3),

as consisting entirely of proceedings of one or other of those kinds, for the purposes of the application of any order made under paragraph 2.

SCHEDULE 12

MINOR AMENDMENTS

Schedule 12
This schedule sets out all the minor amendments that were made to other legislation as a consequence of this Act.

The Custody of Children Act 1891 (c. 3)

1. The Custody of Children Act 1891 (which contains miscellaneous obsolete provisions with respect to the custody of children) shall cease to have effect.

The Children and Young Persons Act 1933 (c. 12)

2. In section 1(2)(a) of the Children and Young Persons Act 1933 (cruelty to persons under sixteen), after the words "young person" there shall be inserted ", or the legal guardian of a child or young person,".

3. Section 40 of that Act shall cease to have effect.

The Education Act 1944 (c. 31)

4. In section 40(1) of the Education Act 1944 (enforcement of school attendance), the words from "or to imprisonment" to the end shall cease to have effect.

The Marriage Act 1949 (c. 76)

5. – (1) In section 3 of the Marriage Act 1949 (consent required to the marriage of a child by common licence or superintendent registrar's certificate), in subsection (1) for the words "the Second Schedule to this Act" there shall be substituted "subsection (1A) of this section".

(2) After that subsection there shall be inserted-

"(1A) The consents are-

- (a) subject to paragraphs (b) to (d) of this subsection, the consent of-
  - (i) each parent (if any) of the child who has parental responsibility for him; and
  - (ii) each guardian (if any) of the child;
- (b) where a residence order is in force with respect to the child, the consent of the person or persons with whom he lives, or is to live, as a result of the order (in substitution for the consents mentioned in paragraph (a) of this subsection);
- (c) where a care order is in force with respect to the child, the consent of the local authority designated in the order (in addition to the consents mentioned in paragraph (a) of this subsection);
- (d) where neither paragraph (b) nor (c) of this subsection applies but a residence order was in force with respect to the child immediately before he reached the age of sixteen, the consent of the person or persons with whom he lived, or was to live, as a result of the order (in substitution for the consents mentioned in paragraph (a) of this subsection).

(1B)   In this section

"guardian of a child",

"parental responsibility",

"residence order" and

"care order" have the same meaning as in the Children Act 1989.

The Births and Deaths Registration Act 1953 (c. 20)

6. – (1) Sections 10 and 10A of the Births and Deaths Registration Act 1953 (registration of father, and re-registration, where parents not married) shall be amended as follows.

(2) In sections 10(1) and 10A(1) for paragraph (d) there shall be substituted-

- (d) at the request of the mother or that person on production of-
  - (i) a copy of a parental responsibility agreement made between them in relation to the child; and
  - (ii) a declaration in the prescribed form by the person making the request stating that the agreement was made in compliance with section 4 of the Children Act 1989 and has not been brought to an end by an order of a court; or
- (e) at the request of the mother or that person on production of-
  - (i) a certified copy of an order under section 4 of the Children Act 1989 giving that person parental responsibility for the child; and
  - (ii) a declaration in the prescribed form by the person making the request stating that the order has not been brought to an end by an order of a court;

> or
>
> (f) at the request of the mother or that person on production of-
>
>> (i) a certified copy of an order under paragraph 1 of Schedule 1 to the Children Act 1989 which requires that person to make any financial provision for the child and which is not an order falling within paragraph 4(3) of that Schedule; and
>>
>> (ii) a declaration in the prescribed form by the person making the request stating that the order has not been discharged by an order of a court; or
>
> (g) at the request of the mother or that person on production of-
>
>> (i) a certified copy of any of the orders which are mentioned in subsection (1A) of this section which has been made in relation to the child; and
>>
>> (ii) a declaration in the prescribed form by the person making the request stating that the order has not been brought to an end or discharged by an order of a court.

"(3) After sections 10(1) and 10A(1) there shall be inserted-

"(1A) The orders are-

> (a) an order under section 4 of the Family Law Reform Act 1987 that that person shall have all the parental rights and duties with respect to the child;
>
> (b) an order that that person shall have custody or care and control or legal custody of the child made under section 9 of the Guardianship of Minors Act 1971 at a time when such an order could only be made in favour of a parent;
>
> (c) an order under section 9 or 11B of that Act which requires that person to make any financial provision in relation to the child;
>
> (d) an order under section 4 of the Affiliation Proceedings Act 1957 naming that person as putative father of the child.

(4) In section 10(2) for the words "or (d)" there shall be substituted "to (g)".

(5) In section 10(3) for the words from " "relevant order" " to the end there shall be substituted

"parental responsibility agreement" has the same meaning as in the Children Act 1989

(6) In section 10A(2) in paragraphs (b) and (c) for the words "paragraph (d)" in both places where they occur there shall be substituted "any of paragraphs (d) to (g)".

The Army Act 1955 (c. 18)

7. In section 151 of the Army Act 1955 (deductions from pay for maintenance of wife or child), in subsection (1A)(a) for the words "in the care of a local authority in England or Wales" there shall be substituted "being looked after by a local authority in England or Wales (within the meaning of the Children Act 1989)".

8. – (1) Schedule 5A to that Act (powers of court on trial of civilian) shall be amended as follows.

(2) For paragraphs 7(3) and (4) there shall be substituted-

(3) While an authorisation under a reception order is in force the order shall (subject to sub-paragraph (4) below) be deemed to be a care order for the purposes of the Children Act 1989, and the authorised authority shall be deemed to be the authority designated in that deemed care order.

(3A) In sub-paragraph (3) above

"care order" means a care order which is not an interim care order under section 38 of the Children Act 1989.

(4) The Children Act 1989 shall apply to a reception order which is deemed to be a care order by virtue of sub-paragraph (3) above as if sections 31(8) (designated local authority), 91 (duration of care order etc.) and 101 (effect of orders as between different jurisdictions) were omitted.

(3) In sub-paragraph (5)(c) for the words from "attains" to the end there shall be substituted "attains 18 years of age".

(4) In paragraph 8(1) for the words "Children and Young Persons Act 1969" there shall be substituted "Children Act 1989".

The Air Force Act 1955 (c. 19)

9. Section 151(1A) of the Air Force Act 1955 (deductions from pay for maintenance of wife or child) shall have effect subject to the amendment that is set out in paragraph 7 in relation to section 151(1A) of the Army Act 1955.

10. Schedule 5A to that Act (powers of court on trial of civilian) shall have effect subject to the amendments that are set out in paragraph 8(2) to (4) in relation to Schedule 5A to the Army Act 1955.

The Sexual Offences Act 1956 (c. 69)

11. In section 19(3) of the Sexual Offences Act 1956 (abduction of unmarried girl under eighteen from parent or guardian) for the words "the lawful care or charge of" there shall be substituted "parental responsibility for or care of".

12. In section 20(2) of that Act (abduction of unmarried girl under sixteen from parent or guardian) for the words "the lawful care or charge of" there shall be substituted "parental responsibility for or care of".

13. In section 21(3) of that Act (abduction of defective from parent or guardian) for the words "the lawful care or charge of" there shall be substituted "parental responsibility for or care of".

14. In section 28 of that Act (causing or encouraging prostitution of, intercourse with, or indecent assault on, girl under sixteen) for subsections (3) and (4) there shall be substituted-

(3) The persons who are to be treated for the purposes of this section as responsible for a girl are (subject to subsection (4) of this section)-

(a) her parents;

(b) any person who is not a parent of hers but who has parental responsibility for her; and

(c) any person who has care of her.

(4) An individual falling within subsection (3)(a) or (b) of this section is not to be treated as responsible for a girl if-

(a) a residence order under the Children Act 1989 is in force with respect to her and he is not named in the order as the person with whom she is to live; or

(b) a care order under that Act is in force with respect to her.

15. Section 38 of that Act (power of court to divest person of authority over girl or boy in case of incest) shall cease to have effect.

16. – (1) In section 43 of that Act (power to search for and recover woman detained for immoral purposes), in subsection (5) for the words "the lawful care or charge of" there shall be substituted "parental responsibility for or care of".

(2) In subsection (6) of that section, for the words "section forty of the Children and Young Persons Act 1933" there shall be substituted "Part V of the Children Act 1989".

17. After section 46 of that Act there shall be inserted-

Meaning of "parental responsibility".

46A. In this Act

"parental responsibility" has the same meaning as in the Children Act 1989.

The Naval Discipline Act 1957 (c. 53)

18. Schedule 4A to the Naval Discipline Act 1957 (powers of court on trial of civilian) shall have effect subject to the amendments that are set out in paragraph 8(2) to (4) in relation to Schedule 5A to the Army Act 1955.

The Children and Young Persons Act 1963 (c. 37)

19. Section 3 of the Children and Young Persons Act 1963 (children and young persons beyond control) shall cease to have effect.

The Children and Young Persons Act 1969 (c. 54)

20. In section 5 of the Children and Young Persons Act 1969 (restrictions on criminal proceedings for offences by young persons), in subsection (2), for the words "section 1 of this Act" there shall be substituted " Part IV of the Children Act 1989".

21. After section 7(7) of that Act (alteration in treatment of young offenders, etc.) there shall be inserted-

(7B) An order under subsection (7)(c) of this section shall not require a person to enter into a recognisance-

(a) for an amount exceeding œ1,000; or
(b) for a period exceeding-
  (i) three years; or
  (ii) where the young person concerned will attain the age of eighteen in a period shorter than three years, that shorter period.

(7C) Section 120 of the Magistrates' Courts Act 1980 shall apply to a recognisance entered into in pursuance of an order under subsection (7)(c) of this section as it applies to a recognisance to keep the peace.

22. In section 12A of that Act (young offenders) for subsections (1) and (2) there shall be substituted-

(1) This subsection applies to any supervision order made under section 7(7) of this Act unless it requires the supervised person to comply with directions given by the supervisor under section 12(2) of this Act.

23. After that section there shall be inserted-

12AA. – (1) Where the conditions mentioned in subsection (6) of this section are satisfied, a supervision order may impose a requirement ("a residence requirement") that a child or young person shall live for a specified period in local authority accommodation.

(2) A residence requirement shall designate the local authority who are to receive the child or young person and that authority shall be the authority in whose area the child or young person resides.

(3) The court shall not impose a residence requirement without first consulting the designated authority.

(4) A residence requirement may stipulate that the child or young person shall not live with a named person.

(5) The maximum period which may be specified in a residence requirement is six months.

(6) The conditions are that-

(a) a supervision order has previously been made in respect of the child or young person;
(b) that order imposed-
  (i) a requirement under section 12A(3) of this Act; or
  (ii) a residence requirement;
(c) he is found guilty of an offence which-
  (i) was committed while that order was in force;
  (ii) if it had been committed by a person over the age of twenty-one, would have been punishable with imprisonment; and

(iii) in the opinion of the court is serious; and

(d) the court is satisfied that the behaviour which constituted the offence was due, to a significant extent, to the circumstances in which he was living,

except that the condition in paragraph (d) of this subsection does not apply where the condition in paragraph (b)(ii) is satisfied.

(7) For the purposes of satisfying itself as mentioned in subsection (6)(d) of this section, the court shall obtain a social inquiry report which makes particular reference to the circumstances in which the child or young person was living.

(8) Subsection (7) of this section does not apply if the court already has before it a social inquiry report which contains sufficient information about the circumstances in which the child or young person was living.

(9) A court shall not include a residence requirement in respect of a child or young person who is not legally represented at the relevant time in that court unless-

(a) he has applied for legal aid for the purposes of the proceedings and the application was refused on the ground that it did not appear that his resources were such that he required assistance; or

(b) he has been informed of his right to apply for legal aid for the purposes of the proceedings and has had the opportunity to do so, but nevertheless refused or failed to apply.

(10) In subsection (9) of this section-

(a) "the relevant time" means the time when the court is considering whether or not to impose the requirement; and

(b) "the proceedings" means-
(i) the whole proceedings; or
(ii) the part of the proceedings relating to the imposition of the requirement.

(11) A supervision order imposing a residence requirement may also impose any of the requirements mentioned in sections 12, 12A, 12B or 12C of this Act.

(12) In this section

"social inquiry report" has the same meaning as in section 2 of the Criminal Justice Act 1982.

24. – (1) In section 15 of that Act (variation and discharge of supervision orders), in subsections (1)(a), (2A), (3)(e) and (4) after the word "12A", in each place where it occurs, there shall be inserted "12AA".

(2) In subsection (4) of that section for the words "(not being a juvenile court)" there shall be substituted "other than a juvenile court".

25. – (1) In section 16 of that Act (provisions supplementary to section 15), in subsection (3) for the words "either direct" to the end there shall be substituted-

(i) direct that he be released forthwith; or

(ii) remand him.

(2) In subsection (4) of that section-

    (a) in paragraph (a) for the words "an interim order made by virtue of" there shall be substituted "a remand under";

    (b) in paragraph (b) for the words "makes an interim order in respect of" there shall be substituted "remands", and

    (c) for the words "make an interim order in respect of" there shall be substituted "remand".

(3) In subsections (5)(b) and (c) and (6)(a) after the word "12A", in each place where it occurs, there shall be inserted "12AA".

26. For section 23 of that Act (remand to care of local authorities etc.) there shall be substituted-

23. – (1) Where a court-

    (a) remands or commits for trial a child charged with homicide or remands a child convicted of homicide; or

    (b) remands a young person charged with or convicted of one or more offences or commits him for trial or sentence,

and he is not released on bail, then, unless he is a young person who is certified by the court to be of unruly character, the court shall remand him to local authority accommodation.

(2) A court remanding a person to local authority accommodation shall designate the authority who are to receive him and that authority shall be the authority in whose area it appears to the court that-

    (a) he resides; or

    (b) the offence or one of the offences was committed.

(3) Where a person is remanded to local authority accommodation, it shall be lawful for any person acting on behalf of the designated authority to detain him.

(4) The court shall not certify a young person as being of unruly character unless-

    (a) he cannot safely be remanded to local authority accommodation; and

    (b) the conditions prescribed by order made by the Secretary of State under this subsection are satisfied in relation to him.

(5) Where the court certifies that a young person is of unruly character, it shall commit him-

    (a) to a remand centre, if it has been notified that such a centre is available for the reception from the court of such persons; and

    (b) to a prison, if it has not been so notified.

(6) Where a young person is remanded to local authority accommodation, a court may, on the application of the designated authority, certify him to be of unruly character

in accordance with subsection (4) of this section (and on so doing he shall cease to be remanded to local authority accommodation and subsection (5) of this section shall apply).

(7) For the purposes of subsection (6) of this section,

"a court" means-

(a) the court which remanded the young person; or
(b) any magistrates' court having jurisdiction in the place where that person is for the time being,

and in this section

"court" and

"magistrates' court" include a justice.

(8) This section has effect subject to-

(a) section 37 of the Magistrates' Courts Act 1980 (committal to the Crown Court with a view to a sentence of detention in a young offender institution); and
(b) section 128(7) of that Act (remands to the custody of a constable for periods of not more than three days),

but section 128(7) shall have effect in relation to a child or young person as if for the reference to three clear days there were substituted a reference to twenty-four hours.

27. – (1) In section 32 of that Act (detention of absentees), for subsection (1A) there shall be substituted the following subsections-

(1A) If a child or young person is absent, without the consent of the responsible person-

(a) from a place of safety to which he has been taken under section 16(3) of this Act; or
(b) from local authority accommodation-
　(i) in which he is required to live under section 12AA of this Act; or
　(ii) to which he has been remanded under section 23(1) of this Act,

he may be arrested by a constable anywhere in the United Kingdom or Channel Islands without a warrant.

(1B) A person so arrested shall be conducted to-

(a) the place of safety;
(b) the local authority accommodation; or
(c) such other place as the responsible person may direct,

at the responsible person's expense.

(1C) In this section

"the responsible person" means the person who made the arrangements under section 16(3) of this Act or, as the case may be, the authority designated under section 12AA or 23 of this Act.

(2) In subsection (2B) of that section for the words "person referred to in subsection (1A)(a) or (b) (as the case may be) of this section" there shall be substituted "responsible person".

28. In section 34(1) of that Act (transitional modifications of Part I for persons of specified ages)-

    (a) in paragraph (a), for the words "13(2) or 28(4) or (5)" there shall be substituted "or 13(2)"; and

    (b) in paragraph (e), for the words "section 23(2) or (3)" there shall be substituted "section 23(4) to (6)".

29. In section 70(1) of that Act (interpretation)-

    (a) after the definition of "local authority" there shall be inserted-
"local authority accommodation" means accommodation provided by or on behalf of a local authority (within the meaning of the Children Act 1989) "; and

    (b) in the definition of "reside" for "12(4) and (5)" there shall be substituted "12B(1) and (2)".

30. In section 73 of that Act (extent, etc.)-

    (a) in subsection (4)(a) for "32(1), (3) and (4)" there shall be substituted "32(1) to (1C) and (2A) to (4)"; and

    (b) in subsection (6) for "32(1), (1A)" there shall be substituted "32(1) to (1C)".

The Matrimonial Causes Act 1973 (c. 18)

31. For section 41 of the Matrimonial Causes Act 1973 (restrictions on decrees for dissolution, annulment or separation affecting children) there shall be substituted-

41. – (1) In any proceedings for a decree of divorce or nullity of marriage, or a decree of judicial separation, the court shall consider-

    (a) whether there are any children of the family to whom this section applies; and

    (b) where there are any such children, whether (in the light of the arrangements which have been, or are proposed to be, made for their upbringing and welfare) it should exercise any of its powers under the Children Act 1989 with respect to any of them.

(2) Where, in any case to which this section applies, it appears to the court that-

    (a) the circumstances of the case require it, or are likely to require it, to exercise any of its powers under the Act of 1989 with respect to any such child;

    (b) it is not in a position to exercise that power or (as the case may be) those powers without giving further consideration to the case; and

(c) there are exceptional circumstances which make it desirable in the interests of the child that the court should give a direction under this section,

it may direct that the decree of divorce or nullity is not to be made absolute, or that the decree of judicial separation is not to be granted, until the court orders otherwise.

(3) This section applies to-

(a) any child of the family who has not reached the age of sixteen at the date when the court considers the case in accordance with the requirements of this section; and

(b) any child of the family who has reached that age at that date and in relation to whom the court directs that this section shall apply.

32. In section 42 of that Act, subsection (3) (declaration by court that party to marriage unfit to have custody of children of family) shall cease to have effect.

33. In section 52(1) of that Act (interpretation), in the definition of "child of the family", for the words "has been boarded-out with those parties" there shall be substituted "is placed with those parties as foster parents".

The National Health Service Act 1977 (c. 49)

34. In Schedule 8 to the National Health Service Act 1977 (functions of local social services authorities), the following sub-paragraph shall be added at the end of paragraph 2-

(4A) This paragraph does not apply in relation to persons under the age of 18.

The Child Care Act 1980 (c. 5)

35. Until the repeal of the Child Care Act 1980 by this Act takes effect, the definition of

"parent" in section 87 of that Act shall have effect as if it applied only in relation to Part I and sections 13, 24, 64 and 65 of that Act (provisions excluded by section 2(1)(f) of the Family Law Reform Act 1987 from the application of the general rule in that Act governing the meaning of references to relationships between persons).

The Education Act 1981 (c. 60)

36. The following section shall be inserted in the Education Act 1981, after section 3-

3A. – (1) A local authority may make such arrangements as they think fit to enable any child in respect of whom they maintain a statement under section 7 to attend an establishment outside England and Wales which specialises in providing for children with special needs.

(2) In subsection (1) above

"children with special needs" means children who have particular needs which would be special educational needs if those children were in England and Wales.

(3) Where an authority make arrangements under this section with respect to a child, those arrangements may, in particular, include contributing to or paying-

  (a) fees charged by the establishment;
  (b) expenses reasonably incurred in maintaining him while he is at the establishment or travelling to or from it;
  (c) those travelling expenses;
  (d) expenses reasonably incurred by any person accompanying him while he is travelling or staying at the establishment.

(4) This section is not to be taken as in any way limiting any other powers of a local education authority.

The Child Abduction Act 1984 (c. 37)

37. – (1) Section 1 of the Child Abduction Act 1984 (offence of abduction by parent, etc.) shall be amended as follows.

(2) For subsections (2) to (4) there shall be substituted-

(2) A person is connected with a child for the purposes of this section if-

  (a) he is a parent of the child; or
  (b) in the case of a child whose parents were not married to each other at the time of his birth, there are reasonable grounds for believing that he is the father of the child; or
  (c) he is a guardian of the child; or
  (d) he is a person in whose favour a residence order is in force with respect to the child; or
  (e) he has custody of the child.

(3) In this section

"the appropriate consent", in relation to a child, means-

  (a) the consent of each of the following-
    (i) the child's mother;
    (ii) the child's father, if he has parental responsibility for him;
    (iii) any guardian of the child;
    (iv) any person in whose favour a residence order is in force with respect to the child;
    (v) any person who has custody of the child; or
  (b) the leave of the court granted under or by virtue of any provision of Part II of the Children Act 1989; or
  (c) if any person has custody of the child, the leave of the court which awarded custody to him.

(4) A person does not commit an offence under this section by taking or sending a child out of the United Kingdom without obtaining the appropriate consent if-

(a) he is a person in whose favour there is a residence order in force with respect to the child, and

(b) he takes or sends him out of the United Kingdom for a period of less than one month.

(4A) Subsection (4) above does not apply if the person taking or sending the child out of the United Kingdom does so in breach of an order under Part II of the Children Act 1989.

(3) In subsection (5) for the words from "but" to the end there shall be substituted-

(5A) Subsection (5)(c) above does not apply if-

(a) the person who refused to consent is a person-
(i) in whose favour there is a residence order in force with respect to the child; or
(ii) who has custody of the child; or

(b) the person taking or sending the child out of the United Kingdom is, by so acting, in breach of an order made by a court in the United Kingdom.

(4) For subsection (7) there shall be substituted-

(7) For the purposes of this section-

(a) "guardian of a child",
"residence order" and
"parental responsibility" have the same meaning as in the Children Act 1989; and

(b) a person shall be treated as having custody of a child if there is in force an order of a court in the United Kingdom awarding him (whether solely or jointly with another person) custody, legal custody or care and control of the child.

(5) In subsection (8) for the words from "or voluntary organisation" to "custodianship proceedings or" there shall be substituted "detained in a place of safety, remanded to a local authority accommodation or the subject of".

38. – (1) In section 2 of that Act (offence of abduction of child by other persons), in subsection (1) for the words from "Subject" to "above" there shall be substituted "Subject to subsection (3) below, a person, other than one mentioned in subsection (2) below."

(2) For subsection (2) of that section there shall be substituted-

(2) The persons are-

(a) where the father and mother of the child in question were married to each other at the time of his birth, the child's father and mother;

(b) where the father and mother of the child in question were not married to each other at the time of his birth, the child's mother; and

(c) any other person mentioned in section 1(2)(c) to (e) above.

(3) In proceedings against any person for an offence under this section, it shall be a defence for that person to prove-

(a) where the father and mother of the child in question were not married to each other at the time of his birth-
(i) that he is the child's father; or
(ii) that, at the time of the alleged offence, he believed, on reasonable grounds, that he was the child's father; or
(b) that, at the time of the alleged offence, he believed that the child had attained the age of sixteen.

39. At the end of section 3 of that Act (construction of references to taking, sending and detaining) there shall be added "and"

(d) references to a child's parents and to a child whose parents were (or were not) married to each other at the time of his birth shall be construed in accordance with section 1 of the Family Law Reform Act 1987 (which extends their meaning).

40. – (1) The Schedule to that Act (modifications of section 1 for children in certain cases) shall be amended as follows.

(2) In paragraph 1(1) for the words "or voluntary organisation" there shall be substituted "within the meaning of the Children Act 1989".

(3) For paragraph 2(1) there shall be substituted-

(1) This paragraph applies in the case of a child who is-

(a) detained in a place of safety under section 16(3) of the Children and Young Persons Act 1969; or
(b) remanded to local authority accommodation under section 23 of that Act.

(4) In paragraph 3(1)-

(a) in paragraph (a) for the words "section 14 of the Children Act 1975" there shall be substituted "section 18 of the Adoption Act 1976"; and
(b) in paragraph (d) for the words "section 25 of the Children Act 1975 or section 53 of the Adoption Act 1958" there shall be substituted "section 55 of the Adoption Act 1976".

(5) In paragraph 3(2)(a)-

(a) in sub-paragraph (i), for the words from "order or," to "Children Act 1975" there shall be substituted "section 18 order or, if the section 18 order has been varied under section 21 of that Act so as to give parental responsibility to another agency", and
(b) in sub-paragraph (ii), for the words "(c) or (e)" there shall be substituted "or (c)".

(6) At the end of paragraph 3 there shall be added-

"(3) Sub-paragraph (2) above shall be construed as if the references to the court included, in any case where the court is a magistrates' court, a reference to any magistrates' court acting for the same area as that court".

(7) For paragraph 5 there shall be substituted-

"5. In this Schedule-

(a) "adoption agency" and "adoption order" have the same meaning as in the Adoption Act 1976; and
(b) "area", in relation to a magistrates' court, means the petty sessions area (within the meaning of the Justices of the Peace Act 1979) for which the court is appointed."

The Foster Children (Scotland) Act 1984 (c. 56)

41. In section 1 of the Foster Children (Scotland) Act 1984 (definition of foster child)-

(a) for the words "he is- (a)" there shall be substituted "(a) he is"; and
(b) the words "for a period of more than 6 days" and the words from "The period" to the end shall cease to have effect.

42. In section 2(2) of that Act (exceptions to section 1), for paragraph (f) there shall be substituted-

"(f) if he has been in that person's care for a period of less than 28 days and that person does not intend to undertake his care for any longer period."

43. In section 7(1) of that Act (persons disqualified from keeping foster children)-

(a) the word "or" at the end of paragraph (e) shall be omitted; and
(b) after paragraph (f) there shall be inserted "or"
(g) he is disqualified from fostering a child privately (within the meaning of the Children Act 1989) by regulations made under section 68 of that Act,

The Disabled Persons (Services, Consultation and Representation) Act 1986 (c. 33)

44. In section 2(5) of the Disabled Persons (Services, Consultation and Representation) Act 1986 (circumstances in which authorised representative has right to visit etc. disabled person), after paragraph (d) there shall be inserted-

"(dd) in accommodation provided by any educational establishment.

"The Legal Aid Act 1988 (c. 34)

45. In paragraph 2 of Part I of Schedule 2 to the Legal Aid Act 1988 (proceedings in magistrates' courts to which the civil legal aid provisions of Part IV of the Act apply), the following sub-paragraph shall be added at the end-

(g) proceedings under the Children Act 1989.

SCHEDULE 13

CONSEQUENTIAL AMENDMENTS

Schedule 13
This schedule deals with consequential amendments to other legislation.

The Wills Act 1837 (c. 26)

1. In section 1 of the Wills Act 1837 (interpretation), in the definition of "will", for the words "and also to a disposition by will and testament or devise of the custody and tuition of any child" there shall be substituted "and also to an appointment by will of a guardian of a child".

The Children and Young Persons Act 1933 (c. 12)

2. In section 1(1) of the Children and Young Persons Act 1933 (cruelty to persons under sixteen) for the words "has the custody, charge or care of" there shall be substituted "has responsibility for".

3. In the following sections of that Act-

   (a) 3(1) (allowing persons under sixteen to be in brothels);
   (b) 4(1) and (2) (causing or allowing persons under sixteen to be used for begging);
   (c) 11 (exposing children under twelve to risk of burning); and
   (d) 25(1) (restrictions on persons under eighteen going abroad for the purpose of performing for profit),

   for the words "the custody, charge or care of" there shall, in each case, be substituted "responsibility for".

4. In section 10(1A) of that Act (vagrants preventing children from receiving education), for the words from "to bring the child" to the end there shall be substituted "to make an application in respect of the child or young person for an education supervision order under section 36 of the Children Act 1989".

5. For section 17 of that Act (interpretation of Part I) there shall be substituted the following section-

17. – (1) For the purposes of this Part of this Act, the following shall be presumed to have responsibility for a child or young person-

   (a) any person who-
      (i) has parental responsibility for him (within the meaning of the Children Act 1989); or
      (ii) is otherwise legally liable to maintain him; and
   (b) any person who has care of him.

(2) A person who is presumed to be responsible for a child or young person by virtue of subsection (1)(a) shall not be taken to have ceased to be responsible for him by reason only that he does not have care of him.

6. – (1) In section 34 of that Act (attendance at court of parent of child or young person charged with an offence etc.), in subsection (1) after the word "offence" there shall be inserted "is the subject of an application for a care or supervision order under Part IV of the Children Act 1989".

(2) In subsection (7) of that section after the words "Children and Young Persons Act 1969" there shall be inserted "or Part IV of the Children Act 1989".

(3) After subsection (7) of that section there shall be inserted-

"(7A) If it appears that at the time of his arrest the child or young person is being provided with accommodation by or on behalf of a local authority under section 20 of the Children Act 1989, the local authority shall also be informed as described in subsection (3) above as soon as it is reasonably practicable to do so.

7. In section 107(1) of that Act (interpretation)-

   (a) in the definition of "guardian", for the words "charge of or control over" there shall be substituted "care of";
   (b) for the definition of legal guardian there shall be substituted-

"legal guardian", in relation to a child or young person, means a guardian of a child as defined in the Children Act 1989

The Education Act 1944 (c. 31)

8. – (1) Section 40 of the Education Act 1944 (enforcement of school attendance) shall be amended as follows.

(2) For subsection (2) there shall be substituted-

(2) Proceedings for such offences shall not be instituted except by a local education authority.

(2A) Before instituting such proceedings the local education authority shall consider whether it would be appropriate, instead of or as well as instituting the proceedings, to apply for an education supervision order with respect to the child.

(3) For subsections (3) and (4) there shall be substituted-

(3) The court-

   (a) by which a person is convicted of an offence against section 37 of this Act; or
   (b) before which a person is charged with an offence under section 39 of this Act,

may direct the local education authority instituting the proceedings to apply for an education supervision order with respect to the child unless the authority, having consulted the appropriate local authority, decide that the child's welfare will be satisfactorily safeguarded even though no education supervision order is made.

(3A) Where, following such a direction, a local education authority decide not to apply for an education supervision order they shall inform the court of the reasons for their decision.

(3B) Unless the court has directed otherwise, the information required under subsection (3A) shall be given to the court before the end of the period of eight weeks beginning with the date on which the direction was given.

(4) Where-

    (a) a local education authority apply for an education supervision order with respect to a child who is the subject of a school attendance order; and

    (b) the court decides that section 36(3) of the Children Act 1989 prevents it from making the order;

the court may direct that the school attendance order shall cease to be in force.

(4) After subsection (4) there shall be inserted-

(5) In this section-

"appropriate local authority" has the same meaning as in section 36(9) of the Children Act 1989; and

"education supervision order" means an education supervision order under that Act.

9. In section 71 of that Act (complaints with respect to independent schools), the following paragraph shall be added after paragraph (d), in subsection (1)-

    (e) there has been a failure, in relation to a child provided with accommodation by the school, to comply with the duty imposed by section 87 of the Children Act 1989 (welfare of children accommodated in independent schools);";

10. After section 114(1C) of that Act (interpretation) there shall be inserted the following subsections-

(1D)   In this Act, unless the context otherwise requires,

"parent", in relation to a child or young person, includes any person-

(a) who is not a parent of his but who has parental responsibility for him, or
(b) who has care of him,

except for the purposes of the enactments mentioned in subsection (1E) of this section, where it only includes such a person if he is an individual.

(1E) The enactments are-

    (a) sections 5(4), 15(2) and (6), 31 and 65(1) of, and paragraph 7(6) of Schedule 2 to, the Education (No. 2) Act 1986; and

    (b) sections 53(8), 54(2), 58(5)(k), 60 and 61 of the Education Reform Act 1988.

(1F)   For the purposes of subsection (1D) of this section-

(a) "parental responsibility" has the same meaning as in the Children Act 1989; and

(b) in determining whether an individual has care of a child or young person any absence of the child or young person at a hospital or boarding school and any other temporary absence shall be disregarded.

The National Assistance Act 1948 (c. 29)

11. – (1) In section 21(1)(a) of the National Assistance Act 1948 (persons for whom local authority is to provide residential accommodation) after the word "persons" there shall be inserted "aged eighteen or over".

(2) In section 29(1) of that Act (welfare arrangements for blind, deaf, dumb and crippled persons) after the words "that is to say persons" and after the words "and other persons" there shall, in each case, be inserted "aged eighteen or over".

The Reserve and Auxiliary Forces (Protection of Civil Interests) Act 1951 (c. 65)

12. For section 2(1)(d) of the Reserve and Auxiliary Forces (Protection of Civil Interests) Act 1951 (cases in which leave of the appropriate court is required before enforcing certain orders for the payment of money), there shall be substituted-

(d) an order for alimony, maintenance or other payment made under sections 21 to 33 of the Matrimonial Causes Act 1973 or made, or having effect as if made, under Schedule 1 to the Children Act 1989."

The Mines and Quarries Act 1954 (c. 70)

13. In section 182(1) of the Mines and Quarries Act 1954 (interpretation), in the definition of "parent", for the words from "or guardian" to first "young person" there shall be substituted "of a young person or any person who is not a parent of his but who has parental responsibility for him (within the meaning of the Children Act 1989)".

The Administration of Justice Act 1960 (c. 65)

14. In section 12 of the Administration of Justice Act 1960 (publication of information relating to proceedings in private), in subsection (1) for paragraph (a) there shall be substituted-

(a) where the proceedings-
   (i) relate to the exercise of the inherent jurisdiction of the High Court with respect to minors;
   (ii) are brought under the Children Act 1989; or
   (iii) otherwise relate wholly or mainly to the maintenance or upbringing of a minor;

The Factories Act 1961 (c. 34)

15. In section 176(1) of the Factories Act 1961 (interpretation), in the definition of "parent", for the words from "or guardian" to first "young person" there shall be substituted "of a child or young person or any person who is not a parent of his but who has parental responsibility for him (within the meaning of the Children Act 1989)".

The Criminal Justice Act 1967 (c. 80)

16. In section 67(1A)(c) of the Criminal Justice Act 1967 (computation of sentences of imprisonment passed in England and Wales) for the words "in the care of a local authority" there shall be substituted "remanded to local authority accommodation."

The Health Services and Public Health Act 1968 (c. 46)

17. – (1) In section 64(3)(a) of the Health Services and Public Health Act 1968 (meaning of "relevant enactments" in relation to power of Minister of Health or Secretary of State to provide financial assistance), for sub-paragraph (xix) inserted by paragraph 19 of Schedule 5 to the Child Care Act 1980 there shall be substituted-

"(xx) the Children Act 1989."

(2) In section 65(3)(b) of that Act (meaning of "relevant enactments" in relation to power of local authority to provide financial and other assistance), for sub-paragraph (xx) inserted by paragraph 20 of Schedule 5 to the Child Care Act 1980 there shall be substituted-

"(xxi) the Children Act 1989.

The Social Work (Scotland) Act 1968 (c. 49)

18. In section 2(2) of the Social Work (Scotland) Act 1968 (matters referred to social work committee) after paragraph (j) there shall be inserted-

"(k) section 19 and Part X of the Children Act 1989,

19. In section 5(2)(c) of that Act (power of Secretary of State to make regulations) for the words "and (j)" there shall be substituted "to (k)".

20. In section 21(3) of that Act (mode of provision of accommodation and maintenance) for the words "section 21 of the Child Care Act 1980" there shall be substituted "section 23 of the Children Act 1989".

21. In section 74(6) of that Act (parent of child in residential establishment moving to England or Wales) for the words from "Children and Young Persons Act 1969" to the end there shall be substituted "Children Act 1989, but as if section 31(8) were omitted".

22. In section 75(2) of that Act (parent of child subject to care order etc. moving to Scotland), for the words "Children and Young Persons Act 1969" there shall be substituted "Children Act 1989".

23. In section 86(3) of that Act (meaning of ordinary residence for purpose of adjustments between authority providing accommodation and authority of area of residence), the words "the Child Care Act 1980 or" shall be omitted and after the words "education authority" there shall be inserted "or placed with local authority foster parents under the Children Act 1989".

The Civil Evidence Act 1968 (c. 64)

24. In section 12(5)(b) of the Civil Evidence Act 1968 (findings of paternity etc. as evidence in civil proceedings - meaning of "relevant proceedings") for sub-paragraph (iv) there shall be substituted-

> (iv) paragraph 23 of Schedule 2 to the Children Act 1989.

The Administration of Justice Act 1970 (c. 31)

25. In Schedule 8 to the Administration of Justice Act 1970 (maintenance orders for purposes of Maintenance Orders Act 1958 and the 1970 Act), in paragraph 6 for the words "section 47 or 51 of the Child Care Act 1980" there shall be substituted "paragraph 23 of Schedule 2 to the Children Act 1989".

The Local Authority Social Services Act 1970 (c. 42)

26. – (1) In Schedule 1 to the Local Authority Social Services Act 1970 (enactments conferring functions assigned to social service committee)-

(a) in the entry relating to the Mental Health Act 1959, for the words "sections 8 and 9" there shall be substituted "section 8"; and
(b) in the entry relating to the Children and Young Persons Act 1969, for the words "sections 1, 2 and 9" there shall be substituted "section 9".

(2) At the end of that Schedule there shall be added-

"Children Act 1989.

The whole Act, in so far as it confers functions on a local authority within the meaning of that Act.

Welfare reports.

Consent to application for residence order in respect of child in care.

Family assistance orders.

Functions under Part III of the Act (local authority support for children and families).

Care and supervision.

Protection of children.

Functions in relation to community homes, voluntary homes and voluntary organisations, registered children's homes, private arrangements for fostering children, child minding and day care for young children.

Inspection of children's homes on behalf of Secretary of State.

Research and returns of information.

Functions in relation to children accommodated by health authorities and local education authorities or in residential care, nursing or mental nursing homes or in independent schools."

The Chronically Sick and Disabled Persons Act 1970 (c. 44)

27. After section 28 of the Chronically Sick and Disabled Persons Act 1970 there shall be inserted-

"28A. This Act applies with respect to disabled children in relation to whom a local authority have functions under Part III of the Children Act 1989 as it applies in relation to persons to whom section 29 of the National Assistance Act 1948 applies."

The Courts Act 1971 (c. 23)

28. In Part I of Schedule 9 to the Courts Act 1971 (substitution of references to Crown Court), in the entry relating to the Children and Young Persons Act 1969, for the words "Sections 2(12), 3(8), 16(8), 21(4)(5)" there shall be substituted "Section 16(8).".

The Attachment of Earnings Act 1971 (c. 32)

29. In Schedule 1 to the Attachment of Earnings Act 1971 (maintenance orders to which that Act applies), in paragraph 7, for the words "section 47 or 51 of the Child Care Act 1980" there shall be substituted "paragraph 23 of Schedule 2 to the Children Act 1989".

The Tribunals and Inquiries Act 1971 (c. 62)

30. In Schedule 1 to the Tribunals and Inquiries Act 1971 (tribunals under direct supervision of the Council on Tribunals) for paragraph 4 there shall be substituted-

"Registration of voluntary homes and children's homes under the Children Act 1989.

4. Registered Homes Tribunals constituted under Part III of the Registered Homes Act 1984.

The Local Government Act 1972 (c. 70)

31. – (1) In section 102(1) of the Local Government Act 1972 (appointment of committees) for the words "section 31 of the Child Care Act 1980" there shall be substituted "section 53 of the Children Act 1989".

(2) In Schedule 12A to that Act (access to information: exempt information), in Part III (interpretation), in paragraph 1(1)(b) for the words "section 20 of the Children and Young Persons Act 1969" there shall be substituted "section 31 of the Children Act 1989".

The Employment of Children Act 1973 (c. 24)

32. – (1) In section 2 of the Employment of Children Act 1973 (supervision by education authorities), in subsection (2)(a) for the words "guardian or a person who has actual custody of" there shall be substituted "any person responsible for".

(2) After that subsection there shall be inserted-

"(2A) For the purposes of subsection (2)(a) above a person is responsible for a child-

(a) in England and Wales, if he has parental responsibility for the child or care of him; and
(b) in Scotland, if he is his guardian or has actual custody of him.

The Domicile and Matrimonial Proceedings Act 1973 (c. 45)

33. – (1) In Schedule 1 to the Domicile and Matrimonial Proceedings Act 1973 (proceedings in divorce etc. stayed by reference to proceedings in other jurisdiction), paragraph 11(1) shall be amended as follows-

(a) at the end of the definition of "lump sum" there shall be added "or an order made in equivalent circumstances under Schedule 1 to the Children Act 1989 and of a kind mentioned in paragraph 1(2)(c) of that Schedule";
(b) in the definition of "relevant order", at the end of paragraph (b), there shall be added "or an order made in equivalent circumstances under Schedule 1 to the Children Act 1989 and of a kind mentioned in paragraph 1(2)(a) or (b) of that Schedule";
(c) in paragraph (c) of that definition, after the word "children)" there shall be inserted "or a section 8 order under the Children Act 1989"; and
(d) in paragraph (d) of that definition for the words "the custody, care or control" there shall be substituted "care".

(2) In paragraph 11(3) of that Schedule-

(a) the word "four" shall be omitted; and
(b) for the words "the custody of a child and the education of a child" there shall be substituted "or any provision which could be made by a section 8 order under the Children Act 1989".

The Powers of Criminal Courts Act 1973 (c. 62)

34. In Schedule 3 to the Powers of Criminal Courts Act 1973 (the probation and after-care service and its functions), in paragraph 3(2A) after paragraph (b) there shall be inserted-

and

(c) directions given under paragraph 2 or 3 of Schedule 3 to the Children Act 1989".

The Rehabilitation of Offenders Act 1974 (c. 53)

35. – (1) Section 7(2) of the Rehabilitation of Offenders Act 1974 (limitations on rehabilitation under the Act) shall be amended as follows.

(2) For paragraph (c) there shall be substituted-

(c) in any proceedings relating to adoption, the marriage of any minor, the exercise of the inherent jurisdiction of the High Court with respect to minors or the provision by any person of accommodation, care or schooling for minors;
(cc) in any proceedings brought under the Children Act 1989;

(3) For paragraph (d) there shall be substituted-

(d) in any proceedings relating to the variation or discharge of a supervision order under the Children and Young Persons Act 1969, or on appeal from any such proceedings

The Domestic Proceedings and Magistrates' Courts Act 1978 (c. 22)

36. For section 8 of the Domestic Proceedings and Magistrates' Courts Act 1978 (orders for the custody of children) there shall be substituted-

8.   Where an application is made by a party to a marriage for an order under section 2, 6 or 7 of this Act, then, if there is a child of the family who is under the age of eighteen, the court shall not dismiss or make a final order on the application until it has decided whether to exercise any of its powers under the Children Act 1989 with respect to the child.

37. In section 19(3A)(b) (interim orders) for the words "subsections (2) and" there shall be substituted "subsection".

38. For section 20(12) of that Act (variation and revocation of orders for periodical payments) there shall be substituted-

(12) An application under this section may be made-

(a) where it is for the variation or revocation of an order under section 2, 6, 7 or 19 of this Act for periodical payments, by either party to the marriage in question; and
(b) where it is for the variation of an order under section 2(1)(c), 6 or 7 of this Act

for periodical payments to or in respect of a child, also by the child himself, if he has attained the age of sixteen.

39. – (1) For section 20A of that Act (revival of orders for periodical payments) there shall be substituted-

20A. – (1) Where an order made by a magistrates' court under this Part of this Act for the making of periodical payments to or in respect of a child (other than an interim maintenance order) ceases to have effect-

(a) on the date on which the child attains the age of sixteen, or
(b) at any time after that date but before or on the date on which he attains the age of eighteen,

the child may apply to the court which made the order for an order for its revival.

(2) If on such an application it appears to the court that-

(a) the child is, will be or (if an order were made under this subsection) would be receiving instruction at an educational establishment or undergoing training for a trade, profession or vocation, whether or not while in gainful employment, or
(b) there are special circumstances which justify the making of an order under this subsection,

the court shall have power by order to revive the order from such date as the court may specify, not being earlier than the date of the making of the application.

(3) Any order revived under this section may be varied or revoked under section 20 in the same way as it could have been varied or revoked had it continued in being.

40. In section 23(1) of that Act (supplementary provisions with respect to the variation and revocation of orders) for the words "14(3), 20 or 21" there shall be substituted "20" and for the words "section 20 of this Act" there shall be substituted "that section".

41. – (1) In section 25 of that Act (effect on certain orders of parties living together), in subsection (1)(a) for the words "6 or 11(2)" there shall be substituted "or 6".

(2) In subsection (2) of that section-

(a) in paragraph (a) for the words "6 or 11(2)" there shall be substituted "or 6"; and
(b) after paragraph (a) there shall be inserted "or".

42. In section 29(5) of that Act (appeals) for the words "sections 14(3), 20 and 21" there shall be substituted "section 20".

43. In section 88(1) of that Act (interpretation)-

(a) in the definition of "child", for the words from "an illegitimate" to the end there shall be substituted "a child whose father and mother were not married to each other at the time of his birth"; and

(b) in the definition of "child of the family", for the words "being boarded-out with those parties" there shall be substituted "placed with those parties as foster parents".

The Magistrates' Courts Act 1980 (c. 43)

44. – (1) In section 59(2) of the Magistrates' Courts Act 1980 (periodical payments through justices' clerk) for the words "the Guardianship of Minors Acts 1971 and 1973" there shall be substituted "(or having effect as if made under) Schedule 1 to the Children Act 1989".

(2) For section 62(5) of that Act (payments to children) there shall be substituted-

(5) In this section references to the person with whom a child has his home-

(a) in the case of any child who is being looked after by a local authority (within the meaning of section 22 of the Children Act 1989), are references to that local authority; and

(b) in any other case, are references to the person who, disregarding any absence of the child at a hospital or boarding school and any other temporary absence, has care of the child.

The Supreme Court Act 1981 (c. 54)

45. – (1) In section 18 of the Supreme Court Act 1981 (restrictions on appeals to Court of Appeal)-

(a) in subsection (1)(h)(i), for the word "custody" there shall be substituted "residence"; and

(b) in subsection (1)(h)(ii) for the words "access to", in both places, there shall be substituted "contact with".

(2) In section 41 of that Act (wards of court), the following subsection shall be inserted after subsection (2)-

"(2A) Subsection (2) does not apply with respect to a child who is the subject of a care order (as defined by section 105 of the Children Act 1989).

(3) In Schedule 1 to that Act (distribution of business in High Court), for paragraph 3(b)(ii) there shall be substituted-

"(ii) the exercise of the inherent jurisdiction of the High Court with respect to minors, the maintenance of minors and any proceedings under the Children Act 1989, except proceedings solely for the appointment of a guardian of a minor's estate;"

The Armed Forces Act 1981 (c. 55)

46. In section 14 of the Armed Forces Act 1981 (temporary removal to, and detention in, place of safety abroad or in the United Kingdom of service children in need of care and control), in subsection (9A) for the words "the Children and Young

Persons Act 1933, the Children and Young Persons Act 1969" there shall be substituted "the Children Act 1989".

The Civil Jurisdiction and Judgments Act 1982 (c. 27)

47. In paragraph 5(a) of Schedule 5 to the Civil Jurisdiction and Judgments Act 1982 (maintenance and similar payments excluded from Schedule 4 to that Act) for the words "section 47 or 51 of the Child Care Act 1980" there shall be substituted "paragraph 23 of Schedule 2 to the Children Act 1989".

The Mental Health Act 1983 (c. 20)

48. – (1) For section 27 of the Mental Health Act 1983 (children and young persons in care of local authority) there shall be substituted the following section-

"27. Where-

   (a) a patient who is a child or young person is in the care of a local authority by virtue of a care order within the meaning of the Children Act 1989; or
   (b) the rights and powers of a parent of a patient who is a child or young person are vested in a local authority by virtue of section 16 of the Social Work (Scotland) Act 1968,

the authority shall be deemed to be the nearest relative of the patient in preference to any person except the patient's husband or wife (if any).

(2) Section 28 of that Act (nearest relative of minor under guardianship, etc.) is amended as mentioned in sub-paragraphs (3) and (4).

(3) For subsection (1) there shall be substituted-

"(1) Where-

   (a) a guardian has been appointed for a person who has not attained the age of eighteen years; or
   (b) a residence order (as defined by section 8 of the Children Act 1989) is in force with respect to such a person,

the guardian (or guardians, where there is more than one) or the person named in the residence order shall, to the exclusion of any other person, be deemed to be his nearest relative."

(4) For subsection (3) there shall be substituted-

"(3) In this section "guardian" does not include a guardian under this Part of this Act."

(5) In section 131(2) of that Act (informal admission of patients aged sixteen or over) for the words from "notwithstanding" to the end there shall be substituted "even though there are one or more persons who have parental responsibility for him (within the meaning of the Children Act 1989)".

The Registered Homes Act 1984 (c. 23)

49. – (1) In section 1(5) of the Registered Homes Act 1984 (requirement of registration) for paragraphs (d) and (e) there shall be substituted-

"(d) any community home, voluntary home or children's home within the meaning of the Children Act 1989."

(2) In section 39 of that Act (preliminary) for paragraphs (a) and (b) there shall be substituted-

"(a) the Children Act 1989."

The Mental Health (Scotland) Act 1984 (c. 36)

50. For section 54 of the Mental Health (Scotland) Act 1984 (children and young persons in care of local authority) there shall be substituted the following section-

"54. Where-

(a) the rights and powers of a parent of a patient who is a child or young person are vested in a local authority by virtue of section 16 of the Social Work (Scotland) Act 1968; or

(b) a patient who is a child or young person is in the care of a local authority by virtue of a care order made under the Children Act 1989,

the authority shall be deemed to be the nearest relative of the patient in preference to any person except the patient's husband or wife (if any)."

The Matrimonial and Family Proceedings Act 1984 (c. 42)

51. In section 38(2)(b) of the Matrimonial and Family Proceedings Act 1984 (transfer of family proceedings from High Court to county court) after the words "a ward of court" there shall be inserted "or any other proceedings which relate to the exercise of the inherent jurisdiction of the High Court with respect to minors".

The Police and Criminal Evidence Act 1984 (c. 60)

52. In section 37(14) of the Police and Criminal Evidence Act 1984 (duties of custody officer before charge) after the words "Children and Young Persons Act 1969" there shall be inserted "or in Part IV of the Children Act 1989".

53. – (1) In section 38 of that Act (duties of custody officer after charge), in subsection (6) for the words from "make arrangements" to the end there shall be substituted "secure that the arrested juvenile is moved to local authority accommodation".

(2) After that subsection there shall be inserted-

"(6A) In this section

"local authority accommodation" means accommodation provided by or on behalf of a local authority (within the meaning of the Children Act 1989).

(6B) Where an arrested juvenile is moved to local authority accommodation under subsection (6) above, it shall be lawful for any person acting on behalf of the authority to detain him.

(3) In subsection (8) of that section for the words "Children and Young Persons Act 1969" there shall be substituted "Children Act 1989".

54. In section 39(4) of that Act (responsibilities in relation to persons detained) for the words "transferred to the care of a local authority in pursuance of arrangements made" there shall be substituted "moved to local authority accommodation".

55. In Schedule 2 to that Act (preserved powers of arrest) in the entry relating to the Children and Young Persons Act 1969 for the words "Sections 28(2) and" there shall be substituted "Section".

The Surrogacy Arrangements Act 1985 (c. 49)

56. In section 1(2)(b) of the Surrogacy Arrangements Act 1985 (meaning of "surrogate mother", etc.) for the words "the parental rights being exercised" there shall be substituted "parental responsibility being met".

The Child Abduction and Custody Act 1985 (c. 60)

57. – (1) In section 9(a) and 20(2)(a) of the Child Abduction and Custody Act 1985 (orders with respect to which court's powers suspended), for the words "any other order under section 1(2) of the Children and Young Persons Act 1969" there shall be substituted "a supervision order under section 31 of the Children Act 1989".

(2) At the end of section 27 of that Act (interpretation), there shall be added-

(4) In this Act a decision relating to rights of access in England and Wales means a decision as to the contact which a child may, or may not, have with any person.

"(3) In Part I of Schedule 3 to that Act (orders in England and Wales which are custody orders for the purposes of the Act), for paragraph 1 there shall be substituted-

"1. The following are the orders referred to in section 27(1) of this Act-

(a) a care order under the Children Act 1989 (as defined by section 31(11) of that Act, read with section 105(1) and Schedule 14);
(b) a residence order (as defined by section 8 of the Act of 1989); and
(c) any order made by a court in England and Wales under any of the following enactments-
(i) section 9(1), 10(1)(a) or 11(a) of the Guardianship of Minors Act 1971;
(ii) section 42(1) or (2) or 43(1) of the Matrimonial Causes Act 1973;
(iii) section 2(2)(b), 4(b) or (5) of the Guardianship Act 1973 as applied by section 34(5) of the Children Act 1975;
(iv) section 8(2)(a), 10(1) or 19(1)(ii) of the Domestic Proceedings and Magistrates Courts Act 1978;

(v) section 26(1)(b) of the Adoption Act 1976.

"The Disabled Persons (Services, Consultation and Representation) Act 1986 (c. 33)

58. In section 1(3) of the Disabled Persons (Services, Consultation and Representation) Act 1986 (circumstances in which regulations may provide for the appointment of authorised representatives of disabled persons)-

(a) in paragraph (a), for the words "parent or guardian of a disabled person under the age of sixteen" there shall be substituted-
"(i) the parent of a disabled person under the age of sixteen, or
(ii) any other person who is not a parent of his but who has parental responsibility for him"; and
(b) in paragraph (b), for the words "in the care of" there shall be substituted "looked after by".

59. – (1) Section 2 of that Act (circumstances in which authorised representative has right to visit etc. disabled person) shall be amended as follows.

(2) In subsection (3)(a) for the words from second "the" to "by" there shall be substituted "for the words "if so requested by the disabled person" there shall be substituted "if so requested by any person mentioned in section 1(3)(a)(i) or (ii)"."

(3) In subsection (5) after paragraph (b) there shall be inserted-

"(bb) in accommodation provided by or on behalf of a local authority under Part III of the Children Act 1989, or

(4) After paragraph (c) of subsection (5) there shall be inserted-

"(cc) in accommodation provided by a voluntary organisation in accordance with arrangements made by a local authority under section 17 of the Children Act 1989, or

60. In section 5(7)(b) of that Act (disabled persons leaving special education) for the word "guardian" there shall be substituted "other person who is not a parent of his but who has parental responsibility for him".

61. – (1) In section 16 of that Act (interpretation) in the definition of "disabled person", in paragraph (a) for the words from "means" to "applies" there shall be substituted "means-

(i) in the case of a person aged eighteen or over, a person to whom section 29 of the 1948 Act applies, and
(ii) in the case of a person under the age of eighteen, a person who is disabled within the meaning of Part III of the Children Act 1989".

(2) After the definition of "parent" in that section there shall be inserted-

"parental responsibility" has the same meaning as in the Children Act 1989."

(3) In the definition of "the welfare enactments" in that section, in paragraph (a) after the words "the 1977 Act" there shall be inserted "and Part III of the Children Act 1989".

(4) At the end of that section there shall be added-

"(2) In this Act any reference to a child who is looked after by a local authority has the same meaning as in the Children Act 1989."

The Family Law Act 1986 (c. 55)

62. – (1) The Family Law Act 1986 shall be amended as follows.

(2) Subject to paragraphs 63 to 71, in Part I-

    (a) for the words "custody order", in each place where they occur, there shall be substituted "Part I order";

    (b) for the words "proceedings with respect to the custody of", in each place where they occur, there shall be substituted "Part I proceedings with respect to"; and

    (c) for the words "matters relating to the custody of", in each place where they occur, there shall be substituted "Part I matters relating to".

(3) For section 42(7) (general interpretation of Part I) there shall be substituted-

"(7) In this Part-

    (a) references to Part I proceedings in respect of a child are references to any proceedings for a Part I order or an order corresponding to a Part I order and include, in relation to proceedings outside the United Kingdom, references to proceedings before a tribunal or other authority having power under the law having effect there to determine Part I matters; and

    (b) references to Part I matters are references to matters that might be determined by a Part I order or an order corresponding to a Part I order."

63. – (1) In section 1 (orders to which Part I of the Act of 1986 applies), in subsection (1)-

    (a) for paragraph (a) there shall be substituted-

"(a) a section 8 order made by a court in England and Wales under the Children Act 1989, other than an order varying or discharging such an order"; and

    (b) for paragraph (d) there shall be substituted the following paragraphs-

"(d) an order made by a court in England and Wales in the exercise of the inherent jurisdiction of the High Court with respect to children-

      (i) so far as it gives care of a child to any person or provides for contact with, or the education of, a child; but

      (ii) excluding an order varying or revoking such an order;

    (e) an order made by the High Court in Northern Ireland in the exercise of its jurisdiction relating to wardship-

      (i) so far as it gives care and control of a child to any person or provides for the education of or access to a child; but

(ii) excluding an order relating to a child of whom care or care and control is (immediately after the making of the order) vested in the Department of Health and Social Services or a Health and Social Services Board.

(2) In subsection (2) of that section, in paragraph (c) for "(d)" there shall be substituted "(e)".

(3) For subsections (3) to (5) of that section there shall be substituted-

(3) In this Part,

"Part I order"-

(a) includes any order which would have been a custody order by virtue of this section in any form in which it was in force at any time before its amendment by the Children Act 1989; and

(b) (subject to sections 32 and 40 of this Act) excludes any order which would have been excluded from being a custody order by virtue of this section in any such form.

64. For section 2 there shall be substituted the following sections-

"**2**. – (1) A court in England and Wales shall not have jurisdiction to make a section 1(1)(a) order with respect to a child in or in connection with matrimonial proceedings in England and Wales unless the condition in section 2A of this Act is satisfied.

(2) A court in England and Wales shall not have jurisdiction to make a section 1(1)(a) order in a non-matrimonial case (that is to say, where the condition in section 2A of this Act is not satisfied) unless the condition in section 3 of this Act is satisfied.

(3) A court in England and Wales shall not have jurisdiction to make a section 1(1)(d) order unless-

(a) the condition in section 3 of this Act is satisfied, or

(b) the child concerned is present in England and Wales on the relevant date and the court considers that the immediate exercise of its powers is necessary for his protection.

2A. – (1) The condition referred to in section 2(1) of this Act is that the matrimonial proceedings are proceedings in respect of the marriage of the parents of the child concerned and-

(a) the proceedings-
  (i) are proceedings for divorce or nullity of marriage, and
  (ii) are continuing;

(b) the proceedings-
  (i) are proceedings for judicial separation,
  (ii) are continuing,
  and the jurisdiction of the court is not excluded by subsection (2) below; or

(c) the proceedings have been dismissed after the beginning of the trial but-

  (i) the section 1(1)(a) order is being made forthwith, or

  (ii) the application for the order was made on or before the dismissal.

(2) For the purposes of subsection (1)(b) above, the jurisdiction of the court is excluded if, after the grant of a decree of judicial separation, on the relevant date, proceedings for divorce or nullity in respect of the marriage are continuing in Scotland or Northern Ireland.

(3) Subsection (2) above shall not apply if the court in which the other proceedings there referred to are continuing has made-

 (a) an order under section 13(6) or 21(5) of this Act (not being an order made by virtue of section 13(6)(a)(i)), or

 (b) an order under section 14(2) or 22(2) of this Act which is recorded as being made for the purpose of enabling Part I proceedings to be taken in England and Wales with respect to the child concerned.

(4) Where a court-

 (a) has jurisdiction to make a section 1(1)(a) order in or in connection with matrimonial proceedings, but

 (b) considers that it would be more appropriate for Part I matters relating to the child to be determined outside England and Wales,

the court may by order direct that, while the order under this subsection is in force, no section 1(1)(a) order shall be made by any court in or in connection with those proceedings.

"**65.** – (1) In section 3 (habitual residence or presence of child concerned) in subsection (1) for "section 2" there shall be substituted "section 2(2)".

(2) In subsection (2) of that section for the words "proceedings for divorce, nullity or judicial separation" there shall be substituted "matrimonial proceedings".

66. – (1) In section 6 (duration and variation of Part I orders), for subsection (3) there shall be substituted the following subsections-

(3) A court in England and Wales shall not have jurisdiction to vary a Part I order if, on the relevant date, matrimonial proceedings are continuing in Scotland or Northern Ireland in respect of the marriage of the parents of the child concerned.

(3A) Subsection (3) above shall not apply if-

 (a) the Part I order was made in or in connection with proceedings for divorce or nullity in England and Wales in respect of the marriage of the parents of the child concerned; and

 (b) those proceedings are continuing.

(3B) Subsection (3) above shall not apply if-

 (a) the Part I order was made in or in connection with proceedings for judicial separation in England and Wales;

(b) those proceedings are continuing; and

(c) the decree of judicial separation has not yet been granted.

(2) In subsection (5) of that section for the words from "variation of" to "if the ward" there shall be substituted "variation of a section 1(1)(d) order if the child concerned".

(3) For subsections (6) and (7) of that section there shall be substituted the following subsections-

"(6) Subsection (7) below applies where a Part I order which is-

(a) a residence order (within the meaning of the Children Act 1989) in favour of a person with respect to a child,

(b) an order made in the exercise of the High Court's inherent jurisdiction with respect to children by virtue of which a person has care of a child, or

(c) an order-

(i) of a kind mentioned in section 1(3)(a) of this Act,

(ii) under which a person is entitled to the actual possession of a child,

ceases to have effect in relation to that person by virtue of subsection (1) above.

(7) Where this subsection applies, any family assistance order made under section 16 of the Children Act 1989 with respect to the child shall also cease to have effect.

(8) For the purposes of subsection (7) above the reference to a family assistance order under section 16 of the Children Act 1989 shall be deemed to include a reference to an order for the supervision of a child made under-

(a) section 7(4) of the Family Law Reform Act 1969,

(b) section 44 of the Matrimonial Causes Act 1973,

(c) section 2(2)(a) of the Guardianship Act 1973,

(d) section 34(5) or 36(3)(b) of the Children Act 1975, or

(e) section 9 of the Domestic Proceedings and Magistrates' Courts Act 1978;

but this subsection shall cease to have effect once all such orders for the supervision of children have ceased to have effect in accordance with Schedule 14 to the Children Act 1989.

67. For section 7 (interpretation of Chapter II) there shall be substituted-

"7. In this Chapter-

(a) "child" means a person who has not attained the age of eighteen;

(b) "matrimonial proceedings" means proceedings for divorce, nullity of marriage or judicial separation;

(c) "the relevant date" means, in relation to the making or variation of an order-

(i) where an application is made for an order to be made or varied, the date of the application (or first application, if two or more are determined together), and

(ii) where no such application is made, the date on which the court is considering whether to make or, as the case may be, vary the order; and

(d) "section 1(1)(a) order" and

"section 1(1)(d) order" mean orders falling within section 1(1)(a) and (d) of this Act respectively.

"**68.** In each of the following sections-

(a) section 11(2)(a) (provisions supplementary to sections 9 and 10),
(b) section 13(5)(a) (jurisdiction ancillary to matrimonial proceedings),
(c) section 20(3)(a) (habitual residence or presence of child),
(d) section 21(4)(a) (jurisdiction in divorce proceedings, etc.), and
(e) section 23(4)(a) (duration and variation of custody orders),

for "4(5)" there shall be substituted "2A(4)".

69. In each of the following sections-

(a) section 19(2) (jurisdiction in cases other than divorce, etc.),
(b) section 20(6) (habitual residence or presence of child), and
(c) section 23(5) (duration and variation of custody orders),

for "section 1(1)(d)" there shall be substituted "section 1(1)(e)".

70. In section 34(3) (power to order recovery of child) for paragraph (a) there shall be substituted-

"(a) section 14 of the Children Act 1989".

71. – (1) In section 42 (general interpretation of Part I), in subsection (4)(a) for the words "has been boarded out with those parties" there shall be substituted "is placed with those parties as foster parents".

(2) In subsection (6) of that section, in paragraph (a) after the word "person" there shall be inserted "to be allowed contact with or".

The Local Government Act 1988 (c. 9)

72. In Schedule 1 to the Local Government Act 1988 (competition) at the end of paragraph 2(4) (cleaning of buildings: buildings to which competition provisions do not apply) for paragraph (c) there shall be substituted-

"(c) section 53 of the Children Act 1989."

Amendments of local Acts

73. – (1) Section 16 of the Greater London Council (General Powers) Act 1981 (exemption from provisions of Part IV of the Act of certain premises) shall be amended as follows.

(2) After paragraph (g) there shall be inserted-

"(gg) used as a children's home as defined in section 63 of the Children Act 1989".

(3) In paragraph (h)-

> (a) for the words "section 56 of the Child Care Act 1980" there shall be substituted "section 60 of the Children Act 1989";
> (b) for the words "section 57" there shall be substituted "section 60"; and
> (c) for the words "section 32" there shall be substituted "section 53".

(4) In paragraph (i), for the words "section 8 of the Foster Children Act 1980" there shall be substituted "section 67 of the Children Act 1989".

74. – (1) Section 10(2) of the Greater London Council (General Powers) Act 1984 (exemption from provisions of Part IV of the Act of certain premises) shall be amended as follows.

(2) In paragraph (d)-

> (a) for the words "section 56 of the Child Care Act 1980" there shall be substituted "section 60 of the Children Act 1989";
> (b) for the words "section 57" there shall be substituted "section 60"; and
> (c) for the words "section 31" there shall be substituted "section 53".

(3) In paragraph (e), for the words "section 8 of the Foster Children Act 1980" there shall be substituted "section 67 of the Children Act 1989".

(4) In paragraph (l) for the words "section 1 of the Children's Homes Act 1982" there shall be substituted "section 63 of the Children Act 1989".

SCHEDULE 14

TRANSITIONALS AND SAVINGS

Schedule 14
This schedule sets out the provisions to cover the transitional period when the Children Act 1989 came into force. It is therefore of very little relevance now.

Pending proceedings, etc

1 – (1) [Subject to sub-paragraphs (1A) and (4)], nothing in any provision of this Act (other than the repeals mentioned in sub-paragraph (2)) shall affect any proceedings which are pending immediately before the commencement of that provision.

(1A) Proceedings pursuant to section 7(2) of the Family Law Reform Act 1969 (committal or wards of court to care of local authority) or in the exercise of the High Court's inherent jurisdiction with respect to children which are pending in relation to a child who has been placed or allowed to remain in the care of a local authority shall not be treated as pending proceedings after 13th October 1992 for the purposes of this Schedule if no final order has been made by that date pursuant to section 7(2) of the 1969 Act or in the exercise of the High Court's inherent jurisdiction in respect of the child's care.

(2) The repeals are those of–

    (a) section 42(3) of the Matrimonial Causes Act 1973 (declaration by court that party to marriage unfit to have custody of children of family); and

    (b) section 38 of the Sexual Offences Act 1956 (power of court to divest person of authority over girl or boy in cases of incest).

(2) For the purposes of the following provisions of this Schedule, any reference to an order in force immediately before the commencement of a provision of this Act shall be construed as including a reference to an order made after that commencement in proceedings pending before that commencement.

(3) Sub-paragraph (3) is not to be read as making the order in question have effect from a date earlier than that on which it was made.

(4) An order under section 96(3) may make such provision with respect to the application of the order in relation to proceedings which are pending when the order comes into force as the Lord Chancellor considers appropriate.

2. Where, immediately before the day on which Part IV comes into force, there was in force an order under section 3(1) of the Children and Young Persons Act 1963 (order directing a local authority to bring a child or young person before a [youth court] under section 1 of the Children and Young Persons Act 1969), the order shall cease to have effect on that day.

Custody Orders, etc

Cessation of declarations of unfitness, etc

3. Where, immediately before the day on which Parts I and II come into force, there was in force–

    (a) a declaration under section 42(3) of the Matrimonial Causes Act 1973 (declaration by court that party to marriage unfit to have custody of children of family); or

    (b) an order under section 38(1) of the Sexual Offences Act 1956 divesting a person of authority over a girl or boy in a case of incest;

    the declaration or, as the case may be, the order shall cease to have effect on that day.

The Family Law Reform Act 1987 (c. 42)

Conversion of orders under section 4

4. Where, immediately before the day on which Parts I and II come into force, there was in force an order under section 4(1) of the Family Law Reform Act 1987 (order giving father parental rights and duties in relation to a child), then, on and after that day, the order shall be deemed to be an order under section 4 of this Act giving the father parental responsibility for the child.

Orders to which paragraphs 6 to 11 apply

5 – (1) In paragraphs 6 to 11 'an existing order' means any order which–

(a) is in force immediately before the commencement of Parts I and II;
(b) was made under any enactment mentioned in sub-paragraph (2);
(c) determines all or any of the following–
    (i) who is to have custody of a child;
    (ii) who is to have care and control of a child;
    (iii) who is to have access to a child;
    (iv) any matter with respect to a child's education or upbringing; and
(c) is not an order of a kind mentioned in paragraph 15(1).

(2) The enactments are–

(a) the Domestic Proceedings and Magistrates' Courts Act 1978;
(b) the Children Act 1975;
(c) the Matrimonial Causes Act 1973;
(d) the Guardianship of Minors Acts 1971 and 1973;
(e) the Matrimonial Causes Act 1965;
(e) the Matrimonial Proceedings (Magistrates' Courts) Act 1960.

(2) For the purposes of this paragraph and paragraphs 6 to 11 'custody' includes legal custody and joint as well as sole custody but does not include access.

Parental responsibility of parents

6 – (1) Where–

(a) a child's father and mother were married to each other at the time of his birth; and
(b) there is an existing order with respect to the child,

each parent shall have parental responsibility for the child in accordance with section 2 as modified by sub-paragraph (3).

(2) Where–

(a) a child's father and mother were not married to each other at the time of his birth; and

(b) there is an existing order with respect to the child,

section 2 shall apply as modified by sub-paragraphs (3) and (4).

(3) The modification is that for section 2(8) there shall be substituted–

'(8) The fact that a person has parental responsibility for a child does not entitle him to act in a way which would be incompatible with any existing order or any order made under this Act with respect to the child'.

(4) The modifications are that–

(a) for the purposes of section 2(2), where the father has custody or care and control of the child by virtue of any existing order, the court shall be deemed to have made (at the commencement of that section) an order under section 4(1) giving him parental responsibility for the child; and

(b) where by virtue of paragraph (a) a court is deemed to have made an order under section 4(1) in favour of a father who has care and control of a child by virtue of an existing order, the court shall not bring the order under section 4(1) to an end at any time while he has care and control of the child by virtue of the order.

Persons who are not parents but who have custody or care and control

7 – (1) Where a person who is not the parent or guardian of a child has custody or care and control of him by virtue of an existing order, that person shall have parental responsibility for him so long as he continues to have that custody or care and control by virtue of the order.

(2) Where sub-paragraph (1) applies, [Parts I and II and paragraph 15 of Schedule 1] shall have effect as modified by this paragraph.

(3) The modifications are that–

(a) for section 2(8) there shall be substituted–

'(8) The fact that a person has parental responsibility for a child does not entitle him to act in a way which would be incompatible with any existing order or with any order made under this Act with respect to the child';

(b) at the end of section 10(4) there shall be inserted–

'(c) any person who has custody or care and control of a child by virtue of any existing order'; and

(c) at the end of section 34(1)(c) there shall be inserted–

'(cc) where immediately before the care order was made there was an existing order by virtue of which a person had custody or care and control of the child, that person.'

[(d) for paragraph 15 of Schedule 1 there shall be substituted–

'15 Where a child lives with a person as the result of a custodianship order within the meaning of section 33 of the Children Act 1975, a local authority may make contributions to that person towards the cost of the accommodation and maintenance of the child so long as that person continues to have legal custody of that child by virtue of the order.']

Persons who have care and control

8 – (1) Sub-paragraphs (2) to (6) apply where a person has care and control of a child by virtue of an existing order, but they shall cease to apply when that order ceases to have effect.

(2) Section 5 shall have effect as if–

  (a) for any reference to a residence order in favour of a parent or guardian there were substituted a reference to any existing order by virtue of which the parent or guardian has care and control of the child; and

  (b) for subsection (9) there were substituted–

  '(9) Subsections (1) and (7) do not apply if the existing order referred to in paragraph (b) of those subsections was one by virtue of which a surviving parent of the child also had care and control of him.'

(3) Section 10 shall have effect as if for subsection (5)(c)(i) there were substituted–

  '(i) in any case where by virtue of an existing order any person or persons has or have care and control of the child, has the consent of that person or each of those persons'.

(3) Section 20 shall have effect as if for subsection (9)(a) there were substituted 'who has care and control of the child by virtue of an existing order.'

(5) Section 23 shall have effect as if for subsection (4)(c) there were substituted–

  '(c) where the child is in care and immediately before the care order was made there was an existing order by virtue of which a person had care and control of the child, that person.'

(6) In Schedule 1, paragraphs 1(1) and 14(1) shall have effect as if for the words 'in whose favour a residence order is in force with respect to the child' there were substituted 'who has been given care and control of the child by virtue of an existing order'.

Persons who have access

9 – (1) Sub-paragraphs (2) to (4) apply where a person has access by virtue of an existing order.

(2) Section 10 shall have effect as if after subsection (5) there were inserted–

'(5A) Any person who has access to a child by virtue of an existing order is entitled to apply for a contact order.'

(3) Section 16(2) shall have effect as if after paragraph (b) there were inserted–

'(bb) any person who has access to the child by virtue of an existing order.'

(4) Sections 43(11), 44(13) and 46(10), shall have effect as if in each case after

paragraph (d) there were inserted–

'(dd) any person who has been given access to him by virtue of an existing order.'

Enforcement of certain existing orders

10 – (1) Sub-paragraph (2) applies in relation to any existing order which, but for the repeal by this Act of–

(a) section 13(1) of the Guardianship of Minors Act 1971;
(b) section 43(1) of the Children Act 1975; or
(c) section 33 of the Domestic Proceedings and Magistrates' Courts Act 1978,

(provisions concerning the enforcement of custody orders) might have been enforced as if it were an order requiring a person to give up a child to another person.

(2) Where this sub-paragraph applies, the existing order may, after the repeal of the enactments mentioned in sub-paragraph (1)(a) to (c), be enforced under section 14 as if–

(a) any reference to a residence order were a reference to the existing order; and
(b) any reference to a person in whose favour the residence order is in force were a reference to a person to whom actual custody of the child is given by an existing order which is in force.

(2) In sub-paragraph (2) 'actual custody', in relation to a child, means the actual possession of his person.

Discharge of existing orders

11 – (1) The making of a residence order or a care order with respect to a child who is the subject of an existing order discharges the existing order.

(2) Where the court makes any section 8 order (other than a residence order) with respect to a child with respect to whom any existing order is in force, the existing order shall have effect subject to the section 8 order.

(3) The court may discharge an existing order which is in force with respect to a child–

(a) in any family proceedings relating to the child or in which any question arises with respect to the child's welfare; or
(b) on the application of–
(i) any parent or guardian of the child;
(ii) the child himself; or
(ii) any person named in the order.

(3) A child may not apply for the discharge of an existing order except with the leave of the court.

(4) The power in sub-paragraph (3) to discharge an existing order includes the power to discharge any part of the order.

(5) In considering whether to discharge an order under the power conferred by sub-paragraph (3) the court shall, if the discharge of the order is opposed by any party to the proceedings, have regard in particular to the matters mentioned in section 1(3).

Guardians

Existing guardians to be guardians under this Act

12 – (1) Any appointment of a person as guardian of a child which–

(a) was made–
    (i) under sections 3 to 5 of the Guardianship of Minors Act 1971;
    (ii) under section 38(3) of the Sexual Offences Act 1956; or
    (iii) under the High Court's inherent jurisdiction with respect to children; and
(b) has taken effect before the commencement of section 5,

shall (subject to sub-paragraph (2)) be deemed, on and after the commencement of section 5, to be an appointment made and having effect under that section.

(2) Where an appointment of a person as guardian of a child has effect under section 5 by virtue of sub-paragraph (1)(a)(ii), the appointment shall not have effect for a period which is longer than any period

(3) specified in the order.

Appointment of guardian not yet in effect

13. Any appointment of a person to be a guardian of a child–

(a) which was made as mentioned in paragraph 12(1)(a)(i); but
(b) which, immediately before the commencement of section 5, had not taken effect,

shall take effect in accordance with section 5 (as modified, where it applies, by paragraph 8(2)).

14 Persons deemed to be appointed as guardians under existing wills

For the purposes of the Wills Act 1837 and of this Act any disposition by will and testament or devise of the custody and tuition of any child, made before the commencement of section 5 and paragraph 1 of Schedule 13, shall be deemed to be an appointment by will of a guardian of the child.

Children in Care

Children in compulsory care

15 – (1) Sub-paragraph (2) applies where, immediately before the day on which Part IV comes into force, a person was–

(a) in care by virtue of–
   (i) a care order under section 1 of the Children and Young Persons Act 1969;
   (ii) a care order under section 15 of that Act, on discharging a supervision order made under section 1 of that Act; or
   (iii) an order or authorisation under section 25 or 26 of that Act;
(b) ...
(c) in care–
   (i) under section 2 of the Child Care Act 1980; or
   (ii) by virtue of paragraph 1 of Schedule 4 to that Act (which extends the meaning of a child in care under section 2 to include children in care under section 1 of the Children Act 1948),
   and a child in respect of whom a resolution under section 3 of the Act of 1980 or section 2 of the Act of 1948 was in force;
(d) a child in respect of whom a resolution had been passed under section 65 of the Child Care Act 1980;
(e) in care by virtue of an order under–
   (i) section 2(1)(e) of the Matrimonial Proceedings (Magistrates' Courts) Act 1960;
   (ii) section 7(2) of the Family Law Reform Act 1969;
   (iii) section 43(1) of the Matrimonial Causes Act 1973; or
   (iv) section 2(2)(b) of the Guardianship Act 1973;
   (v) section 10 of the Domestic Proceedings and Magistrates' Courts Act 1978, (orders having effect for certain purposes as if the child had been received into care under section 2 of the Child Care Act 1980);
(f) in care by virtue of an order made, on the revocation of a custodianship order, under section 36 of the Children Act 1975; ...
(g) in care by virtue of an order made, on the refusal of an adoption order, under section 26 of the Adoption Act 1976 or any order having effect (by virtue of paragraph 1 of Schedule 2 to that Act) as if made under that section[; or
(b) in care by virtue of an order of the court made in the exercise of the High Court's inherent jurisdiction with respect to children.]

(2) Where this sub-paragraph applies, then, on and after the day on which Part IV commences–

(a) the order or resolution in question shall be deemed to be a care order;
(b) the authority in whose care the person was immediately before that commencement shall be deemed to be the authority designated in that deemed care order; and
(c) any reference to a child in the care of a local authority shall include a reference

to a person who is the subject of such a deemed care order,

and the provisions of this Act shall apply accordingly, subject to paragraph 16.

Modifications

16 – (1) Sub-paragraph (2) only applies where a person who is the subject of a care order by virtue of paragraph 15(2) is a person falling within sub-paragraph (1)(a) ... of that paragraph.

(2) Where the person would otherwise have remained in care until reaching the age of nineteen, by virtue of–

(a) section 20(3)(a) or 21(1) of the Children and Young Persons Act 1969; ...
(b) ...

this Act applies as if in section 91(12) for the word 'eighteen' there were substituted 'nineteen'.

(4) ...

(3A) Where in respect of a child who has been placed or allowed to remain in the care of a local authority pursuant to section 7(2) of the Family Law Reform Act 1969 or in the exercise of the High Court's inherent jurisdiction and the child is still in the care of a local authority, proceedings have ceased by virtue of paragraph 1(1A) to be treated as pending, paragraph 15(2) shall apply on 14th October 1992 as if the child was in care pursuant to an order as specified in paragraph 15(1)(e)(ii) or (h) as the case may be.

(5) [Sub-paragraphs (5) and (6) only apply] where a child who is the subject of a care order by virtue of paragraph 15(2) is a person falling within sub-paragraph (1)(e) to [(h)] of that paragraph.

(5) [Subject to sub-paragraph (6),] where a court, on making the order, or at any time thereafter, gave directions [–

(a) under section 4(4)(a) of the Guardianship Act 1973;
(b) under section 43(5)(a) of the Matrimonial Causes Act 1973; or
(c) in the exercise of the High Court's inherent jurisdiction with respect to children,]

as to the exercise by the authority of any powers, those directions shall[, subject to the provisions of section 25 of this Act and of any regulations made under that section,] continue to have effect (regardless of any conflicting provision in this Act [other than section 25]) until varied or discharged by a court under this sub-paragraph.

(6) Where directions referred to in sub-paragraph (5) are to the effect that a child be placed in accommodation provided for the purpose of restricting liberty then the directions shall cease to have effect upon the expiry of the maximum period specified by regulations under section 25(2)(a) in relation to children of his

description, calculated from 14th October 1991.

16A Cessation of wardship where ward in care

[(1)] Where a child who is a ward of court is in care by virtue of–

(a) an order under section 7(2) of the Family Law Reform Act 1969; or

(b) an order made in the exercise of the High Court's inherent jurisdiction with respect to children,

he shall, on the day on which Part IV commences, cease to be a ward of court.

(2) Where immediately before the day on which Part IV commences a child was in the care of a local authority and as a result of an order–

(a) pursuant to section 7(2) of the Family Law Reform Act 1969; or

(b) made in the exercise of the High Court's inherent jurisdiction with respect to children,

continued to be in the care of a local authority and was made a ward of court, he shall on the day on which Part IV commences, cease to be a ward of court.

(2) Sub-paragraphs (1) and (2) do not apply in proceedings which are pending.]]

Children placed with parent etc while in compulsory care

17 – (1) This paragraph applies where a child is deemed by paragraph 15 to be in the care of a local authority under an order or resolution which is deemed by that paragraph to be a care order.

(2) If, immediately before the day on which Part III comes into force, the child was allowed to be under the charge and control of–

(a) a parent or guardian under section 21(2) of the Child Care Act 1980; or

(b) a person who, before the child was in the authority's care, had care and control of the child by virtue of an order falling within paragraph 5,

on and after that day the provision made by and under section 23(5) shall apply as if the child had been placed with the person in question in accordance with that provision.

Orders for access to children in compulsory care

18 – (1) This paragraph applies to any access order–

(a) made under section 12C of the Child Care Act 1980 (access orders with respect to children in care of local authorities); and

(b) in force immediately before the commencement of Part IV.

(2) On and after the commencement of Part IV, the access order shall have effect as an order made under section 34 in favour of the person named in the order.

18A – (1) This paragraph applies to any decision of a local authority to terminate arrangements for access or to refuse to make such arrangements–

(a) of which notice has been given under, and in accordance with, section 12B of the Child Care Act 1980 (termination of access); and

(b) which is in force immediately before the commencement of Part IV.

(2) On and after the commencement of Part IV, a decision to which this paragraph applies shall have effect as a court order made under section 34(4) authorising the local authority to refuse to allow contact between the child and the person to whom notice was given under section 12B of the Child Care Act 1980.]

19 – (1) This paragraph applies where, immediately before the commencement of Part IV, an access order made under section 12C of the Act of 1980 was suspended by virtue of an order made under section 12E of that Act (suspension of access orders in emergencies).

(2) The suspending order shall continue to have effect as if this Act had not been passed.

(3) If–

(a) before the commencement of Part IV; and

(b) during the period for which the operation of the access order is suspended,

the local authority concerned made an application for its variation or discharge to an appropriate juvenile court, its operation shall be suspended until the date on which the application to vary or discharge it is determined or abandoned.

Children in voluntary care

20 – (1) This paragraph applies where, immediately before the day on which Part III comes into force–

(a) a child was in the care of a local authority–
   (i) under section 2(1) of the Child Care Act 1980; or
   (ii) by virtue of paragraph 1 of Schedule 4 to that Act (which extends the meaning of references to children in care under section 2 to include references to children in care under section 1 of the Children Act 1948); and

(b) he was not a person in respect of whom a resolution under section 3 of the Act of 1980 or section 2 of the Act of 1948 was in force.

(2) Where this paragraph applies, the child shall, on and after the day mentioned in sub-paragraph (1), be treated for the purposes of this Act as a child who is provided with accommodation by the local authority under Part III, but he shall cease to be so treated once he ceases to be so accommodated in accordance with the provisions of Part III.

(3) Where–

(a) this paragraph applies; and

(b) the child, immediately before the day mentioned in sub-paragraph (1), was (by virtue of section 21(2) of the Act of 1980) under the charge and control of a person falling within paragraph 17(2)(a) or (b),

the child shall not be treated for the purposes of this Act as if he were being looked after by the authority concerned.

Boarded out children

21 – (1) Where, immediately before the day on which Part III comes into force, a child in the care of a local authority–

  (a) was–
    (i) boarded out with a person under section 21(1)(a) of the Child Care Act 1980; or
    (ii) placed under the charge and control of a person, under section 21(2) of that Act; and
  (b) the person with whom he was boarded out, or (as the case may be) placed, was not a person falling within paragraph 17(2)(a) or (b),

on and after that day, he shall be treated (subject to sub-paragraph (2)) as having been placed with a local authority foster parent and shall cease to be so treated when he ceases to be placed with that person in accordance with the provisions of this Act.

(2) Regulations made under section 23(2)(a) shall not apply in relation to a person who is a local authority foster parent by virtue of sub-paragraph (1) before the end of the period of twelve months beginning with the day on which Part III comes into force and accordingly that person shall for that period be subject–

  (a) in a case falling within sub-paragraph (1)(a)(i), to terms and regulations mentioned in section 21(1)(a) of the Act of 1980; and
  (b) in a case falling within sub-paragraph (1)(a)(ii), to terms fixed under section 21(2) of that Act and regulations made under section 22A of that Act,

as if that Act had not been repealed by this Act.

Children in care to qualify for advice and assistance

22. Any reference in Part III to a person qualifying for advice and assistance shall be construed as including a reference to a person within the area of the local authority in question who is under twenty-one and who was, at any time after reaching the age of sixteen but while still a child–

  (a) a person falling within–
    (i) any of paragraphs (a) to [(h)] of paragraph 15(1); or
    (ii) paragraph 20(1); or
  (b) the subject of a criminal care order (within the meaning of paragraph 34).

Emigration of children in care

23. Where–

    (a) the Secretary of State has received a request in writing from a local authority that he give his consent under section 24 of the Child Care Act 1980 to the emigration of a child in their care; but

    (b) immediately before the repeal of the Act of 1980 by this Act, he has not determined whether or not to give his consent,

section 24 of the Act of 1980 shall continue to apply (regardless of that repeal) until the Secretary of State has determined whether or not to give his consent to the request.

Contributions for maintenance of children in care

24 – (1) Where, immediately before the day on which Part III of Schedule 2 comes into force, there was in force an order made (or having effect as if made) under any of the enactments mentioned in sub-paragraph (2), then, on and after that day–

    (a) the order shall have effect as if made under paragraph 23(2) of Schedule 2 against a person liable to contribute; and

    (b) Part III of Schedule 2 shall apply to the order, subject to the modifications in sub-paragraph (3).

(2) The enactments are–

    (a) section 11(4) of the Domestic Proceedings and Magistrates' Courts Act 1978;

    (b) section 26(2) of the Adoption Act 1976;

    (c) section 36(5) of the Children Act 1975;

    (d) section 2(3) of the Guardianship Act 1973;

    (e) section 2(1)(h) of the Matrimonial Proceedings (Magistrates' Courts) Act 1960,

(provisions empowering the court to make an order requiring a person to make periodical payments to a local authority in respect of a child in care).

(3) The modifications are that, in paragraph 23 of Schedule 2–

    (a) in sub-paragraph (4), paragraph (a) shall be omitted;

    (b) for sub-paragraph (6) there shall be substituted–

'(6) Where–

    (a) a contribution order is in force;

    (b) the authority serve a contribution notice under paragraph 22; and

    (c) the contributor and the authority reach an agreement under paragraph 22(7) in respect of the contribution notice,

the effect of the agreement shall be to discharge the order from the date on which it is agreed that the agreement shall take effect'; and

    (c) at the end of sub-paragraph (10) there shall be inserted–

'and

(c) where the order is against a person who is not a parent of the child, shall be made with due regard to–

    (i) whether that person had assumed responsibility for the maintenance of the child, and, if so, the extent to which and basis on which he assumed that responsibility and the length of the period during which he met that responsibility;

    (ii) whether he did so knowing that the child was not his child;

    (ii) the liability of any other person to maintain the child.'

Supervision Orders

25 – (1) This paragraph applies to any supervision order–

(a) made–

    (i) under section 1(3)(b) of the Children and Young Persons Act 1969; or

    (ii) under section 21(2) of that Act on the discharge of a care order made under section 1(3)(c) of that Act; and

(b) in force immediately before the commencement of Part IV.

(2) On and after the commencement of Part IV, the order shall be deemed to be a supervision order made under section 31 and–

(a) any requirement of the order that the child reside with a named individual shall continue to have effect while the order remains in force, unless the court otherwise directs;

(b) any other requirement imposed by the court, or directions given by the supervisor, shall be deemed to have been imposed or given under the appropriate provisions of Schedule 3.

(3) Where, immediately before the commencement of Part IV, the order had been in force for a period of [six months or more], it shall cease to have effect at the end of the period of six months beginning with the day on which Part IV comes into force unless–

(a) the court directs that it shall cease to have effect at the end of a different period (which shall not exceed three years);

(b) it ceases to have effect earlier in accordance with section 91; or

(c) it would have ceased to have had effect earlier had this Act not been passed.

(4) Where sub-paragraph (3) applies, paragraph 6 of Schedule 3 shall not apply.

(5) Where, immediately before the commencement of Part IV, the order had been in force for less than six months it shall cease to have effect in accordance with section 91 and paragraph 6 of Schedule 3 unless–

(a) the court directs that it shall cease to have effect at the end of a different period (which shall not exceed three years); or

(b) it would have ceased to have had effect earlier had this Act not been passed.

Other supervision orders

26 – (1) This paragraph applies to any order for the supervision of a child which was in force immediately before the commencement of Part IV and was made under–

(a) section 2(1)(f) of the Matrimonial Proceedings (Magistrates' Courts) Act 1960;
(b) section 7(4) of the Family Law Reform Act 1969;
(c) section 44 of the Matrimonial Causes Act 1973;
(d) section 2(2)(a) of the Guardianship Act 1973;
(e) section 34(5) or 36(3)(b) of the Children Act 1975;
(f) section 26(1)(a) of the Adoption Act 1976; or
(h) section 9 of the Domestic Proceedings and Magistrates' Courts Act 1978.

(2) The order shall not be deemed to be a supervision order made under any provision of this Act but shall nevertheless continue in force for a period of one year beginning with the day on which Part IV comes into force unless–

(a) the court directs that it shall cease to have effect at the end of a lesser period; or
(b) it would have ceased to have had effect earlier had this Act not been passed.

Place of Safety Orders

27 – (1) This paragraph applies to–

(a) any order or warrant authorising the removal of a child to a place of safety which–
    (i) was made, or issued, under any of the enactments mentioned in sub-paragraph (2); and
    (ii) was in force immediately before the commencement of Part IV; and
(b) any interim order made under section 23(5) of the Children and Young Persons Act 1963 or section 28(6) of the Children and Young Persons Act 1969.

(2) The enactments are–

(a) section 40 of the Children and Young Persons Act 1933 (warrant to search for or remove child);
(b) section 28(1) of the Children and Young Persons Act 1969 (detention of child in place of safety);
(c) section 34(1) of the Adoption Act 1976 (removal of protected children from unsuitable surroundings);
(c) section 12(1) of the Foster Children Act 1980 (removal of foster children kept in unsuitable surroundings).

(4) The order or warrant shall continue to have effect as if this Act had not been passed.

(5) Any enactment repealed by this Act shall continue to have effect in relation to the order or warrant so far as is necessary for the purposes of securing that the effect of the order is what it would have been had this Act not been passed.

(6) Sub-paragraph (4) does not apply to the power to make an interim order or further interim order given by section 23(5) of the Children and Young Persons Act 1963 or section 28(6) of the Children and Young Persons Act 1969.

(7) Where, immediately before section 28 of the Children and Young Persons Act 1969 is repealed by this Act, a child is being detained under the powers granted by that section, he may continue to be detained in accordance with that section but subsection (6) shall not apply.

Recovery of Children

28. The repeal by this Act of subsection (1) of section 16 of the Child Care Act 1980 (arrest of child absent from compulsory care) shall not affect the operation of that section in relation to any child arrested before the coming into force of the repeal.

29 – (1) This paragraph applies where–

(a) a summons has been issued under section 15 or 16 of the Child Care Act 1980 (recovery of children in voluntary or compulsory care); and
(b) the child concerned is not produced in accordance with the summons before the repeal of that section by this Act comes into force.

(2) The summons, any warrant issued in connection with it and section 15 or (as the case may be) section 16, shall continue to have effect as if this Act had not been passed.

30. The amendment by paragraph 27 of Schedule 12 of section 32 of the Children and Young Persons Act 1969 (detention of absentees) shall not affect the operation of that section in relation to–

(a) any child arrested; or
(b) any summons or warrant issued,

under that section before the coming into force of that paragraph.

Voluntary Organisations: Parental Rights Resolutions

31 – (1) This paragraph applies to a resolution–

(a) made under section 64 of the Child Care Act 1980 (transfer of parental rights and duties to voluntary organisations); and
(b) in force immediately before the commencement of Part IV.

(2) The resolution shall continue to have effect until the end of the period of six months beginning with the day on which Part IV comes into force unless it is brought to an end earlier in accordance with the provisions of the Act of 1980 preserved by this paragraph.

(3) While the resolution remains in force, any relevant provisions of, or made under, the Act of 1980 shall continue to have effect with respect to it.

(4) Sub-paragraph (3) does not apply to–

    (a) section 62 of the Act of 1980 and any regulations made under that section (arrangements by voluntary organisations for emigration of children); or

    (b) section 65 of the Act of 1980 (duty of local authority to assume parental rights and duties).

(4) Section 5(2) of the Act of 1980 (which is applied to resolutions under Part VI of that Act by section 64(7) of that Act) shall have effect with respect to the resolution as if the reference in paragraph (c) to an appointment of a guardian under section 5 of the Guardianship of Minors Act 1971 were a reference to an appointment of a guardian under section 5 of this Act.

Foster Children

32 – (1) This paragraph applies where–

    (a) immediately before the commencement of Part VIII, a child was a foster child within the meaning of the Foster Children Act 1980; and

    (b) the circumstances of the case are such that, had Parts VIII and IX then been in force, he would have been treated for the purposes of this Act as a child who was being provided with accommodation in a children's home and not as a child who was being privately fostered.

(2) If the child continues to be cared for and provided with accommodation as before, section 63(1) and (10) shall not apply in relation to him if–

    (a) an application for registration of the home in question is made under section 63 before the end of the period of three months beginning with the day on which Part VIII comes into force; and

    (b) the application has not been refused or, if it has been refused–

        (i) the period for an appeal against the decision has not expired; or

        (ii) an appeal against the refusal has been made but has not been determined or abandoned.

(3) While section 63(1) and (10) does not apply, the child shall be treated as a privately fostered child for the purposes of Part IX.

Nurseries and Child Minding

33 – (1) Sub-paragraph (2) applies where, immediately before the commencement of Part X, any premises are registered under section 1(1)(a) of the Nurseries and Child-Minders Regulation Act 1948 (registration of premises, other than premises wholly or mainly used as private dwellings, where children are received to be looked after).

(2) During the transitional period, the provisions of the Act of 1948 shall continue to have effect with respect to those premises to the exclusion of Part X.

(3) Nothing in sub-paragraph (2) shall prevent the local authority concerned from

registering any person under section 71(1)(b) with respect to the premises.

(4) In this paragraph 'the transitional period' means the period ending with–

(a) the first anniversary of the commencement of Part X; or
(b) if earlier, the date on which the local authority concerned registers any person under section 71(1)(b) with respect to the premises.

34 – (1) Sub-paragraph (2) applies where, immediately before the commencement of Part X–

(a) a person is registered under section 1(1)(b) of the Act of 1948 (registration of persons who for reward receive into their homes children under the age of five to be looked after); and
(b) all the children looked after by him as mentioned in section 1(1)(b) of that Act are under the age of five.

(2) During the transitional period, the provisions of the Act of 1948 shall continue to have effect with respect to that person to the exclusion of Part X.

(3) Nothing in sub-paragraph (2) shall prevent the local authority concerned from registering that person under section 71(1)(a).

(4) In this paragraph 'the transitional period' means the period ending with–

(a) the first anniversary of the commencement of Part X; or
(b) if earlier, the date on which the local authority concerned registers that person under section 71(1)(a).

Children accommodated in Certain Establishments

35. In calculating, for the purposes of section 85(1)(a) or 86(1)(a), the period of time for which a child has been accommodated any part of that period which fell before the day on which that section came into force shall be disregarded.

Criminal Care Orders

36 – (1) This paragraph applies where, immediately before the commencement of section 90(2) there was in force an order ('a criminal care order') made–

(a) under section 7(7)(a) of the Children and Young Persons Act 1969 (alteration in treatment of young offenders etc); or
(b) under section 15(1) of that Act, on discharging a supervision order made under section 7(7)(b) of that Act.

(2) The criminal care order shall continue to have effect until the end of the period of six months beginning with the day on which section 90(2) comes into force unless it is brought to an end earlier in accordance with–

(a) the provisions of the Act of 1969 preserved by sub-paragraph (3)(a); or
(b) this paragraph.

(3) While the criminal care order remains in force, any relevant provisions–

    (a) of the Act of 1969; and
    (b) of the Child Care Act 1980,

shall continue to have effect with respect to it.

(4) While the criminal care order remains in force, a court may, on the application of the appropriate person, make–

    (a) a residence order;
    (b) a care order or a supervision order under section 31;
    (c) an education supervision order under section 36 (regardless of subsection (6) of that section); or
    (d) an order falling within sub-paragraph (5),

and shall, on making any of those orders, discharge the criminal care order.

(5) The order mentioned in sub-paragraph (4)(d) is an order having effect as if it were a supervision order of a kind mentioned in section 12AA of the Act of 1969 (as inserted by paragraph 23 of Schedule 12), that is to say, a supervision order–

    (a) imposing a requirement that the child shall live for a specified period in local authority accommodation; but
    (b) in relation to which the conditions mentioned in [subsection (6)] of section 12AA are not required to be satisfied.

(5) The maximum period which may be specified in an order made under sub-paragraph (4)(d) is six months and such an order may stipulate that the child shall not live with a named person.

(6) Where this paragraph applies, section 5 of the Rehabilitation of Offenders Act 1974 (rehabilitation periods for particular sentences) shall have effect regardless of the repeals in it made by this Act.

(8) In sub-paragraph (4) 'appropriate person' means–

    (a) in the case of an application for a residence order, any person (other than a local authority) who has the leave of the court;
    (b) in the case of an application for an education supervision order, a local education authority; and
    (c) in any other case, the local authority to whose care the child was committed by the order.

Miscellaneous

Consents under the Marriage Act 1949 (c. 76)

37 – (1) In the circumstances mentioned in sub-paragraph (2), section 3 of and Schedule 2 to the Marriage Act 1949 (consents to marry) shall continue to have effect regardless of the amendment of that Act by paragraph 5 of Schedule 12.

(2) The circumstances are that–

   (a) immediately before the day on which paragraph 5 of Schedule 12 comes into force, there is in force–
   (i) an existing order, as defined in paragraph 5(1); or
   (ii) an order of a kind mentioned in paragraph 16(1); and
   (b) section 3 of and Schedule 2 to the Act of 1949 would, but for this Act, have applied to the marriage of the child who is the subject of the order.

The Children Act 1975 (c. 72)

38. The amendments of other enactments made by the following provisions of the Children Act 1975 shall continue to have effect regardless of the repeal of the Act of 1975 by this Act–

   (a) section 68(4), (5) and (7) (amendments of section 32 of the Children and Young Persons Act 1969); and
   (b) in Schedule 3–
   (i) paragraph 13 (amendments of Births and Deaths Registration Act 1953);
   (ii) paragraph 43 (amendment of Perpetuities and Accumulations Act 1964);
   (iii) paragraphs 46 and 47 (amendments of Health Services and Public Health Act 1968); and
   (iii) paragraph 77 (amendment of Parliamentary and Other Pensions Act 1972).

The Child Care Act 1980 (c. 5)

39. The amendment made to section 106(2)(a) of the Children and Young Persons Act 1933) by paragraph 26 of Schedule 5 to the Child Care Act 1980 shall continue to have effect regardless of the repeal of the Act of 1980 by this Act.

Legal aid

40. The Lord Chancellor may by order make such transitional and saving provisions as appear to him to be necessary or expedient, in consequence of any provision made by or under this Act, in connection with the operation of any provisions of the Legal Aid Act 1988 (including any provision of that Act which is amended or repealed by this Act). ...

SCHEDULE 15

REPEALS

Schedule 15
This schedule is a table of the Acts and sections of Acts that were repealed, and are therefore no longer in force as legislation, as a consequence of the Children Act 1989. It can be seen from the table that a number of Acts were repealed in their entirety as the Children Act 1989 brought together many previous acts and codified them.

Chapter	Short title	Extent of repeal
1891 c. 3.	The Custody of Children Act 1891.	The whole Act.
1933 c. 12.	The Children and Young Persons Act 1933.	In section 14(2), the words from "may also" to "together, and".
		In section 34(8), "(a)" and the words from "and (b)" to the end.
		Section 40.
		In section 107(1), the definitions of "care order" and "interim order".
1944 c. 31.	The Education Act 1944.	In section 40(1), the words from "or to imprisonment" to the end.
		In section 114(1), the definition of parent.
1948 c. 53.	The Nurseries and Child-Minders Regulation Act 1948.	The whole Act.
1949 c. 76.	The Marriage Act 1949.	In section 3(1), the words "unless the child is subject to a custodianship order, when the consent of the custodian and, where the custodian is the husband or wife of a parent of the child of that parent shall be required".

Chapter	Short title	Extent of repeal
		Section 78(1A). Schedule 2.
1956 c. 69.	The Sexual Offences Act 1956.	Section 38.
1959 c. 72.	The Mental Health Act 1959.	Section 9.
1963 c. 37.	The Children and Young Persons Act 1963.	Section 3.
		Section 23. In section 29(1), the words "under section 1 of the Children and Young Persons Act 1969 or".
		Section 53(3).
		In Schedule 3, paragraph 11.
1964 c. 42.	The Administration of Justice Act 1964.	In section 38, the definition of "domestic court".
1968 c. 46.	The Health Services and Public Health Act 1968.	Section 60. In section 64(3)(a), sub-paragraphs (vi), (vii), (ix) and (xv).
		In section 65(3)(b), paragraphs (vii), (viii) and (x).
1968 c. 49.	The Social Work (Scotland) Act 1968.	Section 1(4)(a). Section 5(2)(d).
		In section 86(3), the words "the Child Care Act 1980 or".
		In Schedule 8, paragraph 20.
1969 c. 46.	The Family Law Reform Act 1969.	Section 7.
1969 c. 54.	The Children and Young Persons Act 1969.	Sections 1 to 3.
		In section 7, in subsection (7) the words "to subsection (7A) of this section and", paragraph (a) and the words from "and subsection (13) of section 2 of this Act" to the end; and subsection (7A).

Chapter	Short title	Extent of repeal
		Section 7A.
		In section 8(3), the words from "and as if the reference to acquittal" to the end.
		In section 9(1), the words "proceedings under section 1 of this Act or".
		Section 11A.
		Section 14A.
		In section 15, in subsection (1) the words "and may on discharging the supervision order make a care order (other than an interim order) in respect of the supervised person"; in subsection (2) the words "and the supervision order was not made by virtue of section 1 of this Act or on the occasion of the discharge of a care order"; in subsection (2A), the words "or made by a court on discharging a care order made under that subsection"; and in subsection (4), the words "or made by a court on discharging a care order made under that section".
		In section 16, in subsection (6)(a), the words "a care order or"; and in subsection (8) the words "or, in a case where a parent or guardian of his was a party to the proceedings on an application under the preceding section by virtue of an order under section 32A of this Act, the parent or guardian".
		In section 17, paragraphs (b) and (c).

Chapter	Short title	Extent of repeal
		Sections 20 to 22.
		Section 27(4).
		Section 28.
		Sections 32A to 32C.
		In section 34(2) the words "under section 1 of this Act or", the words "2(3) or" and the words "and accordingly in the case of such a person the reference in section 1(1) of this Act to the said section 2(3) shall be construed as including a reference to this subsection".
		In section 70, in subsection (1), the definitions of "care order" and "interim order"; and in subsection (2) the words "21(2), 22(4) or (6) or 28(5)" and the words "care order or warrant".
		In Schedule 5, paragraphs 12(1), 37, 47 and 48.
1970 c. 34.	The Marriage (Registrar General's Licence Act 1970.	In section 3(b), the words from "as amended" to "1969".
1970 c. 42.	The Local Authority Social Services Act 1970.	In Schedule 1, in the entry relating to the Children and Young Persons Act 1969, the words "welfare, etc. of foster children"; the entries relating to the Matrimonial Causes Act 1973, section 44, the Domestic Proceedings and Magistrates' Courts Act 1978, section 9, the Child Care Act 1980 and the Foster Children Act 1980.
1971 c. 3.	The Guardianship of Minors Act 1971.	The whole Act.
1971 c. 23.	The Courts Act 1971.	In Schedule 8, paragraph 59(1).

Chapter	Short title	Extent of repeal
1972 c. 18.	The Maintenance Orders Reciprocal Enforcement Act 1972.	Section 41.
1972 c. 70.	The Local Government Act 1972.	In Schedule 23, paragraphs 4 and 9(3).
1972 c. 71.	The Criminal Justice Act 1972.	Section 51(1).
1973 c. 18.	The Matrimonial Causes Act 1973.	Sections 42 to 44. In section 52(1), the definition of "custody". In Schedule 2, paragraph 11.
1973 c. 29.	The Guardianship Act 1973.	The whole Act.
1973 c. 45.	The Domicile and Matrimonial Proceedings Act 1973.	In Schedule 1, in paragraph 11(1) the definitions of "custody" and "education" and in paragraph 11(3) the word "four".
1973 c. 62.	The Powers of Criminal Courts Act 1973.	In section 13(1), the words "and the purposes of section 1(2)(bb) of the Children and Young Persons Act 1969". In Schedule 3, in paragraph 3(2A), the word "and" immediately preceding paragraph (b).
1974 c. 53.	The Rehabilitation of Offenders Act 1974.	In section 1(4)(b) the words "or in care proceedings under section 1 of the Children and Young Persons Act 1969". In section 5, in subsection 5(e), the words "a care order or"; and in subsection (10) the words "care order or".
1975 c. 72.	The Children Act 1975.	The whole Act.
1976 c. 36.	The Adoption Act 1976.	Section 11(5). Section 14(3).

Chapter	Short title	Extent of repeal
		In section 15, in subsection (1), the words from "subject" to "cases)" and subsection (4).
		Section 26.
		In section 28(5), the words "or the organisation".
		Section 34.
		Section 36(1)(c).
		Section 37(1), (3) and (4).
		Section 55(4).
		In section 57, in subsection (2), the words from "and the court" to the end and subsections (4) to (10).
		In section 72(1), the definition of "place of safety", in the definition of "local authority" the words from " and" to the end and, in the definition of "specified order", the words "Northern Ireland or".
		In Schedule 3, paragraphs 8, 11, 19, 21, and 22.
1977 c. 45.	The Criminal Law Act 1977.	Section 58(3).
1977 c. 49.	The National Health Service Act 1977.	In section 21, in subsection (1)(a) the words "and young children".
		In Schedule 8, in paragraph 1(1), the words from "and of children" to the end; in paragraph 2(2) the words from "or (b) to persons who" to "arrangements"; and in paragraph 3(1) "(a)" and the words from "or (b) a child" to "school age".

Chapter	Short title	Extent of repeal
		In Schedule 15, paragraphs 10 and 25.
1978 c. 22.	The Domestic Proceedings and Magistrates' Courts Act 1978.	Sections 9 to 15.
		In section 19, in subsection (1) the words "following powers, that is to say" and sub-paragraph (ii), subsections (2) and (4), in subsection (7) the words "and one interim custody order" and in subsection (9) the words "or 21".
		In section 20, subsection (4) and in subsection (9) the words "subject to the provisions of section 11(8) of this Act".
		Section 21.
		In section 24, the words "or 21" in both places where they occur.
		In section 25, in subsection (1) paragraph (b) and the word "or" immediately preceding it and in subsection (2) paragraphs (c) and (d).
		Section 29(4).
		Sections 33 and 34.
		Sections 36 to 53.
		Sections 64 to 72.
		Sections 73(1) and 74(1) and (3).
		In section 88(1), the definition of "actual custody".
		In Schedule 2, paragraphs 22, 23, 27, 29, 31, 36, 41 to 43, 46 to 50.

Chapter	Short title	Extent of repeal
1978 c. 28.	The Adoption (Scotland) Act 1978.	In section 20(3)(c), the words "section 12(3)(b) of the Adoption Act 1976 or of". In section 45(5), the word "approved". Section 49(4). In section 65(1), in the definition of "local authority", the words from "and" to the end and, in the definition of "specified order", the words "Northern Ireland or".
1978 c. 30.	The Interpretation Act 1978.	In Schedule 1, the entry with respect to the construction of certain expressions relating to children.
1980 c. 5.	The Child Care Act 1980.	The whole Act.
1980 c. 6.	The Foster Children Act 1980.	The whole Act.
1980 c. 43.	The Magistrates' Courts Act 1980.	In section 65(1), paragraphs (e) and (g) and the paragraph (m) inserted in section 65 by paragraph 82 of Schedule 2 to the Family Law Reform Act 1987. In section 81(8), in the definition of "guardian" the words "by deed or will" and in the definition of "sums adjudged to be paid by a conviction" the words from "as applied" to the end. In section 143(2), paragraph (i). In Schedule 7, paragraphs 78, 83, 91, 92, 110, 116, 117, 138, 157, 158, 165, 166 and 199 to 201.
1981 c. 60.	The Education Act 1981.	In Schedule 3, paragraph 9.

Chapter	Short title	Extent of repeal
1982 c. 20.	The Children's Homes Act 1982.	The whole Act.
1982 c. 48.	The Criminal Justice Act 1982.	Sections 22 to 25.
		Section 27.
		In Schedule 14, paragraphs 45 and 46.
1983 c. 20.	The Mental Health Act 1983.	In section 26(5), paragraph (d) and the word "or" immediately preceding it.
		In section 28(1), the words "(including an order under section 38 of the Sexual Offences Act 1956)".
		In Schedule 4, paragraphs 12, 26(a), (b) and (c), 35, 44, 50 and 51.
1983 c. 41.	The Health and Social Services and Social Security Adjudications Act 1983.	Section 4(1).
		Sections 5 and 6.
		In section 11, in subsection (2) the words "the Child Care Act 1980 and the Children's Homes Act 1982".
		In section 19, subsections (1) to (5).
		Schedule 1.
		In Schedule 2, paragraphs 3, 9 to 14, 20 to 24, 27, 28, 34, 37 and 46 to 62.
		In Schedule 4, paragraphs 38 to 48.
		In Schedule 9, paragraphs 5, 16 and 17.
1984 c. 23.	The Registered Homes Act 1984.	In Schedule 1, in paragraph 5, sub-paragraph (a) and paragraphs 6, 7 and 8.

Chapter	Short title	Extent of repeal
1984 c. 28.	The County Courts Act 1984.	In Schedule 2, paragraph 56.
1984 c. 37.	The Child Abduction Act 1984.	In section 3, the word "and" immediately preceding paragraph (c). In the Schedule, in paragraph 1(2) the words "or voluntary organisation" and paragraph 3(1)(e).
1984 c. 42.	The Matrimonial and Family Proceedings Act 1984.	In Schedule 1, paragraphs 19 and 23.
1984 c. 56.	The Foster Children (Scotland) Act 1984.	In section 1, the words "for a period of more than 6 days" and the words from "The period" to the end. In section 7(1), the word "or" at the end of paragraph (e). In Schedule 2, paragraphs 1 to 3 and 8.
1984 c. 60.	The Police and Criminal Evidence Act 1984.	In section 37(15), the words "and is not excluded from this Part of this Act by section 52 below". Section 39(5). Section 52. In section 118(1), in the definition of parent or guardian, paragraph (b) and the word "and" immediately preceding it. In Schedule 2, the entry relating to section 16 of the Child Care Act 1980. In Schedule 6, paragraphs 19(a) and 22.
1985 c. 23.	The Prosecution of Offences Act 1985.	Section 27.

Chapter	Short title	Extent of repeal
1985 c. 60.	The Child Abduction and Custody Act 1985.	Section 9(c).
		Section 20(2)(b) and (c).
		Section 25(3) and (5).
		In Schedule 3, paragraph 1(2).
1986 c. 28.	The Children and Young Persons (Amendment) Act 1986.	The whole Act.
1986 c. 33.	The Disabled Persons (Services, Consultation and Representation Act 1986.	In section 16, in the definition of "guardian", paragraph (a).
1986 c. 45.	The Insolvency Act 1986.	In section 281(5)(b), the words "in domestic proceedings".
1986 c. 50.	The Social Security Act 1986.	In Schedule 10, paragraph 51.
1986 c. 55.	The Family Law Act 1986.	In section 1(2), in paragraph (a) the words "(a) or" and paragraph (b).
		Section 3(4) to (6).
		Section 4.
		Section 35(1).
		In section 42(6), in paragraph (b) the words "section 42(6) of the Matrimonial Causes Act 1973 or", in paragraph (c) the words "section 42(7) of that Act or" and in paragraph (d) the words "section 19(6) of the Domestic Proceedings and Magistrates' Courts Act 1978 or".
		In Schedule 1, paragraphs 10, 11, 13, 16, 17, 20 and 23.
1987 c. 42.	The Family Law Reform Act 1987.	Section 3.
		Sections 4 to 7.
		Sections 9 to 16.

Chapter	Short title	Extent of repeal
1988 c. 34.	The Legal Aid Act 1988.	In Schedule 2, paragraphs 11, 14, 51, 67, 68, 94 and 95.
		In Schedule 3, paragraphs 11 and 12.
		Section 3(4)(c).
		Section 27.
		Section 28.
		In section 30, subsections (1) and (2).
		In Part I of Schedule 2, paragraph 2(a) and (e).

Index